The Owl's Watchsong

Istanbul has lured travellers for centuries. *The Owl's Watchsong*, by
an author who lived and worked there in the 1950s, is an absorbing,
intimate study of the ancient capital of the Byzantine Emperors and
Turkish Sultans; not only of its Byzantine and Ottoman art and
architecture (palaces, churches, cisterns, hans, mosques and the
great Seraglio) and the waterways of the Golden Horn and the Bosphorus, but also of its daily and nightly life in street, market
and bazaar, and the numerous characters he meets: merchant, actor,
poet, muezzin, spiv, odalisque *et al*. There are also fascinating accounts of life in the harem, Dervish practices, eunuchs, Janissaries,
the prayer marathons of the Stylites, Turkish custom and Islamic
tradition. A new introduction puts the past in more recent
perspective.

J. A. Cuddon is the author of a wide variety of books, including
other travel works, such as the *Companion Guide to Jugoslavia*. He also
has a dozen plays, several novels and numerous essays to his credit,
as well as *A Dictionary of Literary Terms* and the *Dictionary of Sport and
Games*. Between 1982 and 1983 he compiled and edited the *Penguin
Book of Ghost Stories* and *The Penguin Book of Horror Stories*, both published in 1984. He is currently working on a book about his travels in
the Balkans.

The Owl's Watchsong

A Study of Istanbul

J. A. Cuddon

Pardedâri mikunad dar kasr-i-Kâysar ankebût;
Bûm naubat mîzanad dar gumbed-i-Afrasiâb.

The spider spins his web in the Palace of the Cæsars,
And the owl sings her watchsong on the Towers of Afrasiab.

(A verse from Saadi quoted by
Mehmet II, 'The Conqueror',
when he walked through the ruined
palace of the Byzantine emperors.)

CENTURY HUTCHINSON LTD
LONDON

First published in 1960 by
Barrie and Rockliff

© 1960 J. A. Cuddon

This edition first published in 1986 by
Century Hutchinson Ltd, Brookmount House, 62–65 Chandos Place,
London, WC2N 4NW

Century Hutchison Publishing Group (Australia) Pty Ltd
PO Box 496, 16–22 Church Street, Hawthorn, Melbourne, Victoria 3122

Century Hutchinson Group (NZ) Ltd
PO Box 40–086, 32–34 View Road, Glenfield, Auckland 10

Century Hutchinson Group (SA) Pty Ltd
PO Box 337, Berglvei 2012, South Africa

Printed in Great Britain by
Richard Clay (The Chaucer Press) Ltd, Bungay, Suffolk

ISBN 0 7126 9460 9

Introduction

Personal, subjective travel books tend to be in part a voyage of self-discovery, and to re-read such a book is to rediscover aspects of one's self. Much more important for me was a kind of rediscovery of Istanbul.

Much has happened to and in the city since I first went there in the early 1950s. By around 1955 a massive demolition and redevelopment plan was under way in Stamboul, the old and original part of the city. Hundreds of acres of decrepit and ancient houses (many of wood or mud bricks), gardens and miscellaneous buildings were simply razed to the ground. The detritus of centuries was cleared away. It was drastic but, in the interests of health and safety, it needed to be done. What has replaced them is seldom particularly pleasing but it is more efficient.

On the Pera side of the city and up the shores of the Bosphorus there have been extensive modern building developments, and there is the suspension bridge over the Bosphorus. A wonder of plain geometry in grey steel, it crosses the great strait in a single span between Ortaköy and Beylerbey.

In the last thirty years, too, much renovation of antiquities has been achieved. The churches and mosques have been well maintained and the whole place is tidier. Moreover, many trees have grown where there was none before.

I was fortunate to be there in time to see much of it as it has been in, say, 1900; and when I first went it was rather what I had expected to see. As a schoolboy in the 1930s I regularly heard people talking about their visits to Constantinople (as they invariably called it) in late Victorian and then Edwardian times. I assimilated many impressions, saw hundreds of photographs and not a few sketches and paintings. At an impressionable age, therefore, I discovered much about Istanbul, Turkey, the Turks and the Ottoman empire in the most agreeable way.

There was also the influence of my parents. My father fought through the Gallipoli campaign as a subaltern, returned to France for the rest of the war and was later a member of what the War Office called the Black Sea Army. My mother, always an adventurous person and an enterprising traveller, had served as a V.A.D. in Greece and Serbia and after the war was posted to Turkey. My parents met in Istanbul, married there and lived there from 1919 to 1921.

In our house in England we had various Turkish artefacts: copper and pewter ware made by smiths in Istanbul, ceramics, tiles from Iznik, a *sofra*,[1] strings of blue beads worn on the head harness and bridles of horses as protection against the evil eye, and a number of beautiful carpets—from Turkey, Afghanistan and Persia.

By the time I was in my mid-teens I was becoming an addicted armchair traveller. This was an exciting voyage of discovery; but it was 1942, and it seemed that the war might go on for many years. My brother (later to die of wounds in North Africa), other relatives and friends were overseas in the services. Many of us were frustrated, wanting to leave school and do something more enterprising than train with wooden rifles as potential members of the Home Guard. I was obliged to satisfy my longings for danger and adventure vicariously.

In an antiquated school junior library, which contained little published later than 1900, I began to discover the works of Mungo Park, Richard Burton, Livingstone, Speke, Palgrave and Doughty. There were volumes, too, of travels in the Levant and Asia Minor, such as *The Totall Discourse of the Rare Adventures and Painefull Peregrinations, Etc.* by Edward Lithgow and Aaron Hill's *Account of the Present State of the Ottoman Empire.* I unearthed, also (how well I remember my excitement at this find), Sir Francis Galton's *The Art of Travel: Or, Shifts and Contrivances Available in Wild Countries*; a proto 'survival kit' guide much of whose advice remains sound. I cherish the memory of his entry:

MANAGEMENT OF SAVAGES

GENERAL REMARKS.—A frank, joking, but determined manner, joined with an air of showing more confidence in the faith of the natives than you really feel, is the best ... they thoroughly appreciate common sense, truth, and uprightness; and are not half such fools as strangers usually account them.

Later there were the pleasures of H. M. Tomlinson, Robert Byron and Peter Fleming. I enjoyed Byron and Fleming especially; they were so witty and irreverent.

And then there were maps—long an obsessional interest. With these a different kind of calenture of the brains might conjure up steppe, tundra and veldt. With these I would create numberless *paysages intérieures*, over which, well-equipped with porters (and a copy of Galton's *vade mecum*) I would trek under torrid suns, hack through steaming equatorial jungle, scale sierras in quest of lost worlds and tribes, or, like a badly-stuffed bolster, lumber on a camel through the restless wildernesses of the desert.

[1] A *sofra*: a 'dining table', often low, on stool or folding frame. On the whole I have avoided technical terms and Turkish words, but sometimes one has to use them. A short list of these, with a note on Turkish pronunciation, can be found in the appendix.

I also enjoyed the inestimable privilege and bonus of spending the whole of my childhood and youth in the English countryside. In the 1930s and 1940s it was comparatively unspoilt and for the most part unpolluted. As compared with now there were few vehicles about. On a country road in, say, Hampshire, Lancashire or Suffolk a complete day might show perhaps a couple of vans, a motorbike or two, a local bus and three motor cars.

I learned traditional rural skills: to fish, shoot, hunt, ride and poach. It was commonplace to walk 25–30 miles in a day. And for many years I walked, cycled and hitchhiked over broad areas of England and Wales. The discovery of my own country was a marvellous experience.

As soon as the war was over and I had completed my national service and cured myself of an obsessive ambition to become a professional cricketer (it was Leonard Wilkinson, the Lancashire and England leg-break bowler, who convinced me that though I was not without ability I would find it *very* hard work) I took every opportunity to travel by any available means.

Constantinople/Istanbul/Turkey/the Levant had continued to be an integral part of my consciousness. This had led (inevitably I suppose) to an interest in Ottoman history and art and thence to Byzantine history and art. Later was to come the excitement of exploring those regions (especially the Balkans) that formerly comprised the Ottoman empire which at one stage incorporated Jugoslavia, Hungary, Bulgaria, Albania, Greece, the islands of the Eastern Mediterranean, the Levant, Egypt, the North African littoral as far as Morocco and modern Turkey itself—which is a big place: over three times the size of the United Kingdom. At one time the empire's furthest western and eastern frontiers, on the Adriatic and Caspian respectively, were nearly 2000 miles apart.

Over the years Istanbul had become a kind of lodestone and after some exploratory trips in western Europe that was where I set off for.

In the first place I wanted to emulate Patrick Leigh Fermor and walk there. In the end I went on the now defunct 'Orient Express' which 35 years ago still had a touch of class about it. You could get a comfortable berth and restaurant cars were put on at regular intervals. The old magic of intercontinental carriages placarded with sonorous names—VENEZIA, ZAGREB, BEOGRAD, SOFIA, THESSALONIKI—was potent enough. With me, in an Edwardian gladstone which still has some mileage in it, I carried Murray's *Handbook to Constantinople* (1905), a modern *Guide Bleu*, Dwight's *Istanbul Old and New* and Miss Pardoe's *Beauties of the Bosphorus*. It was only a three-day journey from London (as it still is) and when I arrived everything looked extraordinarily familiar. I dumped my belongings at a cheap hotel in Sirkeci and set straight off into the warren of the bazaars.

Much has changed; much has not. Large areas of the city are still a congenial and fascinating muddle, and the cemeteries, which

helped to inspire the somewhat elegiac tone of this book, are as vast
as ever. It remains an important mart and entrepôt through whose
magnificent bazaars passes the copious and varied merchandise of
the East. It remains, too, an exceptionally cosmopolitan place and
this is one of its chief attractions. One may hear something like forty
different languages spoken there, including Ladino, a medieval language brought by the Sephardic Jews from Spain 500 years ago and
still used by the congregations in the synagogues of Balat.

There have been several contenders for the title 'Where East meets
West' and in many respects they still do so in Istanbul. However, I
think that Sarajevo in Bosnia (it still has about eighty mosques and
was a very important city in the Ottoman empire) is actually the
more appropriate site for the disputed conjunction. In its ethno-
graphic museum there is a brass instrument for funnelling linctus
down the throats of ailing camels. At Sarajevo, the long laden camel
trains that, for centuries, had plodded from Turkestan and Balu-
chistan, from Persia, Syria and Arabia, and via Istanbul, came to a
halt. Further north the climate was unsuitable for the camels
because they developed sore throats, bronchitis and other pulmon-
ary afflictions.

Re-reading this book for revision purposes for the first time since I
checked the proofs in 1959 has been a salutary experience. On one
previous occasion I tried to re-read a book of my own after it was
published. I stopped on the third page because I wanted to start
making alterations. I resolved then that I would never repeat the
experiment with anything that I had had printed unless I absolutely
had to.

As I had feared, I found myself re-reading this book with, often
enough, a rueful smile, which occasionally became a grimace. By the
time I was halfway down the second page I wanted to re-write a
sentence. Often I said to myself: that won't do; this shouldn't have
been said at all. Some of the attitudes and opinions I expressed
twenty-eight years ago seem to me to be intolerant; occasionally
arrogant; periodically pretentious and even pompous. These
glimpses of a younger and earlier self were, to be frank, embarras-
ing. It was very tempting to extrude whole paragraphs, to re-write
complete pages—especially the more sententious ones.

It was also tempting to expand. With the benefit of hindsight (plus
much increased knowledge) I regret that I didn't say a good deal
more about Ottoman and Byzantine history and art; and more
about some of the personalities. For example, there is no mention of
Theodore Metochites, Lord High Treasurer in the reign of Andronicus II Palaeologus. A poet, historian, astronomer and philosopher,
he was one of the outstanding men of his age and responsible for the
rebuilding of St Saviour in Chora (where there is a portrait of him).
I left out, too, Sokollu Mehmet, son of an Orthodox priest in Bosnia,
who became a victim of the hated *devşirme* or levy of Christian youth

and eventually rose to become a famous Grand Vizier in the reign of Süleyman the Magnificent. Another omission was the Köprülü family (their mosque is in Divan Yolu, near the 'Burnt Column'), perhaps the most distinguished family in the history of the Ottoman empire. Five of them served as Grand Viziers in the 17th and 18th centuries and in 1659–60 two of them founded a *külliye* and an important library (which survives). And much more might have been said about the great architect Sinan who began his career as an architect in his mid-fifties (before that he had been an engineer) and in the next forty-odd years designed no fewer than 334 buildings (mosques, schools, hospitals, baths, bridges and palaces) across the empire from Budapest to Damascus, before, eventually, dying aged 99. And there is no mention at all, I now see, of the Turkish novelist Yashar Kemal (of whom Paul Theroux gives a vivid sketch in *The Great Railway Bazaar*), nor of the poet Nazim Hikmet, generally regarded as the best poet to write in modern Turkish. For such omissions one can have only regrets.

One of the writer's prime duties is fidelity to the truth so far as he can attain it. The truth is said to be indivisible. In the end I decided to change and add very little and worked on the following principle: *that*, rightly or wrongly, better or worse, was how I saw things at the time; *that* was how I felt at the time.

In writing the book I endeavoured to combine three main elements: the reactions and reports of previous travellers, historical fact and my own experiences and comments. By these means, by using, as it were, three narrative 'cameras', I attempted to suggest a variety of the city's characteristics and to grasp something of its inscape. In the process, following well-established practice, I allowed myself a number of digressive 'essays'.

One of the pleasantest comments I can recall about the original edition came from an old colleague then in his fifties, 'I read a certain "natural history" over the weekend,' he said. 'I enjoyed it. It's a young man's book.' Well, so it was; and so it is; and thus, with its numerous shortcomings, it must remain.

Contents

The author is indebted to Messrs Faber and Faber Ltd. for permission to
reprint an extract from the poem 'The Death of a Toad' by Richard Wilbur,
and to Messrs Eyre and Spottiswoode Ltd. for permission to reprint an extract
from the poem 'Ode to the Confederate Dead' by Allen Tate.

'For a Gentleman to travel to *Constantinople*, and to view the adjacent Countries, is certainly one of the most pleasing Diversions that may be, and which furnishes a man with Observations the most admirable, while he beholds what Nature offers to his Eyes, the most charming that can be imagin'd, in the delectable situation of Places, and what Time has left, in beautiful Ruins, of the Magnificence and Grandeur of the Eastern Emperors.'

(Grelot, *A Late Voyage to Constantinople*. Translated by J. Philips, London, 1683)

Map of Istanbul

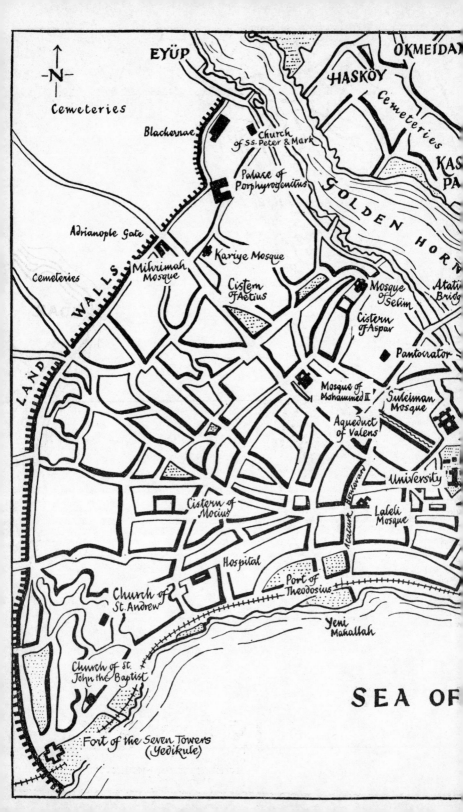

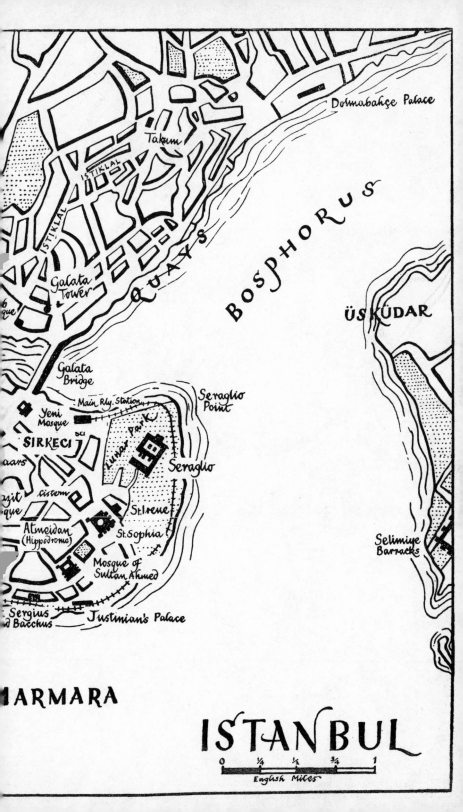

To

Yesanku
A Rare Eastern Lady

CHAPTER ONE

The Golden Horn

THE Harbour of *Constantinople* is the most spacious, the
finest, and the most advantageously situated in the World, it
being the rendezvous of two Seas; and whatever Wind blows,
one may see at all times Vessels sailing into and out, both of
one and the other.

A. DE LA MOTRAYE, *Travels through Europe,*
Asia, and into part of Africa. 3 vols.,
London, 1723

In the dusty blue late afternoon sky a hawk was wheeling. The world
pivoted and tipped in his eye. He jousted in the currents of air, wings
stretched, tilting. . . .

Below slid the enormous reptile, pale brown, winding and slithering
swiftly from the west, through the scattered suburbs, amidst gently
undulating and fertile land, green and ochre, and treed with fig and
plane and cypress. . . .

We had been travelling for three days and now it was nearly over.
People were standing in the corridors of the train. Bags were being
lugged off the racks. Ties were adjusted, complexions touched up. I
stood in the corridor myself and saw the great land-walls in the distance, grey and pale brown: very ancient walls.

Then suddenly buildings crowded in, hedging the eyes, and the
smooth, swift train took us into the city—at a blow. The neat, precise, pentametred tune of the wheels changed, as it had changed a
hundred times in the long journey across Europe . . . anapaest, dactyl.
The undertones leapt up the scale to a hollow roar, the rhythm
went on and the sound echoed and was flung back from the buildings.

The line went all the way round the southern and eastern perimeter of the city close to the sea and there were rapid glimpses of

I

the blue water, the decaying sea-walls, ramshackle wooden houses, squalid cobbled streets, crumbling palaces, domes, minarets. There was a rapid film, quick tracking shots, back projections: a man's legs sticking out from beneath a lorry, a woman arranging her hair in an upstairs room, a donkey reaching for grass, a boy watching, his hand still on the top of a wheel. . . . Scenes of a city shot at random from a moving window.

In the penultimate moments of a long journey disorderly recollections jostle for attention, another camera projects, the sea grass-green and choppy at Dover, heavy rain at Cologne, the jagged jaws of the Alps furry with pine and spruce, the great plains of Serbia and Bulgaria, the minarets of Adrianople ignited by the dawn sun; and the spring that was wound at departure, the spring that has inched its way out fraction by fraction as mile after mile unfolded behind, relaxes and eases to arrival. They are moments of renewal and replenishment and as the metre of the wheels runs gently, rallentando, iamb, spondee, the pace of the heart picks up and quickens. As the busy argument of the pistons resolves to slower and graver pronouncements the limbs acquire a new sense of urgency.

We had arrived. It was pleasant to have returned once again. There are plenty of trains to Istanbul, and the journey takes only half an hour longer than it did in 1900.

★

There were a few men sitting in the café on the waterfront of the Golden Horn near the Marine Arsenal. It was a spacious, gaunt room full of marble-topped tables and chairs and above the counter hung a faded photograph of Mustafa Kemal. On the opposite wall was a reproduction of Bellini's painting of Mehmet 'The Conqueror'. These are the two pictures that one sees most often in Istanbul and Turkey. Some shops contain dozens of them. It is not surprising since they are the two men who accomplished more than anybody else for the nation.

Most of the clients were poor, working men; but probably they were out of work. Their clothes were greasy, crumpled and dirty. The black bristles of two or three days adorned the faces of most of them. Many working men save up their shaves. It costs less, the barbers have hot water and there are many of them.

Of late barbers have become specialists, particularly in the West.

It is only as recently as 1745 that surgeons were separated from barbers by Act of Parliament. It was entitled: 'An Act for making the Surgeons and Barbers of London two distinct and separate Corporations.' In Istanbul they have also changed but more recently. Sir Adolphus Slade, about 1880, remarked that in addition to shaving, cutting hair, trimming, dyeing, and anointing, the barber 'bleeds, draws teeth, and applies leeches, all very adroitly.'[1] Further east than Istanbul they still draw teeth and the methods vary a good deal.

Some of the men were playing cards: interminable games of whist, and each time one played he flung down the card with a violent gesture; a curious trick but quite good-humoured. Others were playing backgammon, sliding and banging the counters, playing it with great speed and skill. Most of the men were Turks and there were one or two Greeks. They all had their little glasses of tea, like pale sherry, beside them. At one table a Turk and a Greek were playing poker. Over the loudspeaker came the usual and everlasting discord of Turkish music: garish and monotonous.

Outside the heat and the sun shimmered on the Golden Horn; the train of the sun wobbling and flickering on the surface. A constant traffic of dozens of different kinds of craft went up and down. In shadows and under trees along the quay-side men lay sprawled in sleep, sweating steadily. Refuse was littered everywhere and exhaled the sour odours drawn out by the sun. Melon-rinds gathered clouds of flies. Cats picked their way deftly and circumspectly among the rubbish. Across the Horn came the hooting of the barges and the steamers. The water slapped against the tethered hulls. Music wailed. It was half-past three. The violet hour.

I sat down in the café and drank two bottles of water to replace moisture, and then lingered over a glass of tea, continually brushing away the flies: little black, persistent flies swarming over the food and on the table-tops. There used to be various talismans on the other side of the city and on the top of a marble column there was the figure of a black fly, made of brass, which by its incessant humming drove away all the flies. This was probably the same column and the same fly as those erected by Apollonius of Tyana, except that his fly is supposed to have been of bronze. But bronze or brass, their potency has long since failed. Apollonius is reputed to have cleared Antioch of scorpions and Constantinople of gnats by the same means, but his charms work no longer. Perhaps we have not enough faith these days.

The ubiquity of flies no doubt gives rise to the Turkish proverb that a fly is small but it is enough to make you sick. It is very true, and they were settling again on sweating faces and hands in the café.

I gazed about aimlessly. It was too hot to bother to think much. I sipped my tea, re-read parts of an old newspaper, dismissed a fly, waved at another, sipped. . . . The proprietor, a cumbersome and corpulent Turk, leaned listlessly over his counter. Periodically he mopped his neck with a cloth. Sip. 'Surrey Champions again.' Fly. 'Danger of Inflation.' I drew off the daily scum of news: the racial riots, the fires, the floods, the revelations of vice, the aberrations of sex, the murders in north London, the rapes in Africa. The after-noon wore on: laden with heat; somnolent. A pattern of sounds settled and established itself: the dissonant moaning of the music and the song; the ticking grandfather clock; the chink of tea-glasses; the suck and slap of water on the swaying boats; the crisp clacking of the backgammon counters; the soft murmur of conversation. I sipped my tea and read a weather forecast for England a fortnight old. It is extraordinary how pleasant the weather is after the crop of unnatural crime and man's inhumanity to man.

The row, when it started, was quite quiet. The Turk playing poker with the Greek said that he had been cheating. The Greek, a short, stocky man, smiled and denied it. The Turk began to explain how it had been done. The Greek, a little more demonstratively, assured him that he was wrong. The proprietor rolled his head in a half-turn and watched without interest, mopping his neck.

The Turk started to explain again, but the Greek courteously and firmly refused to entertain the idea. The Turk, swarthy, with a fine long nose and a cropped skull, was adamant. His expression changed slightly: irritation shadowed it and vanished. A gesture of interest passed through the proprietor's eyes. A man in a corner looked up over his paper and stared.

I sipped my tea and half-listened. 'Middlesex won the toss . . .' The Greek was offering to play with a different pack of cards. The Turk said that he wanted his money back.

I thought of Lord's: the gaudy ties, the sombre pavilion, the ripples of applause, the sudden disturbances by the tavern as some drunkard focuses long enough on the score-board to realize that insufficient has happened in his absence and throws out more or less inaccurate advice. I dreamt, remembered hitting a six at Taunton, being umpired out at Abertillery, bowling all day with a hangover at Derby for nothing. The imparities of fortune at cricket are difficult to forget, but for a moment I wished I was not sitting by the Golden Horn. Nostalgia is useless but inescapable. It lays traps. The memory quakes, a crevasse appears, the door swings open and there you are, suddenly, groping for something you would rather have forgotten; and usually it does not concern cricket.

I read. 'Compton began tentatively but soon the old familiar strokes began to flow . . .' I waved a fly away. The proprietor dabbed his neck.

'Cheat,' said the Turk, quite quietly. The Greek did not reply and looked stubborn. The Turk's voice rose a little and the clacking of the backgammon counters next to me stopped abruptly.

'You have two lira of mine,' the Turk was saying.

'It's not true,' replied the Greek.

'Give me my two lira and I will play with you again.'

'But I won it.'

I was reminded of two boys arguing over some chestnuts. By now the proprietor was listening carefully. Another game of backgammon stopped and I forgot about Compton's innings.

'No,' said the Turk loudly, looking about for support. 'You took it. Give me my property.'

'You are imagining it,' replied the Greek.

'Why don't you go home?' said the Turk, leaning forward. The proprietor changed his weight to another foot and listened; brushed away the flies.

'Why don't you Greeks go home?'

'But Mustapha—' began the Greek conciliatory.

'You are always taking things from Turks.'

'Mustapha—'

'There are ninety thousand Greeks in Istanbul, and we don't want you.'

'Mustapha—'

'We don't want you in Cyprus either.'

Suddenly the Greek was angry. 'You liar!' he shouted. 'What's that got to do with it?'

All the whist and the backgammon stopped at once. Across the Horn a hooter eructed: a long-drawn-out bellow.

'That's enough,' said the proprietor, coming round the counter. He had gauged the argument like a thermometer and now the mercury had crossed the red line. The Turk seized the cards and flung the pack at the Greek. A flurry of them struck him in the face. The rest fanned out, slid and fluttered to the floor. He pushed back his chair and rose.

'You liar!' he shouted. The proprietor stepped forward, minatory. 'I don't want trouble—' he began; but the Turk had acted. He jerked the marble table aside and as it fell jumped forward. The Greek dodged behind another table.

'Liar!' he shouted again.

'Swine! Greek!' rejoined the Turk, bounding after him. He fumbled at his waist for a knife. The Greek saw, picked up a chair. The rest of the men were on their feet and crowding towards the door. They remembered September 6th and other occasions. This was how riots started. The proprietor stood irresolute but shouting. The Turk dodged the chair and went for the Greek, knife out. Light jarred on the suddenly exposed blade. The Greek got another chair just in time and rammed it at his opponent. The Turk stumbled and the Greek, who seemed to be unarmed, made for the door. The proprietor ran forward shouting. The Turk followed. The Greek turned, just in time, behind another table. Then he dashed.

The Turk cut him off from the door. The proprietor lumbered after them cursing. A table was pulled over; then another. The marble split.

For about three minutes they raced round the café yelling at one another. They were completely oblivious of anyone else and I sat riveted with fright in my chair. Something unpleasant was bound to happen soon. If the Turk got within striking distance he would certainly stab.

The proprietor bellowed at the men at the door to do something. They did. As if by unanimous impulse, at one stride they were all out of the door. The proprietor went after the Turk. Now they were up in one corner and the Greek was hemmed in.

Very slowly, crouching, breathing heavily, the Turk approached. The Greek watched. His eyes switched from side to side measuring the distances. At any second they would be at grips. Suddenly it was quite silent. The music had stopped. A man was speaking on the wireless. There were just the two men watching one another and the bulky figure of the proprietor tiptoeing to get near the Turk. He carried a lump off one of the marble-topped tables. Everything was poised in a strong but delicate balance. The spring was drawn. It was like the first pressure on a trigger.

Painfully the proprietor edged himself forward clutching the marble. It was like grandmother's steps. The Greek watched for the move.

Suddenly the Turk sensed the silence and looked over his shoulder. The proprietor was upon him. He sprang to one side but the marble was well aimed. The chunk struck him full on the temple. He reeled and fell. The knife glittered downwards and stuck in the floor, quivering. I breathed again and the Greek stepped forward trying to control his gasps.

'He accused me of cheating,' he said.

'I know,' said the proprietor, wiping his neck again and brushing away a fly. 'Were you?'

There was a pause. Then the proprietor, the pent fire and emotion of five minutes exploding into speech, almost shrieked at him, 'Were you?'

Very quietly, with a slight shrug, the Greek answered, 'Yes.'

The proprietor heaved, opened his mouth, changed his mind and then said sharply, 'Get out before the police come.' The Greek went quickly and the proprietor knelt beside the Turk and shook his head. The music came on again. I looked down. 'Middlesex won the toss . . .' It was difficult to read and my hand shook badly when I raised the cooled glass of tea.

★

It seemed an opportune moment to leave also. As I went the Turk came round greatly-sobered.

I strolled northwards and passed two immaculate naval sentries in white who stood erect at the gates of the Arsenal. I wondered if there was anything worth guarding. I bore away to the right, leaving the Jewish suburb of Hasköy and up into the Hebrew golgotha.

The winding track rose steeply. A man on a laden donkey passed. It is easy to feel sorry for donkeys—poor, wretched, abused creatures. As Chesterton put it: 'The tattered outlaw of the earth.' And I thought then how appropriate, what a splendid gesture it was, that Christ should ride upon one.

> Fools! For I also had my hour;
> One far fierce hour and sweet:
> There was a shout about my ears,
> And palms before my feet.

Then came a peasant woman in black; then a lurcher out on the prowl. Soon I had got quite high and from the eminence, as far as I could see, and further, unfolded the graveyards. The brown, arid land stretched away, littered with gravestones, higgled and piggled, at all angles, like almonds stuck in a coffee-coloured mousse, like white posts, like old teeth, the ground was sown with marble monuments and solid, pentagonal, coffin-shaped sarcophagi ornamented with sculpted flowers and inscriptions. Here and there was a shack and the occasional cypress and shrub. Away to the left were the flanks of Hasköy and to the right the Okmeidan (the Place of Arrows): in the past an assembly-point in times of pestilence and earthquake, but better known as a site where the Sultans used to practise shooting with the bow and throwing the spear. Mehmet II is supposed to have taken the statues from St Sophia and set them up there as targets, marble brethren of St Sebastian. In Evliya Efendi's day in the seventeenth century there were springs of clear water and clumps of plane-trees. Further away to the right there is a small mosque, Piyalepaşa, in a declivity where there used to be a Dervish monastery. Craftsmen assembled there for feasts at kitchens which possessed three thousand brass plates. Near by there was a walk where the rose-bushes were the size of apricot-trees and bore finer roses than any in the whole of Arabia and Persia.

I walked northwards for some three miles, getting more and more thirsty. A strong, hot wind blew all the time and the sun was fiercer than ever. Hot winds have marvellous names: sirocco, simoom, samiel, harmattan; and in their syllables the fervid sufflations of fever and exhaustion. In the distance the fine tracery of wireless masts ascended from a clump of huts. They rose like the spindly forms of one of Dali's surrealisms. In such torrid wildernesses temptations materialize among the mind's cliffs and abysses. Hallucinations of ease and luxury gather body. Fortunately you do not have to be a fasting saint macerating the rebellious flesh to think of courtyards and fountains and grapes, iced sherbet and delicious women. Every hour we can give inhibition and desire a holiday and relax among forbidden visions. In the Middle Ages empty and sterile places were appropriately the abode of demons. Nature was supposed to abhor a vacuum and they were always seeking a desert, or a human heart. They might even lodge in a grain of salt. Once a nun swallowed a fiend in a lettuce. St Cyprian found one in a flower. Nowadays they are not so obvious.

Soon I came upon barbed wire—symbol of this century. So many have looked through it aligned in the sights of machine-guns. So many have hung, sieved, on its steel thorns; the lipless skulls have grinned aimlessly over the desolated lands and the wind has shaken and nudged the uniformed skeletons strung like vermin in a game-keeper's larder. Contemporary Mexican painters, and artists such as Sutherland, have managed to communicate wonderfully, if with terrible immediacy, the hinterland of suffering which lies beyond the scourge of barb and thorn. The Crown of Thorns has become a crown of barbed wire.

Eventually, very tired and parched to the point of exasperated anger, I dropped down again towards the Golden Horn, where Hasköy rambles to an indeterminate end, through uneven cratered streets where shacks and new houses and small blocks of flats are dispersed without design. I bought a small water-melon and sat under a fig-tree outside a shanty. It was cooler. Music wailed once again. Children were coming out to play. Skeins of shearwater flew up and down: beautiful, swift black and white birds that skim un-deviatingly at the very surface, their slim legs just cleaving the water. They are pelagic birds and have the curious but prudent habit of laying their single white egg in a hole underground. When young they are clothed in very long down and are fat and succulent; excel-lent to eat in this condition I am told. In the Dardanelles, the Marmara and the Bosphorus there are thousands of them hastening to and fro at a tremendous pace. Their apparent inability to desist makes them seem as if they are in constant and urgent quest and so they are believed to be the souls of the damned.

Never was a water-melon more delicious. Its ice-cold, pink, crisp flesh transformed my whole outlook. I munched and slobbered, bury-ing my teeth to the rind. There is pleasure in gnawing to the very rind. It was so fresh and brittle that it was like devouring a sweet iced meringue. Afterwards I felt in a more amiable state to consider what was before me. It is sad that the body's chemistry is so demand-ing. The most amicable diabetic in the world becomes intolerable when his sugar is overdue.

I whittled away an hour picking out landmarks, minarets, churches, walls, the courses of unseen streets. The sun declined. The flies began to accumulate on the husks of melon. I tried to capture exactly the effect of the sun on the disturbed water. In the valleys it seemed to lie in concave scoops and little gold dishes and then ignite in bubbles and globules of gold on the crests, winking once and winkled out; repetitive and elusive.

There are two explanations for the title of 'Golden Horn', one economic and one aesthetic. Because it was a fine and safe harbour and because so many fish were driven into it and caught in it and because so much money was gained thereby it proved a source of gold. On the other hand, sometimes, when the sun is occident, its beams gild the whole expanse. These facts apart, it is one of the most remarkable waterways in the world: a great hooked prong driven inland for seven miles and splintering at the end. Strabo, the geographer, writing near the time of the birth of Christ, described it thus: 'The Horn, which is close to the walls of the Byzantines, is a gulf that extends towards the west for a distance of sixty stadia; it resembles a stag's horn, for it is split into numerous gulfs—branches, as it were.'[2] Gibbon prefers, almost as accurately, to picture it as being curved like the horn of an ox. The Turks, quite inaccurately, call it the *Haliç*—the canal. But these are minor points. It is deep and beautiful and can refuge many ships. It is also the recipient of a quite gigantic amount of refuse and sewage.

It was into the water, very near to where I was sitting, that the navy of Mehmet II slid finally after being transported overland from the Bosphorus. The entrance to the Horn was sealed off by a boom, so the Sultan assembled his ships at Beşiktaş. Seventy or eighty of them were then dragged on rollers through the valleys behind Galata and Pera. It was an astounding feat, concluded at night, so that the besieged awoke on a May morning in 1453 and found the enemy floating right under their noses in their supposedly invincible port. I once saw a painting of this exploit in the Dolmabahçe Palace. The scene, as depicted by a competent nineteenth-century war painter, was very reminiscent of one of those battles in pre-war tattoos at Aldershot.

The Horn tapers gradually until it reaches the Sweet Waters of Europe which, like its Asian sister, was a favourite resort for promenade and excursions for many years. On Fridays the Turks and Muslims used it and on Sundays the Christians. Until a hundred and fifty years ago the shores on both sides were adorned by an almost unbroken succession of palaces and gardens. The slopes were rich with plane, cypress and willow; orchards were loaded with peaches, apricots and pomegranates. And at the Sweet Waters themselves there were shady meadows and streams crossed by rustic bridges, and *kiosques* and a royal palace.

And there were gardens bright with sinuous rills,
Where blossomed many an incense-bearing tree;
And here were forests ancient as the hills,
Enfolding sunny spots of greenery.

Docks, barracks, oil-tanks and wharves have replaced the palaces and gardens on the shores but at Kagilhaneköy, the village at the Sweet Waters, we can still recapture the languorous afternoons of an ancient ease.

Among the summer-houses and pavilions the Sultan's horses were put out to grass in the spring. People bathed in the streams. Poets celebrated the beauties of the glades famous all over the Near East. Hundreds of herons built their nests among the giant plane-trees and nightingales sang unceasingly, their nocturnes transmuting to aubades.

Musing sadly about these decays, I heard myself addressed—'Efendim'. It is a pleasant title, as pleasing as *signor, sahib* and *mijnheer*, or something remote like *hospodar* or *sagamore*; much more pleasing than 'mister' or *monsieur* or 'comrade', or just plain 'mate' or 'mucker' or 'Jack'. I have never got quite used to 'efendim'. 'Mister' is hardly ever used now except by urchins, and we have to say 'Excuse me' or 'I say'. 'Sir' people take to be servile or old-fashioned or pretentious. This is a pity, and 'madam' is following it out. If you so address a lady under fifty when offering her gloves or a seat she tends to look surprised and if she does not think you are trying to be funny probably assumes that you work in a shop. If young she may even think you are trying to antiquate her, and 'miss' never sounds quite right.

'Efendim', then, it was. A pair of flawless orange and white shoes were followed by a knife-edged pair of electric-blue slacks and an immaculate cream shirt. Above, a battery of white and gold teeth flashed beneath a jet moustache.

'What are you doing?' he said.

'Thinking.'

I find this a useful answer for putting people off.

'I like to think as well,' he said. This is a firm move and the correct pawn. It is an ambiguous if friendly gesture. People who like thinking do not usually interrupt those who are. Conversations at two heights are awkward so I stood up. He began to descend. We both rose again in unison. His fine brown eyes smiled reassuringly—the junior executive of his teeth. I felt I was caught.

'Istanbul is a very beautiful city,' he said, and caressed the sky-line with his finger-tips. I gladly and honestly agreed. He apologized for disturbing me and we negotiated the next round of formalities. He was easy and charming. Turks have excellent manners. I wondered what he was. It is not very easy to guess in the summer when seventy per cent of the men wear corespondent shoes in various pie-bald combinations, royal or pale or cornflower or Prussian blue trousers and white shirts.

We walked back along the Horn chatting. He was, to my surprise, a circus trainer; but also a variety artist, singer, trumpeter, acrobat and so on. I asked him if he were a Muslim and he thought this very amusing and performed there and then to my considerable embarrassment a rather profane pantomime of praying.

It so happened that he belonged to that age-group that grew up under the regime of Kemal Atatürk and it is now noticeable that the young and the old or late middle-aged are the most religious. The practice of religion is gradually returning.

As a result of the separation of Church and State under the republican scheme the *medreses* that gave training for Muslim ministers were closed in 1924 and religious instruction for pupils in lay schools was abolished. In the last ten years colleges for training ministers and for the instruction of pupils have been reintroduced and increased and there is even a Faculty of Divinity at Ankara University.

His caricature of prayer startled me for such demonstrativeness is fairly rare in my brief experience. On the whole, Turks are rather grave, a gravity which many mistake for moroseness and unfriendliness. This is not so. Closely allied with their gravity is a very natural and impressive dignity.

As Turks go, Abdül was volatile and flippant. He had travelled about the world and had a remarkable fund of stories on lion and elephant catching. Time and art had fashioned some of them into collectors' pieces.

We walked back through Hasköy to Tersane where there was once a paradisial garden adorned, according to Evliya, with *kiosques* and stone seats and twelve thousand different kinds of trees. In the Sultan's pavilion they ate matchless oysters washed down with wine. Evliya adds a warning here that oysters taken in the Arsenal gardens without wine are a powerful aphrodisiac. It is extraordinary how diligent man has been in the discovery of aphrodisiacs. Chopped tiger-whiskers is another recipe and I remember once finding at the H.Q. Mess of the Royal Hampshire Regiment numerous tiger-skins and heads on the noses of which not a single whisker remained.

The boat-houses where the imperial barges with their jewelled canopies were kept are still used as wharves. They were unloading charcoal and fruit and timber. Towards the end of the nineteenth century a British naval school was established here but it was not a great success. It cost too much to build ironclads and when built they were never used and their decks were turned into vegetable gardens.

Eventually we reached a café where I was to be shown off as the latest capture. One drink after another was put before me. Relays of food appeared with dreadful regularity. It was very typical Turkish hospitality. They take a great pleasure and pride in entertaining and very often a competition develops. You have only to mention a dish and it is summoned for trial. It is impossible (and rude) to buy things in return.

I became fuller and tighter, lost badly at whist and backgammon, defeated them in an argument about the Koran, sang some Irish songs and, Celtic abandonment conquering Saxon decorum, swore allegiance with the peoples of Islam. Abdul did an acrobatic stunt with some chairs and this was followed by a cockroach race over twenty feet.

The cockroach, which most people find so repulsive, is really, as Fabre pointed out, quite a pleasant creature—but obstinate. Shining magnificently in their black armour, their antennae wavering uncertainly, they were coaxed into starting positions. There were a dozen runners with a man on his hands and knees behind each one. Once they were going they moved at a great pace.

It was like being in Dublin again. The drinks came—green, amber and red: crème de menthe, beer and wine; then *raki* to complete the demolition. I had not drunk so much for months. I felt the years fall away, dissolve, with each new drink. Good resolutions, the doctor's advice, the minatory nibbling of an ulcer, the occasional stammer in the heart—all the obstructions of restraint and good sense and self-abnegation dispersed.

As the cockroaches were returned to the gutter I remembered that I had, the next morning, to go and see some newly revealed mosaics, but even as I remembered it I knew it would not be an appointment that I would be able to keep.

Finally, so I was assured a week later, I attempted at their behest
to teach them the rudiments of cricket in the café, which was cleared
for the purpose, and promised very foolishly to turn out for the local
soccer team the following Saturday. It was a memorable evening—in
so far as it could be remembered. Long before, in 1571, Ouloudji Ali
took refuge in the harbour of Tersane with the remains of his fleet
which had been defeated by John of Austria at Lepanto—that battle
in which Cervantes lost an arm. Afterwards, the Sultan, Selim II,
lay prostrate on the ground for three days and would not eat anything. I lay prostrate for one day and could not eat anything.

★

Great walls, like great roads, are two of the stock signs of empires.
The walls of Stamboul on the Golden Horn side were set back a little
way from the water's edge and were built half-way through the
ninth century by Theophilus. They were about thirty feet high and
were fortified by one hundred and ten towers and were passable by
a large number of gates. Now very little of them survives and nothing at all eastwards from the Ponte Gazi. What remains has been incorporated in the course of many centuries into various buildings,
warehouses and wharfs.

When new, fine walls impress. When decayed, they depress. They
reflect more than most ruins the utter futility of trying to keep things
out. We have now learnt that in war most kinds of defensive wall
are virtually useless, but so long as we consider the usefulness of
things in terms of warfare their inutility is axiomatic. The failure of
the Maginot Line is a classical example of how dangerous a wall can
be, how it leads to a trust in something which is by its very nature
full of fallibility. We can still wonder at Hadrian's defence and at
the Great Wall of China so long as we forget the cost in human life
of building them. But they were, after all, very unsuccessful. It satis-
fies a primitive instinct to build a wall. It pleases the pride of those
who order it and rule behind it. But the ultimate effect of nearly all
defensive walls, all forms of frontier, is merely to create an incentive
to get past them. The frontier has long since been proved to be quite
useless, a ridiculous and expensive superficiality—and a harmful one
at that. The only things that really need a wall are buildings, mountain roads, the sea coast, fruit and nuns. Otherwise it is better on the
whole that people should be able to see that nothing is concealed

from them; or, where something is dangerous, what it is. It is very difficult to resist looking over a wall or through it.

The history of the evolution of nations takes us from the small, primitive, exclusive and endogamous group to the large, civilized, inclusive, exogamous group. During the last century this process received a severe setback. The prophets of nations each claimed that their own was to be the leader and artificer of a new and nobler order. 'The sole idea now fruitful and powerful in Europe', wrote Mazzini, 'is the idea of national liberty.' Italy, of course, was to be the home of liberty. *Ma patrie, ma patrie peut seule sauver le monde,* wrote Michelet fourteen years later. Every nation was exalted above the others. A century later it is easy to see how presumption masquerades as hope and conviction. The process of self-destruction has gone on almost continuously in this time. How extraordinary therefore is it to find an historian so eminent as Sir Lewis Namier writing that 'Freedom is safest in the self-contained community with territorial nationality; and where this has not by some miracle or the grace of God grown up spontaneously, it might perhaps be best secured by a transfer of populations.'

Here, in a sentence and with a noteworthy reference to the miraculous and the grace of God, we have a negation of the whole point of Christianity and an apparent disregard for the efforts of the Hitlers of this world. But nationalism is one of the most irrational of impulses. Sir Arthur Keith, in that remarkable book *A New Theory of Evolution,* concludes gloomily that within the limited period of the next few centuries, nationalism will grow ever stronger. He feels that the desire and need for it is so instinctive, so deeply founded that the process will not cease 'until every nation is integrated into a unity such as was met with in the evolutionary units of primal humanity'. But how can such a process ever 'cease'? It is continually regressive. Those units having been reached, the reverse process starts. The choice appears to lie between destruction and survival. If we follow Namier and justify Keith we embrace ruin. Fortunately there is a stronger impulse than nationalism—sex love; and one almost as strong—religious belief.

The efforts of the architects of the nobler order in the nineteenth century, apart from resulting in a series of unparalleled wars, have helped to separate the world's forces into roughly two groups with a number of peripheral neutrals and ditherers. The three principal ideas and systems now regulating peoples, the three dynamic and proselytizing ideas and systems, are Communism, Democracy and Catholicism. Only the third of these at the moment enjoys universality and is at the moment strongest indeed where it is in a minority and where it is persecuted. It seems possible that this strength and universality, aided by inter-racial marriage, by easier communication as the result of more languages being learnt by more people and by the common need to solve the problem of economic survival, might, perhaps, in the course of two hundred years breed out, dilute as it were, foolish and irrational feelings like patriotism and nationalism. After all, 'The nations', as it is put in Isaiah, 'are as a drop of a bucket, and are counted as the small dust of the balance: behold, he taketh up the isles as a very little thing.'

One evening I heard a programme on the Turkish radio in which people were invited to spit on the map of Britain and I heard people spitting on, or pretending to spit on, the map of Britain. Perhaps there was no map. Perhaps they were just spitting on the floor. Childish though this kind of thing is, it is the product of nationalism. In other countries I have been spat on personally, had stones thrown at me, been gibed at and pointed at by children, been refused at hotels. Once, in a Near Eastern town it took me nearly six hours to find a bed for the night and I tried more than forty hotels before a police officer insisted on giving me his bed for the night while he slept out on the balcony. On another occasion it took me four and a half hours to obtain a room and then it was only achieved through the good offices of a friend. These were minor expressions of nationalism. I happened to be English and the people of the country had been told by their leaders to dislike the English. All these incidents were humbling and salutary. It was a most useful lesson to have learnt.

From the stockade to the fort, from the castle to the walled town, from a series of walled towns to a series of defended frontiers, the microcosm splitting and expanding, splitting and expanding—this process seems to me to have been beneficial and it has meant, in theory, that it has become increasingly difficult to control large numbers of people when they are dispersed over wide areas. But there is the radio. Whenever there is a revolt in the city the first thing the rebels try to do is to capture the radio-station. The radio and the newspaper and, to a certain extent, the television are now the most influential media for the corruption of people's minds. Large concentrations of people in relatively small areas, in other words in big towns, are the most pliable material for mass manipulation and propaganda. The greater the concentration the quicker the herd instinct operates. The individual becomes anonymous in large cities, the mass is the refuge of the rootless. Small, dispersed and rural groups are much less dangerous, but to advocate this leads once again to a multiplication of microcosms which result in greater divisions and separateness. On the other hand local and rural chauvinism is less harmful than national and urban. A world government might eventually modify and break up the large cities, the great bulk of most of which serves no useful purpose, might disperse the huge concentrations of manpower, prevent the peril of herd emotionalism, weaken by separation under an overall unity and eventually show that liberty and nationality are not concordant ideas.

Already, in this century, as M. Camus has pointed out, over seventy million people have been uprooted, enslaved or killed. This is a huge bill of blood and suffering. Either we go on adding to it by following the course of hatred or not loving or we begin at the lowest level, in the smallest unit, to prevent division by any compromise which will ensure the development of unity. Compromise between heads of states will produce nothing. But, after all, Chaucer was lamenting the same situation five and a half centuries ago, in the ballad of *Lak of Stedfastnesse*. At one time, he complains, the world was so steadfast and stable that a man's word was an obligation but now it is so 'fals and deceivable' that word and deed in the end bear no resemblance to each other. A man, he asserts, is regarded as incompetent unless by some conspiracy, some dishonesty, he can 'don his neighbour wrong and oppressioun'. All is lost, he cries, for lack of steadfastness:

> Trouthe is put doun, resoun is holden fable;
> Vertu hath now no dominacioun;
> Pitee exyled, no man is merciable;
> Through covetyse is blent discrecioun.
> The world hath mad a permutacioun
> Fro right to wrong, fro trouthe to fikelnesse,
> That al is lost for lak of stedfastnesse.

Poor Chaucer! How many requiem ballads would he sing today? As I wound my way through the dusty, grey cobbled streets and the decaying buildings and the gaunt warehouses along the shores of the Horn and saw here and there the pathetic stumps of walls, I was looking at the monument to the fall of a city and a civilization and an empire five hundred years ago. It was the 'God-defended city', firmly believed to be invincible. They really thought that God would defend it—but not with a wall.

★

I was hardly aware of leaving the city through the furthest gate in the western corner. Quite casually I realized that I had. The winding cobbled street shaded by huge plane-trees reminded me of a Provençal town. It was something in the atmosphere as well. I walked flanked by decaying buildings at the sides and backs of which the tombstones of the great cemeteries pressed in chaotic and overgrown disarray. Above them, the cypresses, dark and steely blue, imposed some order. A strong north-easterly wind broke on the great combers of the planes.

A mile's walk brought me to Eyüp and the sacred precinct. At some distance the chink and ring of stone-masons' tools revealed its locality. Then the mosque itself came into view: an elegant building of white marble with a large dome and several small and semi-domes. Two minarets guarded it. They were encased with scaffolding and looked very like intercontinental rockets in their gantries ready for launching.

There was little traffic about. Two lorries loaded with white and yellow melons rocked past; three horses and carts; a couple of donkeys, one weighted with grape-filled panniers, the other ridden very slowly by a wizened old Kurd in a sheepskin jacket and homemade, woollen breeches. His bare feet hung down to within a few inches of the ground.

I passed through a small village square. A particularly discordant wireless blared from one of the cafés and a throaty voice warbled and sobbed inconsolably. A man was sousing his head under the fountain. Some boot-blacks sat idle beneath an old green awning. Near them a boy squatted on the pavement grilling corn-cobs on his charcoal brazier. Lazily he extended a thin arm to turn them. It seemed hardly to belong to him. It operated of its own habit. Three women went by in file, their black dresses fluttering like nuns' robes. Each one had an arm up balancing a basket on her head.

The mosque is surrounded by the smaller humps of tombs and the remains of a school, a *medrese* and a kitchen. A number of storks had built their nests, loose faggots of sticks, on the flat edges of the domes. Two or three of these beautiful birds stood by them, elongated and academic, meditating on the activity about and beneath them. The stork, like the heron, is a most pedantic bird. Looking at them I was reminded of the pillar saints—the Stylites.

It was near here one quiet, hot day in late August that I became aware of a curious noise: a strange whispering, the distant sound of a multitude. At length I thought of looking upwards and there, spread across the sky, a huge canopy flecked black and white, at a great height, there were thousands upon thousands of storks. They were flying south-east.

They come up to the north in the spring and return in the early autumn, but before the return the adult birds make a reconnaissance flight to ensure that their passage is free from predatory birds, for they have great battles with eagles and hawks. It was the reconnaissance flight that I saw. After it they come back to collect their young.

In his *Natural History* Pliny tells us that there were vast plains in Asia called Pythonostome where storks assembled. 'They keep up a gabbling noise,' he wrote, 'and tear to pieces the one that happens to arrive last; after which they take their departure.' He goes on to mention that they were never seen after the ides of August. It used to be held that the stork had no tongue and they were so prized for their skill in destroying snakes that in Thessaly it was a capital crime for anyone to kill a stork.[3]

It is a curious fact that Eyüp appears to be the only part of the city where the storks nest and it is Evliya Efendi, the seventeenth-century traveller, who provides the explanation for this. At one time one of the many talismans in the city bore the figure of a stork and once a year, when it uttered a cry, all the storks which had built their nests in the city died instantly. 'To this time,' Evliya goes on, 'not a stork can come and build its nest within the walls of the city—though there are plenty of them in the suburbs of Eyüp.'[4] Plainly it was a more successful talisman than those against the flies and the gnats.

The mosque takes its name from Eyüp Ensari, the standard-bearer and companion in arms of the Prophet. He was killed during the first siege of Constantinople by the Arabs in 670. His tomb is said to have been revealed in a dream to the famous Mollah Akşemsedin during a crisis of the final siege of 1453. Its discovery is said to have revived the flagging energy of the Turkish host. At any rate, after the capture of the city, Mehmet II built the mosque in order to harbour the bones. The whole place used to be held so sacred that no Christian was allowed to live in the neighbourhood. Previous travellers have recorded the hostile reception they received when they approached. As Grosvenor put it rather harshly: '... all the mouldering fanaticism of the Ottoman has concentrated here as in its desperate last asylum.' Now it is otherwise.

Evliya Efendi says that when 'The Conqueror' was laying siege to Constantinople he spent a whole week assisted by his seven saintly companions looking for Eyüp's grave and when Akşemsedin found it he cried aloud: 'Good news, my prince, of Eyüp's tomb.' Then he began to pray and fell into a trance. Some interpreted his trance as a subterfuge to cover his discomfort at not finding the tomb. But he pulled round and, with bloodshot eyes, swore that the grave lay beneath his prayer carpet. Whereupon the whole gathering, including the Sheik and the Sultan and his suite, began to dig as hard as they could and nine feet down they found a square slab of verde antique which proclaimed it to be indeed Eyüp's tomb. Beneath this they found the body wrapped in a saffron-coloured shroud and holding a play-ball in his well-preserved hand. There and then, having replaced the stone, they laid the foundation of the mausoleum.[5]

A fine courtyard, shaded by three enormous plane-trees, lies before the mosque. Here is a fountain for ablutions and the most sacred tomb of all. It is faced with a faïence of blue tiles.

I peered in at it through a small window and this is as near as any layman, as it were, can get to anything so sanctified. They have become very tolerant about this in recent years as they have about a great many things.

Within all was dim and mysterious. It was like looking into an aquarium tank. A magnificent chamber of blue tiles enclosed a shrine encrusted with gold. Rich lamps hung from the ceiling, and ostrich-eggs—symbolic of patience and faith.

All about in the courtyard thousands upon thousands of pigeons covered the ground. They were so numerous that large areas were completely obscured: a grey pullulation. Pedlars were selling little trays of grain for them. The pigeons sounded as if hundreds of people were all gargling softly together. From time to time several hundreds of them would rise as one bird with a great report of wings, circle and settle again, waddling, becking, warbling.

The trunk of one of the plane-trees was hollow and within it an injured stork, one leg weightily encased in plaster of Paris, prodded tentatively at some raw meat. I believe that an old hermit used to live in it, but there is nothing remarkable about that. The plane-tree has been put to a variety of uses and it has always been of high repute in the East. Xerxes was so struck with the beauty of one in Persia that he ordered it to be adorned with collars and bracelets of gold. The plane was that convivial tree under which Socrates and Cicero liked to sit, and Pliny says that one of his friends actually entertained a party of twenty-two people to supper in the trunk of one.

Dozens of cats and an American and his wife so laden with cinematic equipment that they looked like a mobile film unit completed the scene. I noticed one kitten—a poor ailing beast with a body about five inches long and a head the size of a tea-cup. Its pathetic ears stuck out ludicrously and its large eyes, which reflected its fear and the bewilderment of being powerless to survive, were already misting with the film of death. It crept away to be by itself and miaowed inconsolably and unheeded. Death is familiar enough but there was something about that wretched and defenceless creature which made it particularly painful. Even as I looked at it, wondering what I could do and knowing that I could do nothing, it keeled over, wailed minutely and began to expire. I was reminded of that splendid poem by Richard Wilbur—*The Death of a Toad*. The toad, unlike the cat, has always been regarded as an ugly creature, loathed and condemned. Perhaps it has never lost its medieval stigma of being a regular harbourer of demons, not to mention its later alleged function, like that of the cat, as a familiar. Also, of course, the toad, like the salamander, is venomous though passively so. The skin glands, especially those round the neck, secrete a milky fluid to which humans are very susceptible. Eyes and nose are particularly affected, a fact discovered when toads' legs were eaten instead of frogs'. These facts were also known in the Middle Ages which is another reason for the stigma. These things apart, the kitten of Eyüp and the dying toad of Wilbur had much in common. With a leg injured by the power mower he clambers to a final glade:

> He lies
> As still as if he would return to stone,
> And soundlessly attending, dies
> Toward some deep monotone,
>
> Toward misted and ebullient seas
> And cooling shores, toward lost Amphibia's emperies.

Day dwindles, drowning, and at length is gone
In the wide and antique eyes, which still appear
To watch, across the castrate lawn,
The haggard daylight steer.

I looked at the kitten for a long time—until the first fly came.

It was at Eyüp that the Osmanli Sultans were girded with the
sword of Osman, the founder of the dynasty. This ceremony was
performed by the chief of the Mevlevi Dervishes. Many pilgrims used
to go there carrying offerings of amber, incense, aloes, silver and
gold. A good many Muslims still visit it with pious intentions, and
the tourists with cameras.

Here also, for it was an honour to be inhumed near the remains
of the companion of the Prophet, there are constellations of royal
tombs. The mother and two daughters of Selim III lie enclosed by
opulent mother-of-pearl railings, and a son and daughter of Sultan
Abdül Mecit. The bier of the former is adorned by a fez with a
golden tassel. And there are two more children belonging to the
sister of Sultan Abdül Aziz. The mausolea of numerous *Sheiks-ul-
Islam*, Grand Viziers and Chief Eunuchs are scattered about, the
coffins enclosed by gilt railings, clad in coloured arabesques and
decorated with verses from the Koran. Everywhere noble and distinguished bones are garnished with the wealth they could not live
to enjoy. There is also the tomb of the horse of Mehmet II which is
reputed to have the power of curing crippled children.

The bodies were placed two or three feet down in the ground and
with the right side turned towards Mecca. Slabs of marble, open in
the centre and raised, were placed over them. An empty gable-
shaped wooden frame was then put over this. The catafalque was
shrouded by a black or green pall embroidered with gold or silver
thread. Men were distinguished by turbans or fezzes and Sultans
have a spray of heron's feathers in their turbans. The turbans, like
big white knobs, make a startling contrast to the dark green and
deep black palls. The catafalques are invariably surrounded by balus-
trades, usually of cedarwood; and mother-of-pearl is the commonest
inlay. The catafalques are also guarded by large candle-sticks which
bear candles anything up to six feet long. The marble floors are
covered with carpets and from the lofty ceilings hang censers and
rose-water sprinklers encrusted with gems, rich lamps, glass lustres
and ostrich eggs, as in the shrine of Eyüp. On the whole the mausolea

are airy and well-lighted. Sometimes the windows are of stained glass and the walls are hung with inscriptions from the Koran in gold lettering on green or black material. In each of the greater *türbes*, in a silver box, is preserved one of the countless hairs of the Prophet's beard.

Most of the *türbes* are polygonal and in many cases they are octagonal—the eight sides corresponding with the names of Allah, Mohammed and the six *Imams*. The grave of a Sultan or the founder of a mosque is always opposite the door and those of wives and children are arranged about in symmetrical order. The size of the catafalque and the grave is commensurate with the importance of the tenant. Those renowned for their sanctity and their bravery have the largest of all; and of these the most magnificent is that of Mahmut II. Octagonal, of white marble, with seven large windows, it is protected by elaborate iron railings. It is sumptuously furnished with carpets, white silk draperies, glass chandeliers, clocks, armchairs and sofas.

The Muslim reverences the memory of the dead and believes in the efficacy of prayer and in intercession. In days gone by the bushes and foliage about the graves of saints were covered with scraps and rags of clothing which pilgrims had torn from their garments and left there in the belief that the offering would preserve them from sickness and other misfortunes. Occasionally I have still found vestiges of this kind.

Most of the monument stones in the cemeteries are adorned by a fez or a turban like those of the celebrities. The nature of the carved turban reveals the rank of the deceased. When the fez was introduced it was painted scarlet with a blue tassel. The women's steles have a lotus-leaf carved or painted on them. Some graves are covered with marble troughs filled with soil in which to grow flowers, the belief being that their scents are pleasing to the soul when it revisits its tenement. In the city private graves are sometimes covered with wire-trellis cages in which to keep song-birds which bring comfort to the spirit. Both seem to be eminently civilized practices, if a little impractical to those of other faiths.

When Sir Adolphus Slade was in Constantinople he wrote, and quite correctly, that on whatever side you approach the city or its suburbs 'it is through a burial ground; you cannot pass from one quarter to another but through a burial ground; you look out of a window on a burial ground; your only promenades are in the

burial grounds'.⁶ But it must not be thought that the abundance of
tombs and cemeteries is the result of an unhealthy preoccupation
with death and a taste for the macabre on the part of the inhabitants;
not at all. Their attitude towards death is very much healthier than
in most countries. Their acceptance of the inevitable and the will of
God enables them to view death with a degree of equanimity which
is salutary and admirable. The graves of the dead must not be disturbed—this explains the expanse of the yards—and the ever-present
reminders of death in the shapes of its monuments ensure respect
for the departed and prevent graveyards from becoming vales of
tears and the sites of all the lachrymose hypocrisies and rituals which
we meet from place to place and time to time in Christian lands and
among the Jews.

There were numerous plagues and famines, fires and earthquakes
in the city during the period of the Ottoman Empire—as there had
been in the time of Byzantine rule—but these produced no reaction
in the form of 'macabery' and morbidity. Being a great port,
diseases were often carried to it and spread. As it was frequently
besieged and the neighbouring lands devastated, death from hunger
was common. Fires were commonplace, especially during the Turkish
dominion, because so many houses were built of wood. Finally, the
city lies upon a particularly nervous and uneasy portion of the earth's
crust. Let us take a couple of examples from former travellers to
illustrate. While Peter Mundy was there between 1617 and 1620
there 'hapned ... three terrible accidents: a Small earthquake, a
fearfull fire which by report consumed about four thousand houses,
beeing Most small shoppes or boothes of boards; and a Mortell plage
of pestilence, which at the highest consumed above one thousand a
day in that Citty.'⁷ Evliya Efendi thought nothing of such a heavy
loss of life and once remarked laconically that 'Istanbul is so vast a
city that if a thousand die in it, the want of them is not felt in such
an ocean of men.'

Lithgow, who was there a few years earlier, also mentions the
regular earthquakes and refers to one in 1509 in the reign of Beyazit
II when 'more than 13,000 persons were all smothered and dead,
and laid up in heaps unburied'. He goes on to explain how commonly
every third year 'the pestilence is exceeding great in that City, and
after such an odious manner; that those who are infected (before
they die) have the half of their one side rot, and fall away: so that
you may easily discerne the whole intrailes of their bowels'.⁸ A great

many travellers have confirmed the phlegmatic attitude of the Turks towards such holocausts.

But the story is somewhat different in the west of Europe and particularly during certain periods. There is hardly any macabre literature and art surviving from the classical age. Lucian's *Dialogues* and their grim humour—especially the *Dialogue of the Dead*—are exceptions, and it seems generally true that the Near East and the Mediterranean basin are relatively free of this element in art and literature. Spain and Italy can be cited as exceptions but in those lands it was derivative as well as greatly diminished. It is in the north, in France and Germany and the Netherlands particularly, that we find the principal sources and the best and most numerous examples of the macabre.

One of the most depressed periods in the history of Europe, the fifteenth century, is associated with its full flowering. For centuries in medieval literature the frailty of worldly glory was sung to various melodies in which three main motifs may be discerned: the dirge for the great ones of the past, the dreadful spectacle of human beauty in decay, and the dance of death dragging off men and women of all kinds and ages. The first motif was purely elegiac. It was used in Greek poetry, was adopted by the Church Fathers and later pervaded the literature of Christianity and Islam. The transitory nature of life, the vanity of man and human wishes, the inevitability of death and the silence and dust of the grave were celebrated again and again. It is all summed up in that work attributed to St Bernard, *De Contemptu Mundi*:

> Homo miser, cogita: mors omnes compescit.
> Quis est ab initio, qui morti non cessit?
> Quando moriturus est, omnis homo nescit,
> Hic qui vivit hodie, cras forte putrescit.

Gerson made much of the same matter in a sermon; Denis the Carthusian wrote a treatise on the *Four Last Things of Man*; Chastellain wrote a long poem called *Le Pas de la Mort*; and Olivier de la Marche wrote a long lament about all the princesses who had died in his lifetime. Later Deschamps wrote at least four ballads on the same theme; and Villon, in his *Ballade des Dames du Temps Jadis* and the *Ballad of the Lords*, expressed it most finely of all. The equality of everyone before death was repeated again and again. Centuries

earlier Horace had stressed the matter in his first Ode in a now
famous passage:

> Pallida Mors aequo pulsat pede pauperum tabernas
> Regumque turres.

But elegies, catalogues, and dirges of *ubi sunt?* were not enough.
Towards the end of the fourteenth century the conception of death
in art and literature acquired new shapes—spectral and fantastic;
and interest in it achieved its most remarkable expression in the
Dance of Death—the central motif of the macabre: the philosophical
base and ideas of which had been long prepared. The increased
interest in and desire for the concrete, for worms, putrefaction and
horrors, coincided with that desperate age when, as one writer put
it, people came to regard skeletons as 'an integral part of the landscape' and lived on intimate terms with the horrible. The end of
the world which had been forecast at regular intervals for fourteen
centuries was once again predicted by St Vincent de Ferrer.

The great works were Holbein's engravings and the pictures and
verses in the cloisters of the church of the Holy Innocents in Paris.
The Death of the woodcuts of Holbein is too familiar to dwell upon.
Less well known is the Holy Innocents, a remarkable place where
people could take their fill of the macabre. Skulls and bones were
heaped up in the charnel-houses along the cloisters and lay there
'preaching the lesson of equality'. Beneath the cloisters the paintings
showed the simian figure of Death smiling sardonically as it dragged
off its victims. The Innocents was a popular place and amidst the
constant burials and exhumations people shopped, feasts were celebrated, friars preached and prostitutes plied their trade.

It was from these paintings as well as from the work of Holbein
that a great impulse to the macabre spread throughout Europe and
materialized in countless imitations and adaptations. It flourished
until well on into the seventeenth century and then lapsed until the
great recrudescence of the nineteenth.

It was in Istanbul that I once found a splendid example to illustrate the nature of macabre. Under a glass case in the Museum of
Antiquities, not far from the exquisite marble sarcophagus of Alexander the Great, lie the mortal remnants of King Tobit of Sidon.
He was quite a small man, slimly built. Some membranes and flanges
of withered flesh and strings of wiry sinew still adhere to him. Half
of the shining skull is covered by a pelt of dark copper-coloured

hair. It has survived in such a manner that it lies at a rakish angle, like a skull-cap set awry, tilted forward slightly. Beneath, the sockets stare, as they have stared for two and a half thousand years; and beneath them the lipless teeth are exposed in a boisterous laugh. Tobit's appearance is without doubt humorous. Perhaps, if the hair did not look like a skull-cap at an incongruous and tipsy angle, he would look less so. As it is, supine, dead and jocular, he looks perpetually macabre.

That beautiful word 'Islam' means obedience and submission, and it would be alien, I believe, to the spirit of the religion to associate mockery with death. On the other hand the European and Christian attitude has sought to minimize and disperse its horrors by personifying it, by making it grotesque, bizarre, unpredictable, perverse. It seems that the very conjunction of that which is essentially sad, that which is a *memento mori*, and that which, externally at any rate, suggests and implies happiness—as in Tobit's skeleton—helps us to understand why death, in all its liveries, with all its misery, ritual and solemnity, all its atmosphere and traditions and superstitions, is so often a source of an impression or feeling frequently given the name macabre.

I walked back through the miniature necropolis of Eyüp and struck off on a path up the hill-side behind. The ground rose steeply to a brow upon which lies a café made famous by that rather boring poseur Pierre Loti, and named after him. All these low hills and the brown marcid land which lies about and beneath them compose one enormous cemetery, dozens of acres of it, where generations upon generations of Istamboulis lie in 'cold obstruction' and rot. It is not as big as the one on the Asian side but even so it is one of the biggest cemeteries in the world.

The hot blustering wind eased and dropped and I could hear more clearly the shrill philharmonical outpourings of the cicadas. Dismembered by ants when dead, the prey of the fly parasite, the victim of a fungus disease, and the quarry of grasshoppers, birds, cats, dragonflies, beetles and, most dangerous of all, the hunting wasp, the cicada is one of the most luckless creatures. I never hear them without thinking of the hunting wasp, that most efficient pirate that paralyses its victim, carries it to its nest, attaches an egg to the underside of it, seals off the nest and departs. The larva of the wasp when it hatches is thus provided with an abundance of anaesthetized but fresh meat. Having devoured the flesh the grub spins its cocoon in the husk of the cicada's body and sleeps its long winter slumber. What economy there is in this, what repulsive competence. Even man has never contrived anything quite as neat as this. But there is no getting away from it, the cicada is a sucker. Even the gnat is able to get the better of it by laying its eggs in those of the miserable creature. In its larval state it spends most of its life beneath the ground and there is one kind that passes as many as seventeen years under the soil. And after all this its only purpose is to sing for a few weeks—and then be butchered. In fact its whole enormous body is a sounding-board. We may be indifferent to these sad marvels, but it has had its admirers. They were esteemed by the Greeks who kept them in cages, as do the Chinese. But their greatest praiser was Muffet, the sixteenth-century naturalist. 'There is none', he wrote, 'to whom their Musick can seem harsh and unpleasant but is either not well at ease in his minde or his body, and so can be no competent judge of musical strains.'

At Eyüp their reiterative dirge went on. I reached the crown of the hill and looked back. Below lay Eyüp: bulky volumes of black and dark green splashed and pierced with white. The tap and ring of steel on stone drifted to me faintly. Beyond lay the great arm of the Golden Horn, which curved and swung away to my left, and the whole expanse of the city. Wordsworth would have made something of this view—a pendant to the sonnet on Westminster Bridge. Never did sun more beautifully steep. The Horn was pale cyanine, the city a great conurbation of buff, grey and white, a patched plaid reaching in folds to the blue water. The Atatürk Bridge and the Galata Bridge looked like two slim centipedes joining the two halves of it. The city has changed little, from such a vantage point, since Lithgow saw it three hundred and fifty years ago: 'I beheld . . . the Prospect of that little World, the great City of Constantinople; which indeed yeeldeth such an outward splendor to the amazed beholder, of goodly Churches, stately Towers, gallant Steeples, and other such things, whereof now the World make so great accompt, that the whole earth cannot equall it.'[9]

Below I could see the remains of the quay at which the Sultans used to arrive for ceremonial occasions in their gilded barges caparisoned with gold and silk and rowed by twenty-six oarsmen, sometimes by eighty. From one of these the Sultan mounted a horse clad in velvet whose bits were of gem-studded gold.

Some boys were bathing near by, splashing about gaily in the oily, sewage-laden water. Near here also was a popular place for bathing on Fridays, a place which Evliya Efendi described in most curious terms: 'Here the lover and the beloved', he says, 'mingle without restraint, and take delight in embracing each other, swimming in the sea. You fancy you behold the angels of the sea swimming amongst the angels of mankind dressed in blue aprons.'[10]

After a time I walked down the hill again and after a long search found the 'Well of Souls'. If you prayed at this a voice at the bottom answered, telling you where a lost person or thing was to be found. I shouted down into it and my voice came back in a clear, cold echo —*plus ça change ... change ... change.* I dropped a pebble and saw it shatter the pale eye of light at the bottom. The light glanced and shivered in the sudden disturbance. I walked away. I have always had a fear of wells. They are sinister, and it is so easy to fall into them.

NOTES

The references in this book are to those authors who I believe are not very often read. Thus I have omitted references for authors like Gibbon, Horace, Pope, Tennyson, etc.

1. Sir Adolphus Slade, *Travels in Turkey, Greece* etc. 2 vols., London, 1883.

2. Strabo, *Geography.* Loeb Class. Lib., vol. 3.

3. Pliny, *Natural History*, Bk. x, Chap. 31.

4. Evliya Efendi, *Narrative of Travels.* Trans. by J. von Hammer. 2 vols., London, 1834.

5. Ibid.

6. Sir Adolphus Slade, op. cit.

7. Peter Mundy, *Travels.* Hakluyt Society, 2nd Series, vol. 17.

8. Edward Lithgow, *Rare Adventures and Painefull Peregrinations.* London, 1640.

9. Ibid.

10. Evliya Efendi, op. cit.

CHAPTER TWO

The City (I)

FOR indeed outwardly it hath the fairest show, and inwardly in the streets being narrow, and most part covered, the filthiest & deformed buildings in the world; the reason of its beauty, is, because being situate on moderate prospective heights, the universall tectures, a farre off, yeeld a delectable show, the covertures being erected like the backe of a Coach after the Italian fashion with gutterd tyle. But being entred within, there is nothing but a striking deformity, and a loathsome contrived place; without either internal domesticke furniture, or externall decorements of fabricks palatiatly extended. Notwithstanding that for its situation, the delicious wines, & fruits, the temperate climat, the fertile circumjacent fields, and for the Sea Hellespont, and pleasant Asia on the other side: it may truely be called the Paradice of the earth.

EDWARD LITHGOW, *Rare Adventures and Painefull Peregrinations*. London, 1906

I have only been struck by lightning once. A year or two ago I was wheeling a punctured bicycle along a deserted road in Thrace a few miles from Istanbul. It was an arid but quite fruitful 'scape laden with the accumulated heat of many days. The air had become thicker and closer so that I felt that it was compressing itself into space. Each day became more and more inflamed. Soon, but always too late, a day would burst. So it was this day.

I had walked too far. My legs were stiffening, my feet sore. Clammy clothes adhered. The torrid air lay still over the land: land rolling and folded in long lion-coloured swells. Clumps of sunflowers held up their heads with an almost unnatural rigidity. Here and there a cypress stood stiff, like an exclamation mark; black against the yellow and pale-brown grass. In the distance I could see, rising and falling on the horizon, a dusty amber and grey, the great land walls of the city: those that have stood for fifteen centuries. I wondered if I would reach them before the storm broke.

As most people know, lightning can be approximately divided into three categories: fork, sheet and ball. Fork is the commonest; sheet is quite frequent and is only the reflection of a storm; and ball, or globular, is very rare indeed. There are also, for the expert, beaded and streaked.

It has been calculated that there are roughly forty-four million thunder-storms a year round the surface of the earth; which, at the Equator, makes for about one storm per day every five miles. It has also been assessed approximately that more people are killed each year by lightning than by any other natural disturbance: earthquakes, hurricanes, avalanches, etc. It would seem then that the chances of being struck are not inconsiderable, though, of course, the majority of storms and deaths occur in tropical areas. In our colder climates death by lightning is occasional, but by no means uncommon. Thus, I thought myself extraordinarily lucky.

A good deal is known about lightning now, but I still read with a good deal of pleasure the account that Lucretius gave in *De Rerum Natura*: an account based upon sensible observation and interest. 'It is caused', he writes, 'when many seeds of fire have been squeezed out of clouds by their collision. Just as when a stone is struck by stone or steel a light springs out and scatters bright sparks of fire.' He then explains a second way in which 'the clouds bathe the landscape in fleeting brilliance and the lightning is launched on its quivering flight'. When a wind has forced its way into a cloud, he contends, and hollowed and condensed it by eddying round, it is heated by its own movement. 'Everything grows hot with fiery motion', and when it has burst open a murky cloud it scatters seeds of fire pushed out by the force of the explosion. 'These', writes Lucretius, 'cause the zigzag flashes of flame.' In reverberating lines and with fine images he describes the great bulk of thunder-clouds, their caverns overarched by beetling crags. 'When the squally winds have filled these caverns,' he goes on, 'they protest clamorously in their cloudy prison with the roar of caged beasts. This way and that they hurl their menacing growls through the clouds. In search of an outlet they prowl round and round. They dislodge seeds of fire from the clouds and roll together a multitude of them. Soon they are spinning a flame within a hollow furnace, till the cloud bursts and out they tumble in a dazzling flash.'[1]

Some of this, like his treatise on thunderbolts which follows, makes us smile a little today; but, though the secrets are now exposed, lightning and thunder still hold us in awe. It has always seemed to me that there is something particularly magnificent about being struck dead by lightning. It is the kind of exit which should be the prerogative of the great—particularly great malefactors: a fact which the Greeks and Romans understood. Nowadays only imprudent nonentities shuffle off their coils in such a grandiloquent manner: the innocent golfer on the links at the week-end, the labourer trudging home with his tools, the schoolboy on his bicycle. But lightning, in all its terrifying splendour, enhances their demise. There is something bizarre and yet noble in being despatched at a single blow from the sky. It must be the nearest we ever get to Nemesis in the twentieth century; for thousands of people can live through, walk through, stand in, hundreds of storms and remain unscathed. But here and there, capriciously, one is picked out, sniped as it were, cloven and bereft of life at one colossal stroke as if he had received the accolade of an insane seraph.

Pliny, who went into the matter quite thoroughly, tells us that thunder-storms may be compelled or invoked and maintains, surprisingly enough and in the face of all the evidence, that man is the only animal not killed by it. So selective was it that when a lady of high rank in Rome was struck while pregnant it was the foetus that was destroyed, not she. 'All animals', he says, 'fall down on the opposite side to that which has been struck; man, unless he be thrown down on the parts that are struck, does not expire. Those who are struck directly from above sink down immediately. When a man is struck while he is awake, he is found with his eyes closed; when asleep, with them open.'

He is slightly inconsistent about the immunity of man but otherwise his description fitted my own case very adequately. The eagle, the laurel and the seal were the only things never struck in Pliny's day. The eagle was regarded as the bearer of lightning, the laurel was sacred and, according to Suetonius, Augustus—there were many others—always wore a seal-skin to protect himself.[2]

In Thrace, at that time, I knew almost nothing of these things. Until you have actually been struck, lightning is not a subject about which one bothers very much.

Still hoping that I might reach shelter in time I stopped for a brief rest, eased my aching legs and feet. I was annoyed at having gone

so far—and then the puncture. The pleasures of weariness and antici-
pated return were over. I looked back to the north and west. The
clouds had assembled, lofty, banked; the anvil-head growing up over
the blue sky. In the distance slivers of light were dancing and capering
across it. The blades were being forged. Great prongs with innumerable branches plunged downwards like illuminated roots, groping towards the earth. Gradually silence fell. The stridulous concord of the
cicadas diminished. A hawk flew towards the city. Birds went mute.

I pushed on over the pocked track where the white dust lay thick
in miniature dunes. Soon the rolling, withered ground would revive,
the parched grass stir to water.

I began to look for shelter. The silence became heavier, more
insistent. The clouds were moving swiftly now, sinister and certain,
gathering themselves; grey and purple, flecked with white and
scarred with bronze. The hills humped and crouched. The sun went
out suddenly, but still in the distance I could see the long braiding
of gold on the city walls.

Then the thunder spoke for the first time, like the growl of a
marauding beast. The storm had cleared its throat. I felt a little
afraid. I have always been afraid of thunder.

The clouds were racing up behind and over me. The light deep-
ened perceptibly to a sulphurous green, light going down steadily,
dimming. The land changed. The proximity of the storm grew un-
bearable. It was all about and suddenly I felt in the very centre of
it, very isolated and naked. It became quieter, the air and the atmosphere growing taut, delicately strung, a membrane which quivered
every time the thunder grunted. And the small world flinched, waiting for the annunciation of lightning and the roll of drums. There
was no shelter and I stopped and waited, resigned to a soaking.

An abrupt chill wind shuddered the bushes and rasped through
the dying, tawny grass. For a few moments all was poised, like a
great mass balanced on the edge of an abyss.

Then it sprang, the thunder exploded, the lightning sweeping
from its scabbard and ripping open the clouds with a crash like a
splitting mountain and the roar of a falling hill. Two hundred yards
away a tree was cloven as you might split a cane. A hundred yards
nearer there was a detonation in the middle of the road. I seemed to
be in the pupil of the storm, right in the line of a 'stick' of lightning.
I shivered; stood transfixed as the sky quaked. I was sure I was the
next target and there was nothing I could do. Nothing at all.

Suddenly the bicycle and I were united and we shook together. A blue light fizzed and crackled: an aureole which juggled about us for a fractional second. There was a burning smell. Then I felt as if I had been hit by a boulder. The bicycle was wrenched out of my hands.

I was lying on the side of the road when I came round in the pouring rain. My watch had stopped at precisely three o'clock. Nor could I ever make it go again. It was a timeless comment on a narrow escape. The bicycle was bent. It was the rubber handle-grips and my rubber shoes that did the trick.

★

Some time later, still full of wonder at what had happened and feeling very unsteady, my left arm a little numb, I passed beneath the great Adrianople Gate, one of many in the city walls, and that which gives on to the road to Adrianople (the Turkish name is Edirne) two hundred miles away. I took an old apple-green tram down the long, broad, half-cobbled, half-tarmac street, a main thoroughfare which pierces very directly to the very heart of the city. The storm had passed across and was already far over Asia, the rearguard of ragged cloud strewn about a bluer and serener sky.

From the gate the road runs along the spine of the ridge which joins the seven hills. On both sides the ground falls more or less gradually to the Golden Horn on the north and the Sea of Marmara to the south. And from the gate almost to the end of the blunt peninsula which juts into the Bosphorus the city stretches for over three miles, the mass of buildings dominated by a succession, to put it simply, of grey humps and whiter spikes—the mosques.

It was drawing towards evening. The benefaction of rain was drawing out scents, as admiration elicits gentleness and warmth from an ageing woman, as praise exposes the need for kindness and sympathy; scents that had failed, faded away in the persistent pervasions of dust and dry air. Damp cobbles and roofs steamed. A nimbus of vapour clung to the flanks of horses and donkeys. A soft bloom furred masses, and edges were pencilled clear and sharp. The volumes of downy greys and blues were dashed with pale gold of sunlight that seemed newly minted. Manes of cloud were combed out across the western sky, now tinct with rose. It was a tender, pliable evening, and momentarily, by the unexacting indefiniteness, the buxom air, the trams, I was reminded of warm September dusks after rain in Dublin and Delft and Preston.

Coming back into the city like this was similar to a return after a long absence. And it was a pleasant mild shock, navigating slowly through the continuous proliferation of traffic and pedestrians, to see the old genial restaurateur with his craggy face and bulbous nose, perched absurdly on a rickety chair outside his dining-room; his chef's hat as jaunty as ever, his cigarette dangling. He never did any work: occasionally solved a problem or dispersed a crisis, but mostly sat outside and advertised, saluting acquaintances, plucking friends by the sleeve. He claimed a number of customers like that. It seemed a long time since I had been there so I went in. Habit is a good restorer of jarred senses. Busy and industrious, it smooths over the cracks, blocks up the breaches.

I had a *kebab* and some pears in syrup and a bottle of rough wine. I felt gay and irresponsible. Such a thing could never happen again. I told the old restaurateur about it. He listened gravely. 'Yes, of course,' he said, when I had finished, 'lightning is a very dangerous thing. It was lucky you had rubber shoes on.' I suppose I was disappointed, but later I remembered one of La Rochefoucauld's maxims —*Dans l'adversité de nos meilleurs amis, nous trouvons quelque chose qui ne nous déplaît pas.* I was not even one of his best friends and in any case the Muslim's reaction to misfortune is very different from that of other people. Fatalism is no bad thing provided that one can continue to distinguish between accepting with fortitude and giving up through weakness. And at the other extreme tenacity too often turns into sheer stubbornness for the sake of it. Either way, in the end, victory can often be as tasteless as defeat is bitter. If you win, people will find reasons for decrying the achievement, and if you lose they can take a certain pleasure in it, as La Rochefoucauld without, I think, any cynicism but rather with the sharp insight of a man without illusions, points. And in the last analysis, how many people would be welcomed back from the dead? Fortunately we are able to go on thinking that people care for us and, to a certain extent, some do so. But when we die it is just as well, and resurrection always causes complications. It is one of the saddest lessons that we learn, the lesson implicit in much of everyday life, the lesson of the Grand Inquisitor in *The Brothers Karamazov.*

★

From the Seraglio Point and the Column of the Goths to the Marble Tower the sea-walls ran for over six miles. They followed the configurations of the shore and presented wherever possible a direct and short frontage to the Sea of Marmara. They have been repaired and rebuilt countless times in the course of fifteen centuries. There were a hundred and eighty-eight towers and thirteen gates. The strand which lay between them and the sea has now been widened all the way along; and a broad road is being built with a strong sea-wall below it.

Not far from the Gothic Column which rises below the great grey ramparts of the eastern walls of the Seraglio and near to where stood a church dedicated to St Barbara, the patron saint of fortifications, fire-arms and armourers, is the Gate of the Mill. On its northern wall is the following inscription in Greek: 'Possessing Thee, O Christ, a firm wall, King Theophilus, the pious emperor, reared from new foundations this wall, which guard with Thy Might, O Sovereign Ruler, and display to the end of time, standing unshaken and unmoved.' But the supplication has gone unheeded. 'Look on my works, Ye Mighty . . .'

It is true that from here round the long curve of the butt end of the peninsula the walls still remain in a reasonable condition. But from the end of the curve they present a forlorn, a really painful sight. Shattered, collapsed, decayed, they struggle on to the Marble Tower, a long, grey, jagged line of defence, in places completely demolished for several hundreds of yards. They crumble and totter and flake, infinitely old and broken, and pointless and stricken and weary, past all use, past all reclaim.

Time, frost, 'quake, fire, wind, rain, sea, neglect—many, many enemies have corroded and destroyed them. Year by year they grow more desolate. As Shelley put it in *The Revolt of Islam*:

> With hue like that when some great painter dips
> His pencil in the gloom of earthquake and eclipse.

The railway has been driven through them. Houses have been built over them and beneath them and incorporated into them. Windows have been cut in them. Home-made stairways hang on to them. Sewage runs out below them. Refuse flung over has disfigured them. Shacks of tin and wood and cardboard tied and nailed together perch on their parapets. The remnants of some of the towers have been transformed into temporary dwellings in which people have lived for years. Small vegetable gardens grow along their tops. Amidst all their drab, rotting, perilous ramparts hundreds of people live an almost troglodyte existence: the homeless or almost homeless clinging precariously to the disintegrating vestiges of the perimeter of a great city.

Where emperors and empresses dined on marble terraces and Sultans reclined in gilded *kiosques* amidst all the sumptuous luxury of imperial power and wealth, laundry now flaps and men, women and children eke out an exiguous life among garbage and vermin and cockroaches.

On the broadening strand of earth and rubble and boulder which lies between them and the sea other shacks are being erected, and rows and rows of bell-tents provide some shelter for the destitute and for refugees. Istanbul is a city full of exiles: from Albania and Yugoslavia and Bulgaria; from Russia, Armenia and Romania.

They have been going there for nearly half a century, running before revolutions and invasions, escaping from poverty and servitude and oppression, going to a freer land; many of them returning to their own land, many of them descendants of those who had spread over Europe as the great Ottoman empire waxed and expanded.

Once, as I was waiting at dawn for the train to Istanbul to leave from Pythion in the very north of Thrace, a troop of Turkish people who had been expelled from Yugoslavia boarded the coaches. They had nothing but what they carried.

One family was in my compartment: the father a wiry, resilient man and very much the master of his flock; his wife a shell, emaciated, sunken-eyed, dark brown eyes deep in the sockets of her wan wasting face. In black, she crouched in the corner, a beaten, dying woman, the bones of her skeleton pressing through her papery skin. And her terrible eyes would turn and see nothing: defeated, lacklustre, the eyes of the dying and the hopeless and the helpless. She was death—and yet she had given birth to so many.

There were about seven or eight children; the eldest a boy, the apple of his father's eye but half-imbecile; then a daughter, already a withered old woman of sixteen in a rag of a dress. Her nose ran and she coughed and coughed. And then there were all the little ones from about ten to four, like a Giles cartoon incarnate. They had all been dressed somehow, fed somehow, kept alive.

All their possessions were in sacks and old suitcases and cardboard boxes. Soon the smells of earth and poverty filled the compartment.

They were going home. They had been driven out, their land re-
quisitioned. They had nothing really: some hope, a good deal of
courage, self-respect, resource, the best of the human qualities surviving in the endless salvaging of human dignity.

The head of the family kept his brood in order. He talked in a
courteous and dignified manner. He smiled occasionally. He offered
me a cigarette, wanted to know if he could help me in a foreign land.

He already regarded the foreigner as a guest of his country though
he had only just returned to it himself for the first time for forty
years. And therefore, as a guest, I was to be treated with respect
and courtesy and what generosity was available. His cigarette and
his good-will were eloquent.

From time to time his wife would turn her dying eyes, turn her
death-mask beneath the black head-dress, towards him and me and
see nothing. The journey of two hundred miles took twelve hours
and in that time she never spoke.

About half-way along the coast, where the shore juts out, the railway goes inland. Beyond the jut is a large waste area, once known
as the Vegetable Gardens and the site of an ancient port in the time
of Constantine the Great. The vegetable gardens have gone and it
is a port again. There are some wood-yards and many piles of rubble
brought down from demolished houses for building up the coastal road.

One day I paused there as I often needed to in the long walk from
the Seraglio to the Marble Tower. A number of boats were in; just
off-shore. They had brought wood for fuel. Causeways consisting
of single planks nailed to thick posts covered the intervening water.
There was a constant procession of boys and men walking along
them, bent under faggots of wood. Behind, in the wood-yards, the
rasping wail of the power-driven saws went on all day.

There are some places, especially in big cities, where the pulse
throbs low, where the blood of existence, as it were, is thin, as if
the diastole of the distant heart is barely strong enough to reach
them. This ancient port is one of them. Every city has its anal zones,
and this also is one of them.

A ramshackle café had been built up on the uneven, dusty ground.
Paper and garbage lay thick among the tin tables and iron-work
chairs outside. Flies swarmed among the refuse and over the table-
tops. Cats and a dog or two shifted about, senses primed for a titbit.
Some half-amputated elms still wore a thinning rust of leaves. The
second intimation of autumn was in the air.

Workmen were resting: drinking beer and tea and *ayran*—sour milk which comes in little bottles. It is a most delicious and refreshing drink. The men talked of how they would get through the winter, whether or not there would be enough fuel. They were suprisingly cheerful and clean, and the children that were playing about them were likewise. They looked healthy and strong and their skin was good. You would have expected disease.

Away over the city the hawks were wheeling like scraps of charred paper in a wind. One stood high above—a thousand feet perhaps. He floated indolently on the ambient air; turning calmly, leisurely. The serrated wing-tips fluttered for a moment. Then he floated again; dipped, rolled, swung in a long smooth plane. Then stalled and hung again. It was magnificent.

> My heart in hiding
> Stirred for a bird,—the achieve of, the mastery of the thing!

Nothing could have been more soothing, more glorious, in that woebegone sore at the edge of the city. But I had to remember that it was no comfort to the men wondering how they would get through the winter. You have to be reasonably well-fed before you can enjoy the beauties of nature.

Watching the hawk, I recalled once being stuck half-way up a cliff in England on a military exercise. A very long way below I could hear the sea, powerful and sinister, smacking into the rocks and thumping into the caves, and I could see out of the corner of my eye the cliffs running away into the distance like irregular teeth sunk in the grey flesh of the water. The gulls swooped by, dived in fluent curves. Jammed there, paralysed and very afraid, I envied those gulls. I lacked everything.

And I remembered also once at Delphi sitting at the edge of the precipice beneath the village and watching the great white-tailed eagles spiralling on the rising columns of air, rising for two or three thousand feet, turning with extraordinary slowness in long wide curves, not moving their wings at all. Power. Ease. It was unforgettable. And there was the hawk riding above me. Superb. Untrammelled. As I looked he stalled again. The wings buckled, flashed bronze, and he fell humming like a bolt for five hundred feet —then levelling out, gliding again...

I heard a voice calling: 'Mr Cuddon ... Mr Cuddon ... You are back.' I turned, astonished; and there was Metin running towards me. He was as thin and pale as ever. When I first came across him he was the boy of all work in a barber's shop in Sirkeci—a post which he left because of a fight with the owner. He was an independent and determined youth, ambitious, incredibly self-reliant for seventeen, and with the excellent manners of his race. He had the hardiness and resilience which is characteristic of so many Turkish boys and men; characteristics which have always helped them to be splendid soldiers.

Laboriously he was teaching himself English and German and he would grab and adhere to anybody who could speak these tongues. He kept up a copious correspondence by postcard with English-speaking people all over Europe. I was relieved to find that in a year he had made great progress and I no longer had to endure absurd interrogations about Manchester United and Aston Villa (I wonder if some of our professional footballers realize how famous they are?) and Churchill and 'Lawndawn'.

His father was an engineer and he lived with numerous brothers and sisters in a large wooden house the other side of the city near Ayvan Saray. I was asked there for lunch which turned out to be an enormous meal of about a dozen courses. Neither money nor time had been spared. The boys had been washed and brushed and combed and suited and the girls had been preened and titivated and decorated so that they all must have been heartily sick of me before I ever arrived. But they were all charming and Metin could hardly contain himself: host, interpreter, master of ceremonies, expert on Stanley Matthews, the Prime Minister and Piccadilly Circus.

★

Ahead, for the best part of a mile and a half, stretched the new dual carriage-way which they are driving through the city. On both sides of the road for a great distance the ground has been levelled so that you can look as far as the land-walls up an immense avenue, a swathe about three hundred yards wide which has been cut through the city. Not a building has been left standing. It looks as if there has been a series of tremendous air-raids. Desolation.

I had been to look at the Laleli mosque, the 'Tulip Mosque' built in 1763 and after the craze for tulips created by the Sultans. It is a most elegant building, slender and full of light, and owns the tombs of Mustafa III and Selim III, as usual stockaded by mother-of-pearl railings and candelabra and covered by magnificent embroideries.

Then I bore left where the great new road ends. I never see it without thinking of all the attendant devastation and the houses that have been destroyed. Many of them, of course, were uninhabitable and there is much to be said for making a fine new road. There is much more to be said for putting up houses for people to live in first. Curiously enough that is something to which governments often give secondary importance. First of all the 'Party' H.Q., the post office, the municipal buildings, the outward illusions of prosperity. Meanwhile people live in caves and tents.

I walked due west towards that quarter known as Samatya and after prolonged search found the column of Arcadius, or rather its pedestal—a thick block of marble jammed between houses and overgrown. It is about twenty feet high. The whole column used to be a hundred and fifty feet high and marked the site of the forum of Arcadius. It was put up in A.D. 421 and was hollow with a spiral staircase inside leading to the top. Evliya Efendi says that there was a 'fairy-cheeked' female figure of one of the beauties of the age surmounting it which once a year gave out a sound, whereupon thousands of different kinds of birds after flying round and round the image fell to the earth and were caught for food.

I visited a small Greek church set by itself in mounds of waste land. Stringy chickens were scavenging and children played barefoot. You find these wildernesses all over the city loosely joined by straggling 'villages' and dusty tracks. In the winter everything becomes a morass. This was the church of St George and there were dark paintings of him killing the dragon. His armour and spear and helmet were of silver. Near by a long-faced Virgin was also encased in silver. The church was being repainted and a handsome, bearded priest in a black suit and white shirt showed me round. His bun looked incongruous without his robes and tall hat. But nearly all priests look odd in mufti. The Greek clergy have long been forbidden to wear their robes; so, for that matter, have the *Imams*—except in the mosques. As I left he was watching the restoration fund plate to see how much I would put in it.

Gradually I found my way back to the main cobbled road which runs west, diverging from the new carriage-way. I went along winding tracks among derelict houses. Periodically I came across a ruined church or the remains of an overgrown fountain. Down here people were eking out a flimsy existence: no plumbing, no electricity, no sanitation, very little food.

There was little traffic on the main road except for an occasional taxi and lorry. Donkeys and horses and carts were more frequent. I visited two small mosques which were being repaired, as are so many of them—a combination of quickening religious interest and a desire to attract tourists, though the tourists hardly ever visit any but the most famous and accessible. In this part the people had plainly not seen a tourist for a long time.

I passed the Cerrahpaşa hospital. A van was delivering a coffin and I saw it being taken in by a side door. What a place it was to die, dribbling out one's life in an overcrowded hospital in the steamy heat surrounded by decaying houses and shacks, everything already moribund.

Half an hour later the bier passed me on two shafts carried by four men. They went at a brisk pace into a small plane-lined square and dumped the bier outside a mosque. The men bowed, put out their hands palms upwards—a gesture of delivery and submission —touched their temples and went away. The bier, covered with a pale-green cloth, lay there in the square pathetically. A dog walked over to it and sniffed. Somebody threw a shoe and it scampered away.

There were cafés and wooden houses round the square, shops and some boot-blacks in the shade. Men were sitting in the cafés passing the time, passing the time, playing whist and backgammon. The music wailed from the radios.

There was an immense and incredibly old cypress in the courtyard and from it hung an iron chain which was supposed to have been able to detect deceit and robbery. On one occasion a Jewish debtor was brought to the tree by his Turkish creditor. Just before the Jew stood beneath the chain he handed to the Turk a hollow stick in which he had concealed the money he owed. The chain descended and confirmed that the Jew was innocent, whereupon the Jew took back his stick and his money. From that day all trust in the chain's detective powers was lost.

I went into the mosque, Koca Mustafa Paşa, which used to be a church dedicated to St Andrew the Apostle and was then rededicated to St Andrew of Crete. It was cool and quiet inside. A grandfather clock ticked away solemnly and one of the mosque servants sat cross-legged and chanted from his Koran. The voice droned on, rising and falling as he swayed forwards and backwards. When I came out again the bier was still there.

When the Muslim approaches death, people close to him begin to recite the thirty-sixth chapter of the Koran: 'I swear by the Wise Koran that you are put upon a straight path. . . . It is We who will bring back the dead to life. We record the deeds of men and the marks they leave behind: We note all things in a glorious book. . . . The night is another sign for men. From the night We lift the day—and they are plunged in darkness. The sun hastens to its resting-place: its course is laid for it by the Mighty One, the All-knowing. We have ordained phases for the moon, which daily wanes and in the end appears like a bent and withered twig. . . .' The voices chant this, one of the most beautiful of all the chapters in the Koran, as the body lies on the bed, the life beginning to run out. Meanwhile one of the family perfumes the chamber.

After death the corpse's name is sent to the local *Imam* and he and a *muezzin* and the equivalent of the parish beadle repair to the house of the dead. The corpse is washed. Women wash women, for a man may not look upon a woman when she is dead. After the body has been washed in tepid water and soap the *Imam* rubs powdered camphor on the eight parts of the body which come into the most frequent contact with the ground during prayer: knees, hands, feet, nose and forehead. Then the body is wrapped in a long shirt and seamless winding-sheet. Nails and hair are trimmed, but a woman's hair is never cut. Then the bier is fumigated and the body laid on it with the right side towards Mecca.

Burial takes place as quickly as possible, before sunset on the day of death or early on the following day. All the orthodox Muslim divines believe that the dead suffer torments before they are actually in the grave, hence the sooner they are buried the better. Some believe that they suffer torments even when they are in the grave.

Swift burial sometimes leads to prematurity. The Sultan Osman III is supposed to have fallen into a trance from which he woke when he was placed in the grave. But his successor had already been acclaimed and the Grand Vizier gave orders for the grave to be filled.

Speedy burial was also enjoined by the Prophet. 'If the deceased be of the elect,' he said, 'it is meet to convey him with speed to the goal.' On the other hand, 'If he be of those accursed, it is equally meritorious to get rid of him with expedition.'

The bier having been prepared, the *Imam* recites prayers over it and sometimes hired weepers are used to join their lamentations with the family, but not to follow the bier to the grave. The Jews and the Greeks are, of course, far more lachrymose on these occasions.

It is also considered a meritorious act for everybody concerned to help to carry the bier for a few paces, for the Prophet said that he 'that aids in carrying a corpse forty paces towards the grave thereby expiates a mortal sin'.

The body is placed in the ground and planks placed across it to prevent earth from falling on it. Then the chief mourner casts handfuls of mould on to it and the *Imam* says a brief funeral prayer and calls aloud three times the name of the dead and that of his mother.

In wealthy families it used to be the custom to invite theological students to recite the Koran throughout the night in the house of the dead person; and it was the custom for the heirs to perform various acts of charity not mentioned in the will, like the distribution of Korans to schools and orphans, the digging of wells, the erection of fountains and the clothing of destitute children.

But, buried, the corpse is not yet at peace. It still has to undergo the interrogation of the dark inquisitorial angels—Monkir and Nekir.

When I walked out of the square the body was still there, under its green shroud, already in torment, waiting for the *Imam* and the final prayer, the dull thud of the earth on planks and the interrogation of the black angels. A girl was singing from a wireless—'Don't throw bouquets at me'—and in the cafés the men sat sucking at their nargiles, banging down the backgammon counters.

★

Yedikule and its adjacent suburb are famous for their fortress and some tanneries. The land-walls end not far beyond the castle of the seven towers and used to join the sea-walls on the Marmara. Near that spot, jutting out in the water, solitary and superb, is the White Tower.

I have often walked along that southern border of the city which becomes more and more deserted as the end is approached. The White Tower is a point at which to relax. It is made of marble and is wonderfully well constructed. It must have been to last for fifteen hundred years. On the seaward side it is almost unblemished and gleams deep beneath the pale-blue waters. To the landward it is crumbling and amongst its battered ramparts shacks of wood and biscuit tin and corrugated iron have been built by the homeless. Flowers and vegetables straggle about it. Washing garnishes it.

Some distance further a gateway opens in the extreme bastions of the land-walls. The first time I went through it an overpowering stench filled me with nausea. It was a rancid foetidness which defied analysis but was easily explicable. It was the tanneries.

They are very large and the smells of rotting offal and curing hides test the strongest stomachs initially. But so adaptable are the senses that in half an hour disgust is almost replaced by indifference.

Lorries went in and out piled high with fleeces and skins, and in the big drying and tanning barns, steamy with heat and decay and flies, men were working stripped to the waist, their brown arms and torsos smeared and mottled with blood. The skins were stacked in mounds anything up to thirty feet high. It was a paradise for scavenging dogs, and the open ground was covered with heaps of discarded fleece coloured in delicate copper and bronze by the processing.

The tanneries have been there for a long time and before the Turks came the suburb was a lazaretto where people coming to the city and infected by the plague were obliged to pass a week in quarantine. After the conquest it was turned into shops for tanners and butchers and became a large concern with mosques, baths, Dervish monasteries, fountains and accommodation for three hundred and fifty tanners. Most of them were unmarried—very understandably.

Evliya Efendi says that the overwhelming reek prevented people of quality from living there but adds that the inhabitants were so used to it that the scent of a perfumed dandy tended to upset them.[3]

They were a prosperous community, as they still are, a fact for which they were indebted to their patron saint—Ahuran. The story has it that he was once carrying some dog's ordure in his apron and, being asked what he had, he replied shamefacedly, 'Cash.' Dog's droppings were valuable for tanning purposes and their discovery was thus attributed to the saint. Evliya recalls that it was a well-known fact that one tanner was offered 40,000 piastres by some English merchants for his collection of excrement which it had taken him forty years to gather. He refused the offer.

I re-entered the city by the small gate alongside the fortress. A cobbled street wound away among wooden houses. It is a very modest and humble beginning to such a great metropolis. I called at a café I knew—a cool dark cave of a shop with rickety tables and chairs, and walls plastered with nineteenth-century lithographs. There was a picture of the Duke of Windsor there as well, and one of Queen Victoria. By them was the craggy face of Atatürk and the sombre and drooping features of Sultan Abdül Hamit; also, of course, the inevitable reproduction of Bellini's portrait of Mehmet II. In addition, curiously enough, there were a couple of English rural scenes: gloomy oils of pheasant on a heath and deer on a moor. Beneath them two old men sucked away at their nargiles.

The spacious courtyard of the fortress of Yedikule is surrounded by high and immensely thick walls joining the seven great towers. Nearly everything is overgrown: a miniature veldt of tawny grass broken by some small trees covers the area. A truncated minaret sticks up from the ruins of a tiny mosque in the centre.

I sat under the plane-tree near the gatehouse. Above pigeons disputed gently and from isolated pockets small choirs of cicadas sang. In such peace stray extracts from the *Eclogues* come back. I remembered Corydon wandering in the paths trodden by Alexis, under the burning sun,

Sole sub ardenti resonant arbusta cicadis.

Placid, naïve and persistent, the cicadas are the equivalent of bores. It is difficult to be unkind to them. Unlike bores they lend a pleasing background in rural solitude.

Viviparous, usually first noticeable as an adult, but thereafter of any age and class, in many and various sizes, of diverse appearances, rich and poor, sociable, of good intentions, unspectacular as a husband and assiduous as a parent, the bore is always recognizable by its monotonous song.

Like the sparrow and the starling it is gregarious. It thrives best in urban and suburban surroundings. Its special haunts are pubs, clubs, hotel lounges, passenger ships, railway compartments—indeed nearly all public transport—pavilions, touch-lines, art galleries, literary parties, and the houses of the tolerant, the unsuspecting, the deaf and the boring. The bore is at home almost everywhere. In fact it is easier to list those places that it shuns: deserts, jungles, forests and mountain ranges. It mates all the year round and never emigrates.

But, perhaps, to be fair, the distribution could include everybody

—this is a perilous subject and I must be brief—and there may be no archetypal bore, no universal bore. One man may be a bore to a dozen people, and half of those may be bores to him; but there may be another dozen to whom he is not boring at all: and so on.

But most genuine bores have certain qualifications, and the chief ones seem to be egoism and prolixity in speech. With length go digression and reiteration To these may be added pleasure in frequent and usually pointless parenthetical details, a slavish regard for time and place. The bore is usually a reminiscer, for ever drawing upon the dead bonds of experience. He is the converse of an alchemist. You may be sure that given the most hair-raising experience, escaping from a burning 'plane, fleeing from an erupting volcano, eluding a maddened bull elephant, suspended upon a cliff-face, the bore to the manner born will transform these things into anecdotes as tedious as the repetitive patterns of a suburban street. But very few ever undergo an unusual or exciting experience. The places from which they draw and disperse their particular purling tedia are the luke-warm courses of the humdrum.

Bores are importunate, tenacious and long-winded. We cross the street to avoid them, we discard favourite haunts to escape them. We invent absurd pretexts to leave them. They lie in wait like octopuses and batten like lampreys. They are the parasites of friendship, the leeches of love. They can destroy patience like a drill and dry up benevolence like a drought. Some of their favourite subjects are racing, bridge, photography, motor-cars, money and, naturally, themselves.

Silence is hardly ever boring and the bore is a saboteur of silence, a bumbling saboteur it is true, but often an astoundingly successful one. He has the requisite stamina and application. He is an equally successful destroyer of conversation. He is the long-distance talker, the verbal pentathlete. He can crack the vaults of a person's tolerance by sheer pressure. Especially notable ones are professional old boys, those who have devoted their lives to games, some kinds of intellectual, a great many actors, and story-tellers. The story-tellers are particularly dangerous. I once knew a Welshman in the army who, every night, after lights were out, would begin. He always waited for darkness, like a bullfrog. Then he began to tell stories. For an hour or an hour and a half he went on telling stories, filthier and filthier stories, descending steadily the registers of obscenity until he could reach the basest note, as if he wished to strike a chord so foul and discordant that nobody, including himself, would ever tell another dirty story for fear of universal ridicule. Night after night that lowest note always eluded him. He went on until every scab and boil and wound in the flesh of humour had been prised open, picked and squeezed. Then, quite suddenly, he would stop, turn over and go to sleep. His quota was completed. It was as if he had sluiced out the daily agglomerations of sewage in his mind, as if the pits of his own especial fertility had been drained and scoured. He did it for many weeks and as far as I know he never repeated himself. Fortunately such phenomena are rare.

Literature is full of bores—authors and characters. Lydgate, Hoccleve and Barclay, poor fellows, stand high on the list. Gibbon must have become a little tiresome after a time with that podgy forefinger of his thrust accusingly at his audience. Coleridge, for all his brilliance, must have palled somewhat after two or three hours of concentrated Coleridge. Carlyle, with his gravelly and copious manner, effectively blocks all passages to remorse at having put him down unfinished. Swinburne's shrill voice piercing the ear and his treacly poetry cloying the mind made an unusual combination. And he who could withstand Frank Harris must have been more than ordinarily endowed with patience and good-will. As somebody put it—he was invited to everybody's house—once.

There are not so many characters, perhaps for the plain reason that it is very difficult to create them without alienating sympathy and good-will. Polonius is an exception and Hamlet's technique with him is one many of us would like to use. Raphael in *Paradise Lost* becomes a rather tired and boring extension lecturer as he goes dutifully through the long familiar curriculum of the creation. One gets the feeling that besides seeing it actually happen he has also been obliged to speak about it to other Adams and Eves.

More recently H. H. Munro and Mr Aldous Huxley have created immortal bores. Munro's Amblecope in *A Defensive Diamond* is the story-teller *par excellence*: the club-bore out-bored by Treddleford. Amblecope had 'restless, prominent eyes' and a mouth 'ready mobilized for conversational openings'. He was armed with a copy of *Country Life* as an aid to 'conversational ice-breaking'. It is one of Munro's funniest and most acute stories and he provides us with a sure method, if we have the audacity and invention, of disposing of the Amblecopes of this world.

In *Two or Three Graces* Mr Huxley was daring enough to create two: the phlegmatic, bovine bore, Herbert Comfrey; and the high-powered, back-slapping bore, John Peddley. They nibble away at the nerves with excruciating persistence but it is a measure of their author's skill that they never actually become boring.

Much longer ago Horace nearly immortalized the bore in his ninth *Satire*. It is the man whom we pick up like a thistle-head when we least expect it or wish for it. Horace was strolling along the Sacred Way day-dreaming when the bore came up and seized his hand with a 'How are you, my dear chap?' He falls into step, dogs him. Horace tries to shake him off, walks fast and then slow. It is useless. The man prattles on about the city and the streets. Horace says nothing. At last this penetrates. 'You're very keen to be off,' says the bore. Then, and this is the definition almost, the self-condemnation, he adds:

> 'Iamdudum video; sed nil agis; usque tenebo;
> Persequar hinc quo nunc iter est tibi.'

'I've seen that for a long time, but it's no good. I'll stay with you. I'll stay with you until you get to the end of your journey.' Eventually Horace is delivered when the man's opponent in a law-suit appears. Not everyone is so blessed by chance.

The condition of being bored is common enough, and 'Boredom' is an overpopulated country always encroaching upon the confines of 'Peace'. The condition is also a malaise incident to this age. It is a hellish condition. In that diabolically ingenious play *Huis Clos* M. Sartre has created an abode of punishment more terrifying than anything described in the best of the medieval visions of the other world or anything in *Paradise Lost*. Hell, we may surmise, will be full of Amblecopes, Comfreys and Peddleys, but they will not be the harmless and innocent ones. No. The damned will have their vice of tedious prolixity but none of their virtues; and we shall have no tongues to still their eternal reminiscences, no weapon to repel the buttonholing and the everlasting harangues of abortionists, murderers and blackmailers, the ceaseless preoccupations of suicides, the endless anecdotes of sexual pirates. Let us imagine for a moment the perpetual wailing of self-justification, the eternal weeping of tearless eyes, the infinite gnashing of toothless mouths.

One of Johnson's intended works was a vision of the Palace of Sloth. What a book that would have been. We need someone now to write a vision of the Palace of Boredom—lest we should commit the error of thinking that our present lot is too intolerable.

The soporific tunes of Yedikule continued. A smart Parisian couple, looking a little incongruous, came and departed. Then a terrific belch detonated in my ear and brought me to abruptly. A man was approaching. He was youngish and limped, dragging one leg. He eructed again as he smiled at me, and a long rallentando of lesser belches followed. He was wearing some kind of uniform and he plonked himself down beside me and began to talk affably, pausing every so often to emit another salvo of wind. It appeared that he had lost his leg in the war and had waited ten years for a replacement. After a time the repeated upheavals in his unfortunate stomach became irritating and I made a move. He followed. He clearly intended to be my guide.

The path through the long grass led to the Golden Gate, the triumphal arch through which the emperors usually entered the city on state occasions. It used to be gilded and on the outside was adorned with magnificent sculptures representing the Labours of Hercules, the Tortures of Prometheus and similar mythical misfortunes. The entrance is now blocked in.

I explored the two enormous towers which flank it. My guide followed me devotedly. He was as adhesive as Horace's companion. Every few steps another eruption shuddered through him, and to these noises was added the creaking of his artificial leg. As we clambered round the towers he disserted on its defects. At the end of twenty minutes I knew quite a lot about false legs, more than I wished to know, and a good deal more than I had learnt about the fortress.

There were a number of small rooms in the towers and in one of them Sultan Osman II had been murdered. A notice said so in French, English and Turkish. Lest I could not read, my guide repeated the fact carefully. The room was about ten feet by six and had no window—an unpleasant place to be murdered. But a good many Sultans have died at Yedikule, especially when it was held by the Janissaries in revolt. Countless heads have hung and rotted upon its battlements.

In one room there was a round hole in the floor. A cylindrical shaft went down for about forty feet. It was ingeniously lighted by a bulb at the bottom. It was very sinister. This was another execution chamber and the heads went straight down the shaft. In the courtyard there was a well, a very deep one, the Well of Blood. Down this yet other heads were thrown. There was also a small, minor courtyard where it became the custom to pile them up. It may be judged that Yedikule has a sombre record.

When Mehmet II conquered Constantinople he found the fortress in ruins. He had it repaired and it served to house state treasures. Later it was turned into the equivalent of the Tower of London and the Bastille. Ambassadors, diplomats and merchants were commonly locked up in it, and in the eastern tower and on the walls outside it are a number of inscriptions in Latin, Greek and German. One Frenchman was there for nine years. The ghosts of executed envoys and Sultans and Janissaries are reputed to haunt the walls which are now covered with grass and small shrubs and trees. It would not surprise me if it were true. So much blood and murder must taint any ground and leave uneasy spirits revisiting.

As I left, the grave old man who kept the gate was ringing the bell for closing time and my guide dragged his protesting stomach and creaking limb away.

★

From Yedikule it is but a step to the ruin of St John the Baptist of Studion, founded as long ago as A.D. 463. A community of the Sleep-less Monks was attached to it. In a city that was once bulging with monasteries this was, for a time, the chief. It produced a number of Patriarchs and was also a favourite place for emperors to retire. Now it is a pleasant mosque in which it is possible to see some re-mains of the basilica, as one can detect the fine bone structure of a once-beautiful but now emaciated face.

There is much more to be seen, however, flesh as well as bone, at the famous church of St Saviour in the Chora—the Kariye Camii, but now no longer a mosque. Small, shabby, a dusty pink and grey, the remains of a small minaret stuck at one corner, it is tucked away among areas of waste land near the Adrianople Gate. The archaeolo-gists (of the Byzantine Institute of America) have been working there for a long time and they have uncovered, in year after year of patience, skill and care, some splendid paintings and mosaics. A complicated and chequered history has left the church in the hands of the kind of men from whom, I believe, many of us could learn a profitable lesson. They are expert at their work, they seek and find little material reward, except, of course, the revelation and preservation of the works of art entrusted to their care (and this is an inestimable recompense), and they are, so far as I could see, extremely happy. There are not many people, I feel, of whom this can be said. When we find people who are content, materially speaking, with a little, it makes one take stock of the available recipes for a happy life.

Both the inner and the outer narthexes are covered with mosaics most of which are in an excellent state of repair. A tremendous amount of detail has been crammed into a small space; and by a good deal of neck-craning it is possible to pick out many incidents in the life of Our Lord and the time preceding it. The chapel on the epistle side, the south chapel, is full of wall-paintings, chief of which is a fine version of the Harrowing of Hell with an Ethiopian Satan—a not uncommon form in medieval art and literature—prostrate beneath the collapsed gates of his kingdom and the noble figure of a white-robed Christ.[4]

The Kariye is one of the few places in Istanbul where, so to speak, Christ is still triumphant. It was once the greatest city in Christendom, but now the choirs are silent, the sacristies disused, the tabernacles empty. Yet none of these things can be regretted when we remember that Islam and Christianity have learnt to live side by side.

NOTES

1. Lucretius, *De Rerum Natura*. Loeb Class. Lib., Bk. VI.
2. Pliny, *Natural History*, Bk. 11, chap. 52 et seq.
3. Evliya Efendi, op. cit.
4. The work of restoration by the Byzantine Institute continued for many years. The church is now a museum of Byzantine art at the height of its excellence. The present structure and the works of art date from 1315–21. In that period the church was completely rebuilt and redecorated on the orders of Theodore Metochites, the Lord High Treasurer in the reign of Andronicus II Palaeologus. The mosaics are in six groups and deal with the life of Christ and the Blessed Virgin. They are all in the outer and inner narthex and in the nave. The frescoes are all in the parecclesion.

CHAPTER THREE

The Bosphorus

THIS Citie is situated upon a point of firme land advanced
into the channell which comes from *Pontus Euxinus,* or the
blacke Sea, which Geographers call the *Bosphorus* of Thrace.
It is watred of three parts by the Sea: towards the North by a
Gulfe or Arme of the Sea, called the Horne, which the
Bosphorus thrusts into Europe, and make the Haven of Constantinople the goodliest, the deepest, and the most commodious
in Europe: Towards the East it is watred by the extremetie
of the channell or Bosphorus; on the South by the waves of the
Propontique Sea; and upon the South [he means the north] it
hath the firm land of Thrace.

MICHEL BAUDIER OF LANGUEDOC, *The History of the*
Imperiall Estate of the Grand Seigneurs. Trans. by
Edward Grimstone, London 1635

It was a sullen, steamy morning in mid-July. The thermometer had
climbed steadily for a week; the barometer had declined as surely.
Anything above a minimum effort produced a new outbreak of
thick, sticky sweat. The backs of my hands were permanently dewed.
Warm, heavy beads crept and rolled slowly down my back and legs.
Soon my clothes became clammy and stiff, almost resinous.

I walked very leisurely down the long hill through Pera and
Galata. The streets and the buildings were carved in black and
white. The light lay in smears on the cobblestones. Trams took the
steep hill with one continuous vibrating groan. On the other side of
the Horn a nacreous haze of smoke and dust hung over and misted
the bulk and outline of the city. The coppered sun pulsed. A stillness
seemed to descend and to be growing and investing. Trams, buses
and people—everything was moving; but the tempo appeared to be
gradually decreasing. At such times wrongs are imagined and
tempers shift uneasily.

Down at the Galata Bridge the pall thickened. Demolition of a large area was going on. Bulldozers roared and grunted. A crowd was gathering to watch a wall pulled down: the fourth wall of a tall building. It stood like a thin slice, façade of a derelict film-set, windows gaping.

Two bulldozers began to rev up. Whistles blew. Men shouted. The steel cables attached to the wall tightened, quivering. The engine notes rose and rose. The steel grew taut, painfully taut. Expectancy quickened the gathered crowd and the tension of the steel was communicated to them. They became silent and strung as if they were watching a dangerous acrobatic or waiting for the guillotine to fall. The wall trembled.

There is something fascinating about watching big things collapse: trees, buildings, water, avalanches. There is a moment when everything hangs, waiting; when the volume balances itself, as it were, and assembles itself. Tennyson caught the moment and described it perfectly in the distant view of the land of the Lotus-Eaters:

> And like a downward smoke, the slender stream
> Along the cliff to fall and pause and fall did seem.

The engines reached an agonizing, concentrated bass howl. Then the bulldozers lurched forward. Light sprang and bounced from the steel. The wall shuddered momentarily, leaned a little, began to buckle at the top, folded, was poised for a second, paused and then, with what seemed extraordinary slowness, heeled over and slid with a prolonged, shattering, rumbling detonation. Billows of dust proliferated and blossomed upwards.

All strains were broken. The crowd dispersed and moved on.

At the other end of the bridge the same destruction was going on. I was glad to be making a trip up the Bosphorus.

The majority of the boats operate from the Galata Bridge. A floating quay runs down the whole of one side of it and beneath it. On it are the booking-offices and shops, cafés and stalls. There is a ceaseless and dense traffic of pedestrians, endless noise and movement: the gentle shifting of the quay underfoot, the reverberation of trams, buses and cars immediately overhead, the bellowing and shrieking of innumerable sirens, piercing blasts of whistles, and the lower and persistent volumes of peoples, the day-long crying and chanting of vendors and fishermen.

The fishermen moor their rowing-boats at every opportune place.

The boats roll and buck on the constantly fretted water and the
fishermen balance on them barefooted with amazing agility, their
fish cunningly arranged on big wooden trays, and shout their wares.
Some of them have a number of live fish in a can which they throw
out into the boat periodically to compel attention, the luckless creatures springing and flapping, mouths agape and eyes bulging. A man
above shouts his order and at once they are scooped up and crammed
into a bag, alive and wriggling in final desperation. The bag is flung
up; the coins tossed down. The chant continues.

The Bosphorus has always had a great reputation for fish, of
which there are many varieties: porpoise, sword-fish, tunny,
mackerel, pilchard, turbot, brill, sole, plaice, salmon, grey and red
mullet, loufer, gurnard, whiting and smelt; not to mention lobsters
and oysters and their smaller brethren. A considerable income is
derived from them. Polybius, Strabo and Tacitus all refer to the
profits of the fishery which made up the principal revenue of Byzantium. Pliny, who often has a taste for the unusual, explains the
curious behaviour of tunny at some length. Having assured us that
the Black Sea is never entered by any animal that is noxious to fish
except the sea-calf and the small dolphin, he goes on to tell us that
on entering the sea the tunny keep to the shores on the right. This,
he says, is supposed to arise from the fact that they have better sight
with the right eye, their power of vision with either being naturally
very limited. 'In the channel of the Thracian Bosphorus,' he writes,
'... at the narrowest part of the straits which separate Europe from
Asia, there is near Chalcedon, on the Asiatic side, a rock of remarkable whiteness, the whole of which can be seen from the bottom of
the sea at the surface. Alarmed at the sudden appearance of this
rock, the tunnies always hasten in great numbers, and with headlong impetuosity, towards the promontory of Byzantium, which
stands exactly opposite it, and from this circumstance has received
the name of the Golden Horn. Hence it is that all the fishing is at
Byzantium, to the great loss of Chalcedon, although it is only separated from it by a channel a mile in width. They wait, however, for
the blowing of the north wind to leave the Euxine with a favourable
tide, and are never taken until they have entered the harbour of
Byzantium.'[1]

Strabo, earlier, had described much the same process and maintains that they were so plentiful that they could be caught by hand.
Many travellers have commented on the quantity of the fish, and in

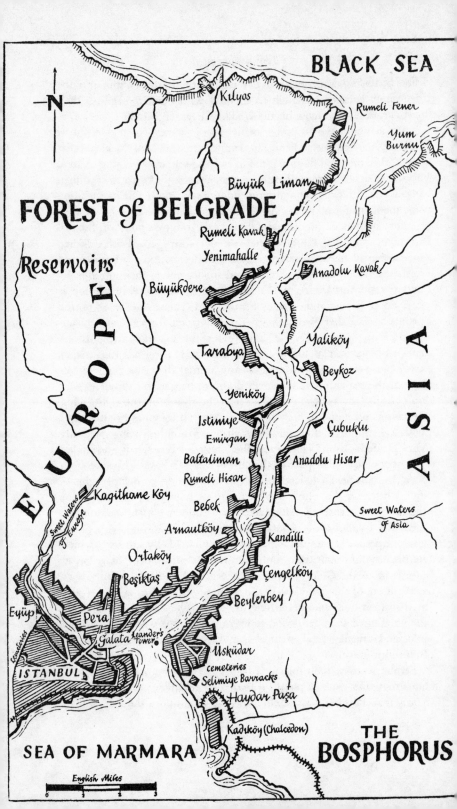

the middle of the sixteenth century Busbecq, in his letters, mentions the densely packed shoals which could be captured by hand. Time and experience have now begun to take their toll.

★

For a time I sat in a small café under the bridge to cool down and have a glass of tea. A handsome grey-haired Kurd with the long nose of his race sat in one corner and sucked methodically at his nargile. When he had finished he dismantled it, cleaned it thoroughly and packed it all away—except for the glass bowl—in an oilskin bag. It seemed that this was his only worldly possession. There was something about him which made me want to talk to him; but I hesitated and he left quickly and I did not have another chance.

As the boat was about to leave there was the usual last-minute, last-second rush as the gates were closing. Men leapt over the widening gap as the boat slid along the quay. There was one ultimate: there is always somebody who risks his life rather than wait half an hour. He was middle-aged and carried a suitcase and a sack. He swung and flung the case and somebody with quick reflexes caught it. Then he sprang and hung on to the side. It was touch—and very nearly go. His sack was heavy with fruit. For some seconds we struggled together trying to heave him over the edge. At one moment he was suspended by one arm. Somehow it was accomplished.

The boat moved swiftly out into the Bosphorus: the Seraglio Point and the Lunar Park on the right and leaving; ahead the coast of Asia hazily brown and green and slashed with white buildings.

Standing out alone in the water nearer the Asian side and built on a rock is the White Tower of Leander. It is misplaced, for as everybody knows Leander was drowned a long way away in the Dardanelles and it is better known for the unhappy daughter of a Sultan who was locked up on the island because of a prophecy that she would die of a snake-bite. Her isolation was in vain. A snake did its work having come in a basket of grapes bought from a passing boat. It is curious how often prophecies come true.

Other strange details are connected with this rock. Alcibiades once built a toll-tower on it and all merchant ships coming from the Black Sea were obliged to pay a fee equal to a tenth of their merchandise. Later a chain, as a fortification, connected the rock with the Seraglio Point and later still a fortress was built on it.

The steamer went out into midstream and steered among big
tankers and trawlermen and countless smaller craft. Merchant ships
and passenger boats lay in a long line by the Galata quays. A weary
and torrid wind generated by the steamer rolled along the decks.
The sun splintered and flashed incandescence from the dark-blue
water.

As befits one of the great waterways of the world the Bosphorus
is always exciting. Scenically it is magnificent and the ceaseless activity in the strait gives it greater importance. Lamartine, a little too
enthusiastically perhaps, wrote that 'there God and Man, Nature
and Art, have together created and placed the most marvellous point
of view which the human eye can contemplate on earth'. If not the
'most marvellous' it must be amongst the first.

It has been given many titles: Philostratus called it, prosaically,
'The Mouth of the Black Sea'; Euripides named it 'The Keys';
Aristotle 'The Doors'; Herodotus 'The Throat'. For the Byzantines
it was 'The Narrows', and for the Crusaders 'The Arm of St
George'. The Turks name it 'Boghaz'. As most people know, it was
one of the mistresses of Zeus, Io, who gave it its name. Io was the
daughter of the first king of Argos and was metamorphosed, through
fear of Hera, into a heifer. Hera, for safe custody, put her under the
command of Argus whom Hermes slew; and the luckless Io then
tormented by a gadfly wandered in frenzy from land to land before
finding peace on the banks of the Nile. In the course of her wandering she swam the strait.

Evliya Efendi, who delights in the narration of the improbable,
tells how Alexander the Great, chained down, near what is now
Galata, a number of magicians and witches from the country of Gog
and Magog by piling mountains upon them. He ordered them to
go to sea during the 'forty winter days' in 'brazen ships' and to
guard the waters surrounding Constantinople. Unfortunately, these
demons carved a passage through the mountains enclosing the Black
Sea so that it broke through into the Bosphorus and drowned the
fiends.

It has always been a swift and perilous passage and often you
can see the big stream of racing waters rushing down from the
Euxine and the counter-currents from the Sea of Marmara contend-
ing with it. Gibbon observes that there were crowds of temples and
votive altars scattered along the banks 'attesting the unskilfulness,
the terrors, and the devotion of the Grecian navigators, who, after

the example of the Argonauts, explored the dangers of the inhospitable Euxine'. Ferries aim well wide of the target and then are caught
and swung, compelled by the powerful sweep and drive of the immense volume. In the days of *caïques* and sailing-craft accidents
were frequent and death common. It was difficult enough to get into
a *caïque* from a landing-stage; impossible to return from midstream.
Lucretius, rather staidly and unrealistically, described it as a sea
'which flows with a uniform tide, maintaining perpetually the single
tenor of its current'. But, like any account of it, this gives no idea.
Many thousands have drowned in its depth and turbulence—both
by design and chance.

Soon the long white marble quay and façade of the Dolmabahçe
Palace came into sight. The quay, fully two hundred yards long,
falls in steps to the lip of the water. Behind it lies an array of ornate
sculpted pillars and railings; beyond that the fine terrace and gardens, then the palace itself: iced pseudo-Baroque.

The imperial barge, more magnificent than anything Cleopatra
ever rode in or Shakespeare dreamt of, used to transport the Sultan
to and from this quay. But it has not been used for many years. A
couple of tin-hatted soldiers patrol the railings. Weed flourishes on
the gravelled terrace.

Of all the many palaces on the Bosphorus and in the city, Dolmabahçe is by far the largest and the most vulgar. Outwardly it is
impressive, from a distance, snow-white and gleaming, splendid; but
within, in lavish lack of proportion, there is an astounding profusion
of opulent crudity. To us, now, it seems an excellent illustration of
the use of wealth without discrimination: the deployment of hard
cash on a gigantic level the results of which impress by sheer bulk
and discordant variety. So fashion and value collaborate to repel.
In perhaps two centuries or less it may be regarded as a masterpiece.
It was built in 1853 and, taken apart, disintegrated, many of the
components would still please and, perhaps, be fashionable. As with
words, it is their mysterious conjunction, the magic of properties
eliciting meaning from each other, the life (and death) they give
each other, that make them offensive (or attractive).

There are many hundreds of rooms, probably thousands; but long
before I had seen a tenth part of them, acute mental indigestion, if
not constipation, had set in. Frescoed alabaster ceilings, alabaster
and marble floors and baths and lavatories, malachite chimney-
pieces, lapis lazuli, verd antique pillars, gigantic cascades of crystal

chandeliers, cataracts of Venetian glass, enormous multi-limbed candelabra, Sèvres china, Waterford glass, Wedgwood pottery, immense pots full of exotic green plants, stained-glass cupolas distilling rich, warm rainbows of ecclesiastical gloom—all crowded upon the eyes in bewildering confusion. There were 'Blue' rooms and 'Green' rooms and 'Red' rooms, huge cliffs of curtains and tapestry, fabulous brocades, forests of drapery, silk, satin and velvet. There were gem-encrusted coffee services, solid-gold chairs and silver tables. The atmosphere was musty, full of the ghosts of stale perfumes. Corridor upon corridor led to chamber after chamber. The walls were laden with hundreds of sombre nineteenth-century battle scenes, melancholy pre-Raphaelite landscapes, portraits of monarchs and nobility. Long heavily carpeted staircases, designed for weak hearts and ballroom gowns, unrolled from floor to floor. Again and again I thought and fervently hoped that there was nothing more to be seen; but I was wrong. New vistas of voluble and drossy wealth and elaborate philistinism unfolded themselves.

The first and last time I visited Dolmabahçe I was unfortunate enough to be attached to a 'cruise' of middle-aged, middle-class, middle-browed American tourists. American tourists have been a joke for a long time. But they are no longer a joke. They should never have been a joke. They are an unforgettable and alarming reality. Two hours' eavesdropping proved one of the most instructive and distressing periods of its kind I can remember. To listen to thirty adults in their fifties and sixties talking and behaving like a group of secondary-modern school children on a visit to Whipsnade is a most enlightening experience; and one not to be repeated.

Murray's guide-book for 1900 says, a little uneasily it seems, that 'the building is a mixture of styles and is overlaid with a profusion of ornament not always in the best taste, but the general effect is not unpleasing to the eye'. If the writer had added 'a quarter of a mile away' nobody could quarrel. But taste is notoriously misleading and, fortunately, it changes. As I say, in perhaps two centuries...

Almost immediately beyond, the steamer stopped at the village of Beşiktaş. The navigation of these ships is haphazard and reckless and the wooden landing-stages endure the roughest treatment. Once again we went in too quickly and a violent collision shook the whole structure. The piles shrieked in protest. The booking-office and the other buildings shuddered. People waiting to embark were thrown off their feet. One of these days a whole stage will collapse and then something may be done about the absurd incompetence of those in command.

Beşiktaş used to be renowned as the resting-place of the stone upon which Jesus was washed after His birth. It also had a reputation for its gardens and for the pride and constancy of its women. From its landing-place the Sacred Camel, blessed by the *Ulema* and laden with offerings for Mecca, was embarked annually for Scutari. Now there is nothing to detain the traveller except the tomb of Barbarossa; and the memory of one of the more imprudent undertakings attempted by various Sultans. Ahmet I ordered a palace to be built in midstream. Everyone in the neighbourhood helped and a pier eight hundred yards long was erected in the water. At the end of it rose the palace. But it lasted only three months. A wild storm from the Black Sea swept everything away. But Sultans were notoriously capricious. When Murat IV was staying at his residence near what is now Dolmabahçe he happened one day to be reading a famous satirical poem by Nefii Efendi called *Shafts* when the ground was struck by lightning. The Sultan, startled out of his wits, threw the book into the sea and gave orders that the author was to be strangled immediately.

Periodically we come across something which reminds us of the astounding stupidity and inhumanity of man. I say 'reminds us' since it is so common that only the unusual can startle. Such an incident, if true, may make us smile—but how futile. Who else has died for quite such an absurd reason? Hundreds of thousands—and for less.

At that moment, watching the passengers jostling for seats, and the boxes of grapes and the chickens and the suitcases being shoved aboard, I became acutely conscious of one's inability to do anything at the right time, or even something useful at the wrong time: a lack of willingness and awareness. We need more saints and men like Signor Dolci, and fewer of our own gardens to cultivate.

The bleak, brassy sun drew out the smells of wood and netting and salt. The propellers thrashed the stilling water again. We drew out and past the little villages of Ortaköy and Arnautköy and then into the splendid bay of Bebek: a small residential town with many luxurious villas and spacious wooden houses at the water's edge and restaurants on piles out into the water. Solid but ageing stilts bent strangely in the pellucid calm, windows and gables wobbled in the inverted sky.

It is a popular place for Istambulis in the summer and I know of few pleasanter ways of passing a summer's evening than sitting at the edge of the darkening water and watching the gold points pricking the deepening purple of the opposite shore, and dining at ease off mullet or lobster and drinking cool white wine. The wooden houses are now diminishing steadily, and many that remain are drab and ramshackle, unpainted and unrepaired. It is only a question of time before they either fall down or are knocked down to make way for the great new road which is being built along the coast by Israel. This is being paid for with sugar.

The wooden *yalis* and *konaks* have a melancholy dignity of their own. Their large and comfortable rooms are filled with the liquefaction of shifting water, liquescent shadows, light glaucous and umber and olive. It is not difficult to imagine those days of ease and relative prosperity when they were filled with rich carpets and voluptuous divans, with veiled and beautiful women, with wealthy and indolent men, with slaves and eunuchs and odalisques, and each garden or small landing-stage with a *caïque*, that most graceful of craft, swaying and dipping idly at the disinterested beck of docile waters. One is inevitably reminded of Venice and Amsterdam and Bruges—especially in the autumn.

An antique Armenian chemist with a taste for the marginal peculiarities of the past told me that at Arnautköy, in the days of Byzantium, the crabs had to abandon the water because of the swiftness of the current and crawl over the land to smooth water and so gradually they wore a deep cleft in the rocks. To this piece of information he added another as interesting and more likely. On the Orthodox Epiphany it was the custom, in the early morning, to celebrate the ceremony of Baptism of Waters. The bishop held a service and then showed a golden cross to the crowd. This was then flung out into the water. Men plunged in to retrieve it. It was, of course, a great distinction to do so and it had the double advantage of a reward in cash as well as an increased reputation for piety.

We were well out in the bay of Bebek, and I was trying to pick out landmarks in the pine-covered hills which rise behind it, when there was a commotion astern. At once everybody craned over the side. There was a violent ringing of bells. The boat began to turn. The passengers all rushed to the port side. The boat listed. Two life-belts sailed out like big quoits. Then I caught sight of what looked like a head in the water about fifty yards away. We swung further

round and the whole hull shuddered at the exertion. The uproar
increased. Men shouted. Women screamed. Several hundred voices
were raised in protest, advice and astonishment. One man stripped
off his jacket and dived from the rails. The blob in the dark-blue
water appeared and disappeared; appeared again. Two arms came
up, wavered for a second: a final gesture as if in benediction. They
vanished. In a few seconds we were close to the spot. Several more
men wrenched off their clothes and leapt in. Pandemonium reigned
for about ten minutes; then suddenly subsided. All was quiet. One
by one the men dragged themselves up by rope and back on board.
They shook themselves like retrievers. It was all over. There was
nothing anyone could do. The Bosphorus is deep—and swift even
when it looks calm. A man next to me turned and spread out his
hands in a gesture of helplessness; then spoke in a voice of gloomy
resignation: 'A suicide.'

After a time we turned and moved on. Three buoys lifted and
dipped on the settling water. Near one of them something caught
my eye—just floating. We passed quite close to it. 'Look!' I shouted
involuntarily. I was almost certain that it was the handsome Kurd's
oilskin bag. But nobody took any notice. It may not have been. I
looked everywhere for him; but I did not see him again.

Soon the boys were running up and down once more with trays
of tea and lemonade and in a few minutes we had reached Rumeli
Hisar: a large and magnificent fortress which dominates the strait
and lies immediately opposite Kandilli and the very much smaller
fort of Anadolu Hisar.

It stands up on a steep slope so that the topmost towers and walls
—these walls are built across and down into a considerable declivity—are much higher than those on the shore. The whole structure
is formidable and in excellent repair.

It was built as long ago as 1452 by Mehmet II, 'The Conqueror', before the capture of Constantinople, despite the opposition of the emperor and against the agreement which the two had
concluded. The emperor complained and sent an embassy. But they
were threatened with being flayed alive and sent packing.

The construction of the castle was an amazing achievement. A
thousand masons and a thousand lime-burners were employed. All
local buildings were pillaged for materials and the whole edifice
was completed in three months: an astounding record in view
of steepness and irregularity of the ground. Mehmet equipped

it with gigantic cannon which could throw stone shot of six hundred-weight. Thus he commanded the Bosphorus and could prevent all passage. Four hundred Janissaries formed the garrison.

After the fall of the city it was turned into a prison. Later, houses were built within it and a self-contained community grew up. According to Miss Pardoe, the nineteenth-century traveller, the inhabitants were forbidden by law to marry outside its precincts. Now there is not very much to see: the broken minaret of the mosque that Mehmet built for his troops, and a number of Byzantine fragments. Paths have been made and stairways cut up the slopes. A lift has even been installed in one of the towers. But it is worth climbing the hill to the topmost point of the battlements to look up the great stretch of the Bosphorus and across into Bithynia.

It was over this part of the strait that Mandrocles of Samos built a bridge for Darius. Herodotus tells us that Darius erected two marble pillars beside it and engraved in Assyrian upon one and in Greek upon the other 'all the peoples he had in his army'. It is believed that there were 700,000 of them.[2]

I disembarked at Rumeli and strolled along the shore to Balta Liman—a little north. A breeze from the Black Sea began to disperse the sultry air. After a quarter of a mile I found a body lying in the road. It was face downwards near the crown. For a moment I was alarmed. Surely it could not be another suicide? I drew closer. It moved. It turned out to be a young brown boy of about fifteen. He wore only a swimming-costume. Perhaps he was an embryo local Gandhi. After I passed him he rose and walked back to the sea.

I sat under some lime-trees in the street of Balta and grew sleepy in the drowsy murmur of the air; then had some fresh mackerel and cool beer. A travelling musician played what seemed to be nostalgic tunes on a mandolin and the afternoon settled easily into a gentle lassitude: the scent of the limes, the hum of honeying industry, the warbling of doves, the leisured noise of donkeys' hooves and cartwheels over cobbled stones.

Slowly approached that hour of the day when the batteries of time run down, the wheels of fortune revolve, diminishing, water is poised between flow and withdrawal, and the day, like an ageing man, reaches the end of its amble and sits for a while—contemplating.

In an old volume about Constantinople I read a tale about a girl called Phidalia who was cursed by her father for disobedience. She was tormented by furies and fled, like Io, over many lands before coming finally to Balta Liman where, in her agony, she threw herself into the Bosphorus. It was then that that stern and stubborn god Poseidon took pity on her, in his own peculiar way, touched her with his trident and converted her into a rock.

Thinking about this I dozed and my torpor grew deeper and more delicious. It was at such a time that the faithful believed the Devil might ensnare one in the 'grune' of sloth. In the late afternoon the warders of the *Castle of Mansoul* became sleepy and then a demon might creep in through one of the gates of the body and settle himself unobserved and begin his subtle work of destruction. Sloth!— a wonderfully onomatopoeic word. Priests, like Chaucer's Parson, were always reminding their flocks of this peril. 'Thanne cometh sompnolence, that is, sloggy slombrynge, which maketh a man be hevy and dul in body and in soule.' How difficult it is to resist 'sloggy slombrynge'. But the Parson is harsh. Against this 'rotenhearted synne of Accidie', he says, '. . . sholde men exercise hemself to doon goode werkes, and manly and vertuously cacchen corage wel to doon'. There is a vigorous rectitude about this which is very dissuasive: an atmosphere of 'Outward Bound' Schools, of crisp young men at military academies and the Jesuit Fathers' régime— and early Mass, cold tubs, sunlight soap, bromide, exercise—all those old-fashioned remedies for the 'brutish stings of the flesh' which never seemed to work. How pleasant it must be to be a sybarite without recrimination and how impossible to answer satisfactorily the brisk opinion of the conscience. It consoles to recall the number of saints who have been libertines but we dare not think how many libertines become saints. Most of us are only too happy to settle for an uneasy compromise and a 'stretch' in Purgatory.

A sudden highly powered roar woke my custodians in time. A Turkish M.T.B. was racing up the Bosphorus. A great white wave curved away from the grey steel prow. It must have been doing forty knots and looked magnificent.

I set off back to Rumeli. I had no courage or opportunity 'wel to doon' but I could take exercise and I clambered up the steep slopes inside the castle once again and marvelled at the stamina and industry which enabled 'The Conqueror's' men to accomplish their feat. It was arduous enough carrying myself and a camera.

Just above the mosque and the little foreshortened minaret a labourer was scything. I watched the fluent strokes and the measured swathes toppling. Then—he stopped; and, facing the south, towards Mecca, closed his eyes, fell upon his knees, spread his arms and, palms upward in a gesture of submission and supplication, began to pray. We were far from any *muezzin* and he did it quite suddenly as if an inward clock and voice had told him that it was the hour. He prayed for perhaps ten minutes, going through the customary ritual of kneeling, touching the forehead to the ground, rising again and so on. His lips moved. His eyes remained closed. It would be diffi-cult to find anything more sincere, less pretentious.

I have seen Muslims pray many times in many unlikely places. After a while one hardly notices. But this man was different. In this unlearned labourer's orisons there was a simplicity and a naïvety which was very affecting. His movements yielded all he had to the divine power. He was passive, obedient and suppliant. He spoke, as it were, directly to God. Every line of his body, each movement of his limbs, was a compliment to his maker; a sacrifice of himself. The man *was* the prayer.

We are not used to this kind of thing in Western Europe and there is nothing in Catholic or Orthodox countries to compare with such open and uninhibited devotion. Of course, when passing shrines and statues and churches the Catholic and the Orthodox make Signs of the Cross and murmur a prayer. It is a routine renewal of spiritual insurance and I have often seen it performed with special fervour in buses on dangerous mountain passes. And when the Angelus rings the workers pause and pray to the Virgin. The *muezzin's* sum-mons is the counterpart of the bell—but the Muslim needs no reminder. He knows—and his humility is of the essence of faith. Nevertheless it does not prevent him from arrogance about other religions.

Less humble but more zealous was the man whom I once saw praying on one of the boats as it travelled down the Bosphorus. He had a small mat with him and as the appeal from some mosque travelled across the water he appeared to make a rapid calculation. Then he oriented himself, as it were, on the spiritual 'beam' of Mecca and tuned to the shifting wavelength of Allah. Thereafter, every time the boat changed its course, so he adjusted his mat that he might remain facing the right direction.

In some Muslim countries even the praying mantis is supposed to turn reverently towards Mecca, and if this seems strange we must remember that St Francis, finding one in its attitude of prayer, actually ordered it to utter praise of God. What is more—it did so. But, as the great Fabre wrote, 'These attitudes of prayer conceal the most atrocious habits. These supplicating arms are lethal weapons; these fingers tell no rosaries but help to exterminate the passer-by.' He might have added that men hide similar habits with comparable piety.

Further north of Balta and Rumeli lies Boyaci Köy, which is full of Greeks and Armenians, and Emirgan. Its small bay is dark with forests of cypress. Immediately north is the largest and finest harbour in the whole strait—Istiniye. Over many centuries it has been used for building ships and a good many battles have taken place there. The Argonauts put up a temple when they escaped from Amycus. But it is especially famous for being near the site where St Daniel the pillar saint practised.

'Stylitism' is one of the more remarkable examples of religious eccentricity. Trances, ecstasy, flagellation, self-mutilation, levitation, starvation, solitude, hair-shirts, fasting, beds of nails—all these have played a part in the sublimation of the flesh and the purifying of the spirit. The Fakirs, naked and encrusted with the dirt of a lifetime, with finger-nails that had grown for as long and become anything up to a foot in length, with hair hanging to their calves, and loaded with weights and chains or bowed irrevocably to the ground, or with withering arms held constantly aloft, or roasting before slow fires, or suspended and swung by hooks embedded in the flesh, have all explored means of subjugating the body and winning some remission. In Christian lands, especially in the East, there were similar tendencies throughout the Middle Ages. Submission to all kinds of restraints became an end in itself. Palladius tells of a hermit in Palestine who lived in a cave on top of a mountain. For twenty-five years he never turned his face to the west. St Gregory of Nazianzus reports of another who stood upright for many years lost in contemplation and without ever lying down. Theodoret claims that he had seen a third who spent ten years in a tub suspended between poles. Thus they acquired reputations and power. They wooed filth and became wedded to discomfort. The task of self-abasement led to the crown of humility.

Later, Blessed Pierre Thomas gave orders that he was to be wrapped in a sack with a cord round his neck and laid on the ground to die. He said that he was to be buried at the entrance to the choir so that everyone might walk over his body—'even the dogs and goats'. One of his disciples went further and, when dying, ordered a heavy chain to be put round his neck. When dead he was to be dragged by his feet naked into the choir, his arms crossed and tied by three ropes to a plank. St Francis, besides preaching to the birds, ate dung. Such activities became fashionable. Ascetics competed to outdo each other in new and more bizarre forms of mortification.

Spiritual marathons have their counterpart in the labours of those who exhibit deformities in glass cages, swallow swords or play pianos and ping-pong for days on end. The desire to excel and be different takes many forms. Lucian somewhere mentions a high column at Hierapolis which a man climbed twice a year in order to speak to the gods. Perhaps it was this example as well as that of the early ascetics that led Simeon Stylites to live on top of a pillar. Whatever the facts of origin it seems to me that on the whole all exercises must take second place to 'Stylitism', of which we have had a modern echo in this century in the shape of pole-squatters.

'Among these heroes of the monastic life,' writes Gibbon, 'the name and genius of Simeon Stylites have been immortalized by the singular invention of an aerial penance.' Simeon, who was born right at the end of the fourth century, lived in the suburbs of Antioch. He worked as a shepherd and then became a monk. Soon he developed a taste for austerities and inordinate extremes. He decided to live alone and underwent the most arduous exercises. He survived a whole Lent without eating or drinking and stood erect for weeks on end. Finally he fixed himself to a rock by a chain. Then he had a column built and lived on that. To start with it was ten feet high; then it was raised to sixty. It is almost as if his ascent measured his spiritual progress. Soon his fame spread over the whole Mediterranean and Near East. His picture was sold in shops as far away as Paris. The Arabs in the desert regarded him as a heavenly creature. I cannot resist quoting Gibbon again who is invariably excellent on subjects like this: '... the Syrian Anachoret resisted the heat of thirty summers, and the cold of as many winters. Habit and exercise instructed him to maintain his dangerous situation without fear or giddiness, and successively to assume the different postures of devotion. He sometimes prayed in an erect attitude, with his outstretched arms in the figure of a cross; but his most familiar practice was that of bending his meagre skeleton from the forehead to the feet; and a curious spectator, after numbering twelve hundred and fourty-four repetitions, at length desisted from the endless account.'

Privation led to disease and an ulcer developed in his thigh. 'This might shorten,' says Gibbon, 'but it could not disturb this celestial life; and the patient Hermit expired, without descending from his column.' Gibbon could not forbear to include a long and characteristic footnote about the ulcer. 'I must not', he writes, 'conceal a piece of ancient scandal concerning the origin of this ulcer. It has been reported that the Devil, assuming an angelic form, invited him to ascend, like Elijah, into a fiery chariot. The saint too hastily raised his foot, and Satan seized the moment of inflicting this chastisement on his vanity.' When Simeon died in 459 he was taken down and transported to Antioch. There he was laid at rest in the principal church. The pillar was preserved and surrounded by an octagonal piazza on the sides of which were built four great basilicas.

Not unnaturally he had a succession of imitators of whom the most famous was Daniel. He lived for eighty-four years and spent thirty-three and a third of those on the top of his pillar near Istiniye. That is to say, he mounted it in 460 and was removed from it in 493. To us now it seems scarcely possible that in his middle and old age a man might survive exposed to the heat of so many summers and to the frosts, rain, snow, gales and hail of so many winters. Given every comfort and protection it would be credible but Daniel mortified himself with rigorous fasts and did exercises that would kill most men of that age in a few months.

Once his pillar was nearly blown down and a Greek biographer gives an account of what must have been a quite extraordinary scene. A terrific storm broke and the supports of the column gave way. Then the whole structure began to sway from side to side while the saint clung tenaciously to the top: like a prophet in a crow's nest. The oscillations grew wider and slower. The saint prayed and eventually a calm fell.

The column consisted of three parts: steps up to the platform at the base, the column itself and the enclosure at the top with a balcony round it. After passing nearly the whole of the fifth century in self-abnegation, prayer and spiritual advice Daniel died. The same biographer gives an account of his removal: 'When they took down the railing they found his knees drawn up to his chest, and his heels and legs to his thighs. And whilst his body was being forcibly straightened, his bones creaked so loudly that we thought his body would be shattered; yet when he was laid out, he was quite entire except that his feet had been worn away by inflammation and the

gnawing of worms. The weight of the hair of his head was divided
into twelve plaits, each of which was four cubits long; likewise his
beard was divided into two and each plait was three cubits long.'
That is to say his hair trailed to the ground and his beard fell below
his knees. His nails also were inordinately long. He must have looked
rather like Nebuchadnezzar who was driven from his kingdom and,
as reported in the Book of Daniel, 'his body was wet with the dew
of heaven . . . his hair was grown like eagle feathers, and his nails
like birds' claws'.

In the following century St Alypius had a pillar near Adrianople.
He actually stood upright for fifty-three years and then his legs
would no longer support him. Paralysed, he lay down on his side and
spent the next fourteen years in that position. The last famous Stylite,
St Luke, had a column at Chalcedon. He acquired a reputation as a
healer. There were many others and even some women, though this
form of asceticism never caught on in the West. In the East cases were
found down to the twelfth century and in the Russian Church until
1461.

We may smile a little now at such extravagant otherworldliness,
but what faith; what endurance, and what humility! As Tennyson
put it in a curious and rather unsuccessful poem of *St Simeon*:

> . . . I Simeon,
> The watcher on the column till the end;
> I, Simeon, whose brain the sunshine bakes;
> I, whose bald brows in silent hours become
> Unnaturally hoar with rime, do now
> From my high nest of penance here proclaim
> That Pontius and Iscariot by my side
> Show'd like fair seraphs.

Yeniköy, once renowned for its biscuit-factories and its execrable
wine, is a place I have seldom visited. More often I have been to
Tarabya and Sariyer—from which you can see the mouth of the
Black Sea. Both are pleasant. One spring morning a policeman
friend on leave and a Yugoslavian woman separated from an alco-
holic English husband drove me to Sariyer. There we took an early
lunch of *kebab* and beer before going on to the sea-coast.

While we were sitting there, digesting, talking and repelling the
more forward flies of the summer, the hour of prayer was an-
nounced. The very small minaret, belonging to a mosque converted

from a house, was only thirty yards away. I could see it and its gallery clearly—but there was no *muezzin*. Unmistakably the cry continued to come from that quarter—a particularly harmonious one. Suddenly an explanation occurred to me. I went over to confirm my suspicion. Through the window of a small room adjoining the minaret I saw the *muezzin*. He was sitting in his shirt-sleeves and warbling into a microphone. I looked up. Over the edge of the balcony hung little loudspeakers.

The Prophet is alleged to have said that *muezzins* may expect to go to Paradise, and whoever serves in that office for seven years would almost certainly be saved from Hell. But there must be some exceptions. The Slothful on the fourth cornice of the *Purgatorio* were punished by practising zeal. They had, very appropriately, to run round and round. The Muslim sentence is not specific; perhaps, for idle criers, running up and down spiral staircases in immense minarets. And surely such a one as this would need it. It is only a matter of time before he installs a gramophone. Later he can pay a boy to play the record.

We have become used to modernization of this kind in America and England—especially in Catholic churches. Nevertheless the majority of words are still inaudible. Sunday after Sunday notices are murmured, gospels and epistles mumbled, sermons mutilated by a complete disregard for the basic principles of elocution. The hungry sheep look up—and are not fed. The level of preaching has deteriorated greatly. In Anglican and Evangelical churches the standards are still quite high and, of course, their clergy have a tradition in preaching. But, for instance, in the seventeenth century men like Donne and Taylor, like many of their predecessors, thought nothing of preaching for two or three hours, often in the open air, to congregations which sometimes amounted to many thousands. And what sermons they were. Closely argued and intricately elaborated, packed with allusion and quotation, they require considerable concentration in reading. How much depended, then, on the delivery. Now we have usually much less than twenty minutes—fortunately—to congregations of a few hundred, in buildings properly acousticated and installed with elaborate 'Tannoy' systems—and still we have to strain our ears.

Generally the art of speaking in public has been and is being neglected, and this seems to me to be a great pity. It is sad that a man with a normal voice—part of whose profession it is to use it—

cannot fill the average church or public building with his words; and absurd that if he is not a natural speaker he is not trained, at any rate to be audible. It ought to be a minimum qualification.

Soon we were moving swiftly in the policeman's high-powered American car, following the bends and folds of the broken coast. Music from the radio faded and returned as we took the corners. Above and on our left, exposed, were the balding crowns of scrub-covered hills. Below them clusters of purple and magenta embossed the dark tiers of cypress. The Judas-trees were in bloom.

In Turkish it is called *erguvan*; *erguvani* means purple. The best place to see them is on the slopes of the Bithynian Olympus. The flowers have an odd acid taste and are mixed with salad and made into fritters. The older herbalists often used to reproduce the tree, and I remember once seeing a wood-cut by Castor Durante which had the figure of Iscariot suspended from one of the branches.

Popular antipathy to Iscariot sometimes takes curious forms and in Corfu, for instance, on the Eve of Easter, the people used to throw down crockery and other missiles into the streets—thus performing an imaginary stoning of the traitor. In Mexico they are even more direct and blow up an effigy filled with crackers and explosives. But it is strange that the greatest of all treacheries should be perpetuated by such a beautiful tree.

Mahmut, the policeman, suddenly quoted some verse. I could not understand it. But it was Omar:

> Alas: that the book of youth is folded up
> And that this fresh purple spring is turned to winter.

At that very moment the book of youth nearly did fold up. We completed two and a half revolutions in the middle of the road and stopped dead. The wireless protested. Somehow a quantity of oil had become spread over the relatively smooth surface of the tarmac. With admirable composure Mahmut reversed and drove on. 'Allah blinked on us,' he observed laconically.

Our jarred pulses were quietening as we passed through the village of Yenimahalle where choirs of nightingales sing their plaintive anthem all night long in the beech and chestnut groves. This is a romantic place, fit for ailing poets. The song of these birds, like that of larks, was always prized by the royalty of the Ottoman empire. There were many professional bird-catchers and in Evliya Efendi's day there was a guild of nightingale dealers five hundred strong. They supplied barbers' shops, as well as grandees, with their catches. They exhibited them in cages studded with onyx and pearls. In a similar fashion they pedalled talking parrots and starlings, some of which, according to Evliya, could recite prayers. In the Imperial Palace there was a Keeper of Nightingales—quite a well-paid post.

The Muslim, or at any rate the Turkish Muslim, has a great respect for and indulgence towards birds and animals, especially kites whose function they believe is to keep cities clean. This indulgence might often be turned to profitable account and it was while reading the letters of Busbecq that I came across what must count as one of the most ingenious methods of earning a living. He saw in the city some bird-catchers under a plane-tree, but they were not selling their birds. On the contrary, the victims were ransomed by passers-by and liberated. It seems to me a most enterprising example of 'spivvery'.

Less humane and, probably, less successful, is a custom among the Turks of Central Asia. When a child is late in learning to speak they give it the tongues of certain birds to eat.

Nearer the mouth of the Black Sea the land became more bleak and the channel narrowed. The shore-line is a graveyard of embassies. Soon cliffs of basalt rose steeply. It is an inhospitable terrain, withered and beaten by centuries of storms. Above, on the barren heights, are the ruins of a number of forts and towers.

We climbed and soon the Black Sea came into view, a notorious sea, innocuously blue and glittering. Foam snarled gently against rock below. In the far distance on pale beaches were tiny brown and white figures like pied sea-birds, and scattered among them red and orange and purple and multi-coloured mushrooms: sunbathers and their umbrellas, the resort of Kilyos. Somewhere up here behind us lived the blind soothsayer Phineus who was plagued by the Harpies. Every time he tried to eat they rushed on him and snatched away the food and covered the area with their stench and excrement. Malnutrition set in but his death was averted by the Argonauts; and to Jason he gave the famous advice that enabled him to pass the Cyanean rocks which guarded the entrance to the Bosphorus and swung together to crush any ship which tried to pass into the Black Sea. Jason did as he was told, released the dove, which the rocks destroyed, and made a dash for it. As we know now the rocks have been still ever since and one of the islands remains. There are other versions of course.

On a rocky promontory a lighthouse stood up like the foresight
on a gun-barrel, and the Black Sea scrolls curled whitely about it.
There have always been lighthouses here for it is a perilous piece of
coast. Most travellers have commented upon them but I prefer
Lithgow's description most of all. He saw a 'Lanthorne higher than
any Steeple, whereon there is a panne full of liquor, that burneth
every night to give warning unto ships.' That was in 1610.[3]

★

There is a fast and frequent service of boats across the Bosphorus
to Kadiköy and from time to time I found it pleasant to pass a day
or two in a more village-like and provincial atmosphere. The far
shore is dominated by the immense barracks of Selimiye: a long
pale-yellow frontage with towers at the angles topped with orange
tiles. Near by is Haydarpaşa, the grey and pseudo-Gothic main
station for the Taurus express, for Baghdad and Damascus. It looks
as if St Dominic's has spawned amidst the ancient sites of the Dervishes; and at a distance it reminds one irresistibly of *The Lanchester
Tradition*, the numberless and nameless Perrins and Traills, and the
common-rooms of England filled with men who have plodded
through stale syllabuses and the tedious reiterations of half a century
of speech days and house finals. Nearby also are the sites of
Florence Nightingale's hospital and the British cemeteries overgrown by grass and disfigured by mouldering gravestones. The
cicadas intone their day-long elegies and the stones dutifully record
their euphemistic epitaphs:

> Row after row with strict impunity
> The headstones yield their names to the element,
> The wind whirrs without recollection;
> In the riven troughs the sprayed leaves
> Pile up, of nature the casual sacrament
> To the seasonal eternity of death;

So wrote Allen Tate in his splendid poem *Ode to the Confederate
Dead*. The English always seem to make the best of corners of
foreign fields; and the Smiths and the Browns and the Davies'
guarded by the stony stares of broken and anonymous angels are
curiously pathetic.

Kadiköy is a typically Turkish town with many wooden houses, little cafés and tree-shaded streets. It was the pitch of Chalcedon, the town of those who were described as blind by the Delphic Oracle because they missed the natural harbour opposite. In the fifth century B.C. it passed into the hands of the Persians. Then it became a Roman base for the wars against Mithridates. Later it was used by the Crusaders. Finally it was occupied by the Ottomans. Now, after the vicissitudes of nearly thirty centuries, it is placid and pretty.

Further up the Bosphorus is Üsküdar (Scutari), the ancient Chrysopolis. Xenophon paused here in the course of his retreat with the 'Ten Thousand' but he tells us nothing about it. During the Byzantine era it followed the fortunes and misfortunes of Constantinople but, being exposed, was severely ravaged by the Persians and Arabs, then occupied by the fourth crusade in 1203. Eventually it fell, like Kadiköy, under Ottoman domination. It used to be a much more populous place. In the seventeenth century Evliya Efendi listed eleven kitchens for the poor, forty-seven convents, eight hundred private baths, eleven caravanserais, five hundred *khans*, sixty-six water-distributing establishments, over two thousand shops, four thousand vineyards and 'three hundred gardens with fragrant flowers'.

From here the annual caravan, having crossed the strait, left for Mecca; and here the caravans from the Middle and Far East unloaded.

There are some beautiful mountains and smaller mosques upon one of which no pigeons ever land. There are a number of explanations for this: all are plausible and none convincing.

Now Üsküdar is best known for its cemeteries, for it has long been the favourite burial-place of the Muslim. The graves of many centuries have accumulated amidst a forest of cypresses watered by streams. Here death rules in a crumbling empire of desolated stone and rampant undergrowth. While over all, mile after mile, trim, black and motionless, the cypresses stand like funeral plumes. In places subsidences and upheavals have disarrayed the tombs and steles ornamented by fezes and turbans, and everything is flung into irrevocable disorder. The ground is sacred, sinister and ghostly. Scorpions and reptiles live in the thick cover. To quote Allen Tate again:

> Autumn is desolation in the plot
> Of a thousand acres where these memories grow
> From the inexhaustible bodies that are not
> Dead, but feed the grass row after rich row.

All day the cicadas clack monotonously and at night the owl tolls. It is a place to suit the morbid and the romantic taste. Occasionally, if you are careless, you may surprise an unsuspecting couple copulating.

Scutari also used to be one of the strongholds of the Dervishes. The ceremony of the Howling Dervishes was no less remarkable than that of the Whirling. They stood, to begin, pressed against one another, shoulder to shoulder. Their eyes remained closed. Then they began to swing slowly from side to side in harmony, holding their right feet still but moving sideways with the left. Gradually the pace and the movement intensified. They began to cry out, to sob, to groan. In time the ecstasy overtook them. They went temporarily mad. Their mouths dripped and frothed with foam. The spectators joined and a kind of spellbound bedlam ensued.

Some fell down. Others beat the floor and howled. Then, as the orgasm waned, children and babies were brought in and laid face downwards on sheepskins. Then the Sheik rose and, supported on each side, walked over the rows of prostrate bodies. This was the blessing of the holy feet.

Prayer was based on the principle of constant repetition: the need for quantity being the will of Allah. At one time they used to torture themselves in the most violent manner by cooling red-hot irons in their flesh and mouths, and by driving knives through their cheeks and arms and legs. These Dervishes also had a custom of chanting every night a petition for divine mercy for those who could not sleep. In their neighbourhood cause and cure must have been identical.

From Üsküdar northwards there are a dozen or more villages loosely linked. The elegant minarets of many small mosques appear and disappear among the thickly wooded shores. The white palaces of Sultans punctuate the course. Gardens and *kiosques,* graceful relics of a now long-distant power and luxury, are scattered about. The villages and wooden houses come to the water's edge; and there are innumerable winding cobbled streets with little shops and work-rooms and countless cafés under the plane-trees, the maple and the acacia; and others with marble-topped tables where you can get a simple and extremely cheap meal of pilaf and meat and beans with inexpensive coarse wine and abundant fruit.

One of the most attractive of these villages is Beylerbey at the toe of Mount Bülgürlü: it is the abode of princes and was a favourite resort of Byzantine emperors and Ottoman Sultans.

I went there one night with two Turkish poets and a singer—
one of the girls from the night-clubs in Pera. We sat in the open at
the very brink of the Bosphorus. In columns and restless gyrations
the gnats spun on the warm air. We sipped glasses of tea for a long
while and talked of the Ottoman empire in the palmy days, if there
were any. But these two men believed that even the last fifty years
of the nineteenth century were palmy compared with the present.
Yet it was a time of false and unstable prosperity. Too many died
to sustain it. But the intellectuals deplored the upheavals of the
twentieth century and aired a musty nostalgia for the nineteenth.
They were Romantics at heart and in purpose. We talked of Byron
and Keats and Tennyson. I discovered that Baudelaire was their
mentor and hero. We watched the gold lights juggling in the swift
black stream, the steamers ablaze passing to and fro, and grew
drowsy in the buxom calmness of the night, sniffing the fishy, salty
smells of the wharves.

At eight o'clock we were summoned to the local open-air theatre
to attend a circumcision party. These originated in religious ceremony and are still held to honour a son. Relatives and friends gather
for the function and the 'victims'—usually about ten years old—are
entertained. They are dressed in embroidered jackets and little
braided pill-box hats of coloured silk or satin.

The booking-office and vestibule of the theatre were combined
and consisted merely of a bulge in a passage. Clumsy and garish
posters of illustrious bosoms and fabulous legs adorned the white-
washed walls. At the curtained entrance we were greeted by Sadi
Tek, a splendid old actor with a bald dome flanked by bushy copses
of whitening hair. An illustrated brochure recording his career was
thrust into my hands. It contained pictures of himself as Othello
and as Hamlet mourning the skull of Yorick. He struck a pose and
declaimed:

'Where be your gibes now? your gambols? your songs? your
flashes of merriment, that were wont to set the table on a roar?
Not one now, to mock your own grinning? Quite chap-fallen?'

Then we were taken into the crowded theatre—formerly a long,
narrow, high-walled garden—with the stage at one end. It also
served as a cinema. Ranged along each side were brass bedsteads
and in the beds, gaily attired and hugely enjoying the occasion, were
the circumcised. It was packed out. On the ramshackle stage a

number of men were doing their best with scenery and eccentric lighting apparatus. They were preparing for a Karagöz show.

Karagöz and his protagonist Hacivat, and many other minor characters, are puppets cut out of hide (camel is quite often used) or parchment and gaily decorated. The heads, arms and legs are movable, but the whole thing is done in profile. The entertainment dates from many centuries back and the principals have not changed much, though novelties have been added: Mickey Mouse, Tarzan, Marlene Dietrich, Greta Garbo and so on. The situations involve kidnapping, raids on Turkish baths, raids on cafés, professional scribes, thieves, henpecked husbands and cockpecked wives. A good deal of improvisation is employed.

After prolonged wrestling with flexes and curtains everything was at last ready and a slapstick comedy was performed accompanied by a commentary wildly distorted by a bronchial loudspeaker. The circumcised howled with glee at each bizarre antic. After that the local band performed. They stood and sat rather self-consciously with melancholy faces and produced what was, to the untutored ear, a hideous uproar. A solo followed and then a girl sang. The loudspeaker system grew worse and worse. The girl's throaty ululations became more strident and more grotesque. It sounded like the love-song of some adenoidal hyena. Conversations went on meanwhile—fortunately. A beautiful girl in the row in front with the exquisite name of 'Stupefied with Desire' passed round a box of sugared fruit to the guests—ourselves. Everybody overflowed with good humour and generosity.

At last we had to catch a boat and after the cacophony of music and laughter and voices it was a great relief to glide mellifluously on the smooth currents of the ebony water and watch the big searchlights of the ferries scything the darkness with great sweeps of light.

Grelot, who was in Constantinople towards the end of the seventeenth century, gives an entertaining account of the same ceremony of circumcision—a considerably more elaborate affair in those days. The master of the house prepared a huge feast and the victim was mounted on a horse or a camel and led in triumph through the village or, if it were a city, that quarter in which his parents lived. His school-fellows and friends waited upon him on foot, 'hollowing and hooping for joy that he is going to be admitted into the number of true *Musselmen*'. After the cavalcade everyone returned to the house and the *Imam* made a 'pithie harange' upon the operation that was to follow. Thus Grelot describes it: '. . . comes a Chir-urgion, who having plac'd the lad upon a *Sopha* or *Turkish* Table, two Servants holding a linnen napkin before him, draws out the Preputium in length as far as he can pull it, and so keeping it from running back, by clapping a pair of little Pincers at the head of the nut, takes off the surplusage with a sharp Razor, and then holds it up in his fingers to be seen by all the Company, who cry out at the same time, *Alla Hecher ia Alla Alla.*'[4]

When a member of the royal house was circumcised the festivities were on a scale equal to the Lord Mayor's Show. To mark that of young Mehmet III *kiosques* were erected, gladiators fought in the Hippodrome and a hundred Greeks recanted their faith. A masque of St George and the Dragon was performed and there was a further masque of castles and elephants. A Greek priest showed a forest of artificial cypresses. The prince appeared in scarlet and gold, black heron's plumes nodding in his turban. He was armed with a jewelled sword and a crystal-headed mace. The aristocratic equiva-lents of sugared fruit were sugar elephants, nine in all, seventeen sugar lions, nineteen leopards, twenty-two horses, four giraffes, twenty-one camels, twenty-five falcons, nine sirens and eleven storks. After the operation his foreskin was sent in a golden cup to his mother, and the knife to his grandmother.

Perhaps most remarkable of all was a pageant strongly reminis-cent of Aldershot Tattoos, and of contemporary interest. Baudier of Languedoc observed it. 'The *Occhiali Bassa* a great Admirall of the Sea,' he writes (in Grimstone's translation), 'exceeded by his indus-trie, the *Vizir's* invention. Hee caused to come rowling into the place, a great Island, admirably well made of boords and pastboord, which represented *Cypres*: Two powerfull Armies held it besieged, the one by Sea and the other by Land: There was artificially seene their descent into the Island, the siege of *Famagouste*, the sallies, skir-mishes, batteries, counter-batteries, mines, counter-mines, breaches, assaults upon assault, fire-workes, and whatsoever the furie of Warre could invent. Sometimes the Turkes were Masters of the Wals, and suddenly the generositie of the Cypriots repulsed them: But time, force, and the want of Succours made them receive the composition which they offered them.'[5] Fluellen would have enjoyed himself at this spectacle.

The Feast of the Circumcision was another important occasion and Evliya Efendi, the seventeenth-century traveller, described the

pyrotechnic display which marked it. 'They let off', he writes, 'some
hundred thousand of rockets of every description, covering the surface of the sea; some of these dive and come up again setting the
whole sea ablaze and causing such commotion among the fish that
they leap out of the water and fall back into the sea.'[6] The Sultans
were great showmen and the festivals usually went on for weeks.

★

There is a small and rather beautiful palace at Beylerbey frequented
in the old days by innumerable kings, queens and princes. There
were sumptuous frescoed rooms, colonnades, fountains, baths—all
now abandoned and neglected. Abdül Aziz who built it in 1865 had
a zoo and diverted himself with troops of ostriches and Bengal tigers.
There were magnificent gardens replete with glades and walks and
running streams. These were laid out in 1639 by Murat IV—a
morose fellow who gave instructions to his minions to shoot at sight
anyone who approached the gardens looking happy and contented.
It was here also that the unfortunate Abdül Hamit II retired from
Salonika to spend his last six years in one of the back rooms. Here
he died lonely and destitute, nursed by one faithful concubine who
read to him from the newspapers hour after hour while one tragedy
after another befell his country.

Sometimes I used to take a boat to Beylerbey and spend the day
walking up the bank towards the Black Sea, pottering among deserted and beautiful precincts.

> . . . desolation saddens all thy green:
> . . . No more thy glassy brook reflects the day,
> But, choked with sedges, works its weedy way;
> Along thy glades, a solitary guest,
> The hollow-sounding bittern guards its nest;
> Amidst thy desert walks the lapwing flies,
> And tires their echoes with unvaried cries.
> Sunk are the bowers in shapeless ruin all,
> And the long grass o'ertops the mouldering wall;

Half an hour brings one to what is known as the Village of Hooks
because a number of anchor-hooks of the Byzantine period were
found there. The Persian gardens, the palaces and the *kiosques* have
all gone. Evliya Efendi says that in his day the inhabitants were a

noisy and quarrelsome lot of people, and, true or not, in the course of one afternoon I saw three fights there, blood being drawn in two. But like sudden storms they were short and soon outlasted themselves. It was there also one day, while sitting in the shadow of a great plane-tree and sipping a glass of iced cherry juice, that I saw something that I had not expected to see in these days.

I was watching idly the progress of an old man up the street towards me. From time to time he bent, picked something up and tucked it into a cranny of the nearest wall. It happened several times but it was not until he was right before me that I realized what he was doing.

In the past it was always the custom among Muslims of the simpler orders, and probably still is in some parts of the world, to rescue any piece of paper or rag or leather or anything which might have the Holy Name upon it. And indeed, for long, paper itself or anything written upon was regarded as almost sacred. It was believed to be dangerous to tread upon such articles lest Allah might be insulted. Similarly an inscription on stone was not to be touched. Amulets and talismans were very common and were often of stone or metal, strips of paper, parchment or leather.

As long ago as the middle of the sixteenth century Seigneur Busbecq, that urbane and learned Frenchman who spent some years in Constantinople as a diplomat, observed the same phenomenon. 'While staying in inns,' he wrote, 'I often happened to notice pieces of paper thrust into the chinks of walls. These aroused my curiosity, and I pulled them out. . . . Afterwards, when I grew more familiar with Turks, I learnt from my friends that the Turks have a great respect for paper, because the name of God may be written upon it. . . .'[7]

But there was another reason for this prudence. When summoned from Purgatory for the Last Judgment, Muslims must pass over a red-hot gridiron and all the paper they have not trampled on will adhere to the soles of their feet and prevent them from being burnt. It was also a crime to sit on the Koran or allow the holy book to lie beneath others. An even greater offence was to allow rose-leaves to lie upon the ground for they believed that the rose sprang from the sweat of Mohammed—as the ancients thought it came from the blood of Venus. But this has not prevented them from making rose-petal and rose-leaf jam which is delicious; almost as delicious as the conserve made from lemon and orange blossom.

Only a little further on is Kandilli, a small village where the
Bosphorus is at its swiftest and most dangerous. Here the stream is
known as the Devil's current. I used to visit Kandilli quite often to
see a professorial friend from the University. On a commanding
point, in a spacious house, with a charming wife and a large family,
he seemed to be progressing towards an ideal existence. Once I
sought to surprise him as a philologist by telling him that Latin is
still spoken in the mountainous and inland districts of Sardinia. 'Yes—
but what kind of Latin?' he retorted scornfully; and to cap it told me
that Gothic was last heard in Constantinople at the end of the seventeenth century. I could not be bothered to ask him what kind of Gothic.

One afternoon we strolled down to the Sweet Waters of Asia
which enter the Bosphorus above Kandilli. A deserted rococo palace
and a fountain lie near a meadow admirably suited for picnic
parties.

At the end of the nineteenth century it was frequented by Ottoman society and in such a place it became possible for gentlemen
and painted mistresses to philander in the language of flowers by
purling streams and fritter away sunny afternoons waited upon by
slaves. Lady Neave once went there dressed as a Turkish lady. Thus
she describes her journey: 'Turks in smartly gilded skiffs followed
the ladies' *caïques* as closely as they dared, but the *caïquegees*,
dressed in flowing white trowsers and richly embroidered zouave
coats, and with the inevitable red fez on their heads, did their best
to keep them at oar's length. When the crowd of boats became too
great to make rowing possible, the only means of progress was by
pushing one's craft forward by hand at the expense of the boats
alongside.'[8]

The river was patrolled by police to make sure that nobody spoke
to the women, and Lady Neave's own escapade ended abruptly
when some prince bestowed too much attention upon a veiled lady
and everybody was sent home. It was here also that she saw Pierre
Loti who lay 'languidly against a pile of multi-coloured silk cushions
trailing his manicured fingers covered with turqoise rings through
the muddy water'. *Eheu fugaces . . .*, and with them, we cannot
greatly regret it, the Pierre Lotis.

Men, of course, were segregated on arrival—at any rate in theory.
They lounged, smoking their *tchibouques* and refreshing themselves
with water-melon and scented sherbert; keeping one eye cocked in
the direction of the ladies.

Not far away rich and beautiful Sultanas paraded gently to and fro among the glades, leaning on silken cushions in the *arabas*. These small carriages were always lined with looking-glasses and adorned with bright awnings and draperies. In one quarter would be gathered the *Pasha's harem* and scattered about were the various retinues and stables of *Beys, Efendis* and *Emirs*, clad in satin, silk and gossamer: in James Macintosh's phrase—'the frivolous work of polished idleness'. They reclined on blue carpets from Persia and crimson rugs from Damascus, attended by servants feeding them with delicacies and holding jewelled mirrors for make-up maintenance work. In and about them weaved vendors of sweetmeats and yoghourt, men carrying pails of ice, water-sellers, and others laden with peaches, grapes and musk melons. There where exhibitors of dancing bears and monkeys, strolling musicians and everlasting relays of negroes with more carpets and private refreshments.

So their days passed as they titivated and preened, making a career of indolence and, when the opportunity offered, indulging in surreptitious affairs which were always dangerous and often sterile. But what else was there for them to do? It was the kind of energetic idleness which Pope would have delighted to satirise. In fact, he writes of something like it in the *Rape of the Lock*:

> Hither the heroes and the nymphs resort,
> To taste awhile the pleasures of a court;
> In various talk th'instructive hours they pass'd,
> Who gave the ball, or paid the visit last;
> One speaks the glory of the British Queen,
> And one describes a charming Indian screen;
> A third interprets motions, looks, and eyes;
> At every word a reputation dies.
> Snuff, or the fan, supply each pause of chat,
> With singing, laughing, ogling, and all that.

Conversation, it seems, as elsewhere, was negligible. They seldom saw or read anything about which they could converse. Intercourse was confined to gossip and intrigue, their own ailments and other people's characters. But these, after all, have always been and still are the essentials of most communication. There are few things that we relish more than a little ingenuous calumny and detraction mixed with some self-pity and hypochondria. We swop rumours about the vice and stupidity of others as we discuss racing and test matches and clothes. How fortunate it is that others never really know what we think of them. How dreadful it would be if we knew what they thought of us. One day, at that 'final calling to the bar' that Sir Thomas Browne spoke of, we shall be expected to expose our hypocrisies and explain our malice. Justification can hardly enter into it. Then the food of our mirth will be flung back in our faces as excrement.

But the Turkish women, poor things, had more excuse. Their lives were circumscribed by custom and taboo, and Miss Pardoe, an indefatigable and very well-brought-up Englishwoman who spent a good deal of time observing Turkish women in the middle of the nineteenth century, is hardly fair with a rather severe and governessy verdict. 'Their habits', she wrote, 'are, generally speaking, most luxurious and indolent, if I except their custom of early rising, which, did they occupy themselves in any useful manner, would be undoubtedly very commendable.'[9] It is extraordinary how people can suggest their character in one sentence. Miss Pardoe, one feels, must have been a spinstered shade of a minor Gibbon; one who kept the key of her chastity belt in the bank.

There is a lot to be said for idleness, disciplined inertia, deliberate, uninhibited inaction; in short, a kind of well-organized Oblomovism. There are far too many people going through the motions of working; far too many actually convinced that what may have started as a pretence without them realizing it is now a reality. The clichés in which the word 'work' occurs are multiple and we hear them every day. Life is divided neatly into sections, temporal vessels which somehow have to be filled, emptied and replenished. It is now axiomatic, according to the admirable Mr Parkinson, that 'work expands to fill the time available for its completion'. People imagine work, invent work. Whole organizations and departments come into existence to deal with work which they themselves are creating. Given certain conditions, eating and sleeping have the same results. People rise later in order to have less time in which to realize that they do not know how, and are not equipped, to use it. People eat and drink more and sit over meals for the same reason. A good many other functions and activities operate in the same way. There is also a corollary to this: the cult of saving time: of travelling more quickly, for instance. But, in fact, little time is saved, lives are often endangered, and when time is saved few know what to do with it. The trap has sprung on themselves. Here, under the guises of efficiency and need, men, without realizing the paradox, extend the compartment for which more work, or the pretence of work, is required in order to fill it . . . and so on. They pursue by acceleration what they hope to escape by postponement. Remove habit, throw some men back on themselves and soon they do not know what to do.

Oblomov, unfortunately, allowed himself to grow physically flabby and mentally impotent. He had practice without theory. What is desirable is extensive and fully occupied, fecund and fruitive leisure. The time will come, has already begun to come, when leisure will be a danger. We either use leisure properly, admit our leisure without restraint or inhibition or excuse, or allow people to make money from preventing us using it, or from preventing the realization that we are not using it.

In 1932 Earl Russell wrote an excellent essay called *In Praise of Idleness* which deserves re-attention. He believed that a great deal of harm was being done to the modern world by a belief in the virtuousness of work. He maintained that the way to happiness lay in an organized diminution of work. He simplifies the matter thus: 'First of all: what is work? Work is of two kinds: first, altering the position of matter at or near the earth's surface relatively to other such matter; second, telling other people to do so. The first kind is unpleasant and ill paid; the second is pleasant and highly paid. The second kind is capable of indefinite extension: there are not only those who give orders, but those who give advice as to what orders should be given. Usually two opposite kinds of advice are given simultaneously by two organized bodies of men; this is called politics. The skill required for this kind of work is not knowledge of the subjects as to which advice is given, but knowledge of the art of persuasive speaking and writing, i.e. of advertising.'

Fewer and fewer people are needed for more and more jobs. Every year now more and more people will have, in practice, less to do and will be doing less; and they will be having longer lives in which to do it. It will become ever more necessary to have some idea of what to do with the time. Unconstructive idleness badly leads to rancour, boredom, resentment, misunderstanding, embitterment, envy . . . there is no end to what it leads. The empty and notionless mind is the most fertile vessel of disaster. Lacking the chance of wasting their time with their hands people must have the opportunities of learning how not to waste their time with their minds.

A man begins to come to terms with himself when he finds he has nothing to do, when he depends entirely, or nearly so, on what goes on in his mind. So long as he is caught up in the immense and stultifying machinery which is always persuading him that he is needed to keep it going, then his opportunities for coming to terms with himself are few.

It is necessary periodically to retreat into the desert, to have silence, and to explore, however unpleasant it may be, the garbage-dump of the mind. In those sinister and gently pullulating depths of corrupt urges and base instincts, in the back-alleys and cul-de-sacs of the city, amidst all that rubbish which is so often swept carefully into a corner, a man can find, perhaps quite accidentally, a reason for his existence. As Ecclesiastes puts it: 'The wisdom of a learned man cometh by opportunity of leisure: and he that hath little business shall become wise.'

Wandering along the shores of the Sweet Waters of Asia the professor and I argued about the workings of a world from which money and all the colossal hypocrisy and snobbery which surrounds it had been removed. Logically, and in theory, if one takes the trouble to follow the notion through all the necessary steps, it seems to be the only answer. Practically, it will probably coincide with the coming of the Kingdom of Heaven. A uniform world currency would, however, be a pace in the right direction.

One thing we agreed upon was that many people like the idea of laziness whereas the Turk really enjoys the act of laziness, or the 'not-act' of laziness. When others are not having recriminations about doing nothing they are pretending to have them or thinking that they ought to. The Turk has his feet up and no qualms. *Dolce far niente* is an excellent counsel.

Kandilli. When I had the chance I looked up Evliya Efendi to see what he has to say about it. He is enthusiastic and evokes an image. 'A river resembling the spring of life which flows from Mount Alemtagh is adorned on both banks with gardens and mills. It is crossed by a wooden bridge, under which pass the boats of lovers, who come here to enjoy the delicious meadows.' He adds prosaically that it is a place 'very well worth seeing'.[10] It still is though now no longer reminiscent of the Cherwell at Oxford on summer afternoons; afternoons when so many resolutions to get good degrees are forgotten and lost in prolonged embraces while the agitations of the water record the progress of passion.

One of the Byzantine emperors was once at Kandilli with his

entourage when the bodies of a Sheik and his ten followers who had been executed in Constantinople came floating by, 'dancing on the waves,' as Evliya put it, 'with their heads in their hands'. The emperor's suite, seeing this, suggested that they must have been unjustly executed and the emperor wept as he saw them floating against the current to the opposite shore of Rumeli Hisar. They were buried on that shore and for ten nights afterwards light was seen pouring down on their graves.

Further north is Çubuklu where the monk Alexander founded a monastery of 'Sleepless Monks' in the fifth century. For the best part of a thousand years they prayed in shifts, thus ensuring a continuous supplication. And a little further lies Beykoz, a large village once famous for its glass-factory, and Incirköy where lived the Grand Vizier of Sultan Ibrahim, an immensely fat man better known in Ottoman history as the man who was torn into a thousand pieces. After he had been dismissed and strangled his body was thrown into the Hippodrome where it remained overnight. The following morning a Janissary saw it and felt sure that the corpse of one so fat would be a good cure for rheumatism. Credulity combined with a desire for entertainment led a large number of people to chop the corpse into pieces which were then sold at ten piastres each. No cures for rheumatism were recorded.

Once I took a donkey from Beykoz to make the journey to the end of the Bosphorus. It was a gentle beast; gentle and idle, but more tractable than Modestine. I was in no hurry and it was pleasant to amble from village to village, to the scarcely concealed curiosity of the inhabitants, until at last I came to the cliffs and capes which jut out into the Black Sea, a sea which led Byron, in that everlasting but not immortal poem *Childe Harold*, to write one of his most unfortunate couplets:

> There's not a sea the passenger e'er pukes in,
> Turns up more dangerous breakers than the Euxine.

I was returning one day, again by donkey, having been to look at the caves and the hundreds of birds' nests which fill the cliffs in that part, when I passed through the remains of the grounds of the old palaces. There were forests of sycamore and glades covered in rich grass and creeper-woven ruins: yet another site of decaying luxury. Ponderous clouds had circled indeterminately all day but the sun had prevailed. Then, at last, as if prolonged impatience had resolved itself into action, the cumbersome burdens of the sky moved purposefully. The sun was put out. The shoulders of the storm reared and expanded, flexing and unflexing. I remembered Thrace. I made as rapidly as the donkey would allow for a neglected *kiosque*, a dry, grey shell with a pagoda roof among trees. It was cool and dark inside like a cave. Some old pictures on the walls shone dully like the dim whiteness of fish through aquarium glass. The boards had rotted and fallen in and small saplings had grown up the walls. Shutters hung from warped casements. As I went in a black snake slid across the crumbling wood and oozed slowly into a crack in the wall.

The glaucous light had settled and overpowered the room. Grimed windows framed by entanglements of cobweb filtered it. All was motionless. Then a fly trapped on the sill began to struggle. I stood there and waited as the last black segment of the snake inched its way through the crack. The yellow light thickened.

Without preface thunder exploded. Rain and hail lashed the flimsy wooden frame; a million lances spearing the swollen air. Slabs and coils of light seemed to splinter in the room, searing my eyes. It was rebounding and leaping all round. Jagged white blades whirled. They looped and curvetted. Fire.

It passed quickly and I stood for a long time in the *kiosque* watching the darkness ebb away and the light stealthily resume its domain, listening to the trickle of water from the guttering and the measured drop falling plumb and true from a leak in the roof. The donkey stood on the veranda and drooped, head down, ears back, abject. There is nothing so resigned, so long-suffering, so utterly indifferent as a donkey in the rain. A dampness and a freshness crept through the air clarifying the mingling smells of old paint and wood and the acrid fragrance of rotten tarred netting. The tunes of the water running, falling, trickling, softened. The donkey lifted its head a couple of inches. One ear leant forward like a signal.

I went out. Away to the east the thunder still snarled fitfully and across the broad green slopes of the hills, of the sycamore, the cypress, the planes, a rainbow plunged its aethereal roots, the hook of dissolving colours laid on the sky like the livid weal of a whip-lash on bruised, soft flesh. A blackbird sang—tentatively; and at the *kiosque* side the ghost of a rose trembled in its rags among the militant thorn.

NOTES

1. Pliny, *Natural History*, Bk. X, Chap. 20.
2. Herodotus, *History*, Bk. IV, Chap. 85.
3. Lithgow, op. cit.
4. Grelot, *A Late Voyage to Constantinople*. Trans. by J. Philips. London, 1683.
5. Michel Baudier of Languedoc, *The History of the Imperiall Estate of the Grand Seigneurs*. Trans. by Edward Grimstone. London, 1635.
6. Evliya Efendi, op. cit.
7. Busbecq, *The Turkish Letters*. Ed. and trans. by E. S. Forster. Oxford, 1927.
8. Lady Neave, *Romance of the Bosphorus*. n.d.
9. Pardoe, *The Beauties of the Bosphorus*. London, 1839.
10. Evliya Efendi, op. cit.

CHAPTER FOUR

The City (II)

'I must needes pensill out the line of her praises at some
length, and tell you truely, wherein her worthinesse consisteth,
and yet may deceive opinion without true judgment.'
THOMAS GAINSFORD, *The Glory of England.*
London, 1618

White and dense mist filled the Bosphorus and the Golden Horn
from bank to bank. It lay thick in the streets. It shifted and curdled
among the roofs, pale spissitude in clots and unravellings, in tufts
and skeins. The city was almost completely submerged. Standing
above it was like being over a long savannah of flocculent cloud.
Here and there a stripe or a darker shade suggested the crowns of
low hills. All was chiaroscuro. A damp freshness pervaded the air.

Behind me Europe still lay in the earth's shadow. In front it was
beginning to thin. The globe was turning at a thousand miles an
hour. In London it was two o'clock in the morning, in Tehran five;
in Lahore six; in Lhasa seven. As the earth spun the great line of
shadow was retreating across Asia.

I looked at my watch. It was one minute past four. In another
hour the edge of the shadow would have gone past, rolling up
behind me. Perhaps one day we shall be able to see it moving across
the earth.

There are times of the day and the night, and the hour before
dawn is one of them, which mark a definite end and a beginning.
Another is the late afternoon. The one before dawn is the strangest.

Then it is that fires decline, and coals drop hollowly. The bearded
spiders spin their webs, and the lunatic moves uneasily in his asylum.
In hospital wards the sleepless and the pained lie at last in torpid

wakefulness. Men mutter in their dreams. The turbines of life hum low. And the tolling of the owls passes from point to point, the melancholy peal of the ancient and the solitary reign.

Silence, which all night has spread its gentle and alleviating pressures, now almost attains to completeness. There are a few moments only when its rule is assured, the hour when the minute is weary from the long pursuit, when clocks falter and time pulls up. In those few moments life is poised. It ebbs away from the dying and renews in the living. We move closer to the confines of the preternatural. The haunting return to fire, monks rise to prayer. 'So hallow'd and so gracious is the time.' The heart stutters and picks up again, and in a thousand darkened rooms clocks buzz and lights go on.

All about and beneath me the city did not exist, wrapped in a gossamer cocoon, draped with frail grey swathes of lawn. It was very quiet.

In a garden down by the Horn a cock crew—no finer flourish of syllables for the day's beginning. Somewhere in Sirkeci another answered: clear, silver-tongued. In some trees near by that stood cut cleanly in half by the edge of mist a bird peeped quickly several times, like morse, then stopped. A chill breeze began to sift and thin the air, the breeze that Virgil and Dante knew as they stood at the foot of the Purgatorial mountain in the Easter dawn:

> L'alba vinceva l'ora mattutina
> che fuggia innanzi, si che di lontano
> conobbi il tremolar della marina.

Quite suddenly the eastern sky turned pale lemon: dawn's left hand. Then low down the horizon suffused and crumpled in pink. Mottled clouds flaked grey. They fumed. Then they were ablaze. The light was brandishing, hammering on the night. Great prongs and bars of it sprang out. The sky was plundered with colour. At any second the sagging doors of darkness would burst open. Then the final eruption and the shadow of the earth rolled back in one gesture. The mist was transfused to a buttery haze, dissolving. Rifts leant open. Rising from them the domes were lassoed with light and the minarets flashed like lance-points.

At that moment, as silence seemed to fall again after the great dissonant fanfare of colour and illumination, very faintly, very distantly, a dim cry, fading and returning, wound across the air. It came again, louder, diminuendo, a tenuous frail voice, the syllables loosening and floating away, still held by the wavering tune, separating. The great prayer of the *muezzin* went out to the dawn like an intimation of immortality . . . *Allâhu ákbar! Lâ ilâha illa' llâh!* 'God is most great. I testify there is no God but Allah. . . .'

After such moments everything is an anticlimax. The brief and intense experience of something beautiful and moving leaves a momentary vacuum in the emotions. Then, the time of unconscious awareness past, joy and perhaps a feeling of exuberance well up to fill it. There is a desire to communicate but it cannot be done and you try in vain to reclaim the quintessential moment when the pure note pierced the dull senses and like a needle ran through the eye of pleasure.

I walked back, down into Sirkeci. On the pavements men, half-sleeping, rolled in newspapers, turned over on their carpets, stretched, rubbed their eyes. Shutters crashed. The first tram ground slowly into life, melancholy, honking through the damp air.

All those first movements of the day, of life, are fascinating to observe: like the crack in the hatching egg, the twitch of the chrysalid, the crumpled frill of the wing, the heaving of the womb. There are so many unconscious gestures then, so many unpremeditated reactions, so many things that can be separated and distinguished. It is perhaps the nearest we ever come to seeing the dead stir to life, the petrified reanimated, blood and warmth flowing through marble. And all the time, light, which we accept so easily and yet which has travelled so far, so quickly, so miraculously, is erasing, roughing in, rounding, sharpening, reassembling shapes on the palimpsest, developing the negative, printing out the huge page of the world.

But, as George Meredith put it, 'Prose can paint evening and moonlight . . . poets are needed to sing the dawn.' Realizing this, I went and had breakfast.

Much later, after I had breakfasted off cherries and cream and cheesy butter and bread and pale milkless tea, after the sun had begun to tower above and after I had pondered rather gloomily on the intransigence of words and, more particularly, on one's inability to manipulate them, I set off to explore. I thought of Gainsford's words which head this chapter—he was writing of Constantinople at the time, not England—and wondered how to avoid the deception of opinion and at the same time how to achieve even an approximate 'true judgment'. How can one convey the character, the quintessence of a city? It seems to me that there is only one possible rule and that is also a starting-point. It is necessary to be alone with it a good deal.

The gender of inanimate objects may be an index to racial attitudes. Ships, cities, the sea, night, motor-cars, machines and engines in English tend to be feminine. They are also functional. On the other hand 'day' is definitely neuter. It might tentatively be concluded that we tend to personify as feminine things which are difficult to understand. It is also significant that of the two Saxon words for women 'wif' is neuter and 'wif-mann' is masculine. English is a very sexless language, and that is enough said. Associations and conditioning are strong and when I visit a city I cannot help beginning to think in terms of feminine characteristics: 'she' is middle-aged or beautiful, or 'her' make-up is running. 'She' has moods, mannerisms; 'she' is mysterious or brash or placid. 'She' can be likened to a duchess or a prostitute. She has limbs, garments and diseases. 'She' smells sweet and foul. 'She' is soft and hard, pliable and brittle, and so on. 'She' can be a *grande dame* like London or a tart like Turin. 'She' can be everything that Robert Burton's mistress was. Somehow one cannot speak with any conviction about 'he' or 'it'.

Istanbul, to adapt Wilde, is like a woman with a past and no future. At least she had, apparently, little or no future until recently. She still has many uses, but that is to be expected. In this case it is inevitable geographically. The real city of the future is Ankara, the capital, which half a century ago was a village. But Istanbul is changing. The pick and the drill, the architect and the stone-mason are about to give her a new lease of life. In ten or fifteen years she may be another modern city. That is to say, blocks of more or less ugly buildings will predominate. Much that is of value archaeologically will be destroyed in the process but human needs must come first. People must have a roof and a fire and some food. Soon the inhabitants will be much better accommodated. Also the mosques and the fountains are being refurbished on a big scale. There will also be fine gardens and parks, and these especially the Turkish people know how to create. There is a noble chance here for some inspired architects, backed by some philanthropical millionaires, to continue it as a great and beautiful city. It is doubtful if the Turkish people will be able to achieve results deserving of general esteem by themselves. They lack the money. They may also, at the moment, lack the taste of their ancestors. The Sinans of this world are not born every day. But it could happen.

★

I walked along past the General Post Office, an imposing but rather drab building about the size of the Bank of England, which also houses the law courts and some of the exceptional number of police that there are in the city. Upstairs there were always rows of more or less hopeless and helpless people waiting to be involved in the rather lugubrious machinery of Turkish justice. Once I visited the Attorney-General there: a most charming man. And all the time minions came and went with much bowing and many 'Efendims'. So much bated breath and whispering humbleness put me in mind of the days of the Sultanate when a nod might chop off twenty heads before breakfast.

Ranged along outside the post office there were always a number of blind men sitting behind tables. They sold stationery, pens, lighter-flints, razor-blades and such miscellaneous needs. Further on, near the Spice Bazaar, in a long line, in the shade of some plane-trees, were the public scribes. When Aaron Hill came here right at the beginning of the eighteenth century he reported that there were thirty thousand scribes, all '*Masters* in the Art of *Penmanship*.'

They sat there day after day like their fellow scribes in other parts of the city, each behind an old-fashioned typewriter. They were rather a scruffy lot and spaced out the messages of the illiterate with a bored condescension. They knew. Their typewriters pro-claimed it. I was reminded of the confessional and, like the priest who grows inured to the weekly quota of sin sieved by the interven-ing gauze, so the scribe is indifferent to the imports of love, business and duty. The keys tapped away like the dry legs of old crickets: the monotonous stock tunes of 'Dear Sir', 'Dearest Boy', 'My Beloved Wife'. How crisp and impersonal the words seem jumping on to the sheet; how coldly begin the urgencies of commerce and heart. In the days of quills and ink in sponges there was some grace in them.

A girl was writing to her husband in the army. An old woman was writing to her son. Perhaps they were far away on manoeuvres in Anatolia. They were telling them about the weather, the increasing prices, the last film they saw, how much they loved them: passion and tenderness mixed inconsequentially with economics and enter-tainment. The voices murmured and the old Underwoods and

Imperials responded gallantly. The long black legs jumped to and back and their black prints pattered across the bare pages.

Soon I reached the edge of the bazaar area; then up a long, steep street solidly lined with shops and swollen with crowds. The bright awnings over the stalls which spilled out from the shops flapped and swayed. Taxis, horses and carts, donkeys, porters wove through the proliferations of bodies. All the way up the middle of the road, by separate islands, were free-lance vendors, their wares spread on flat, round wicker trays: bootlaces, pants, scarves, shopping-baskets. A hundred different voices chanted, shouted, appealed, crooned. The din continued from early morning to late afternoon. Soon one became oblivious of it.

The bazaars are enormous and cover many acres, sprawling along the Golden Horn side of the ridge between the mosques of Nuruosmaniye and Beyazit. They are loosely grouped about the main concentration of *hans*: immense stone, barrack-like buildings of two or three storeys with a courtyard. The stables were on the ground floor and then there were two or three storeys of chambers above to accommodate merchants and servants, etc. Often they had four gates at the cardinal points and the gates were named after the principal trades pursued near the porches. They are incredibly solid structures with enormous iron doors. They are felon-proof and fire-proof and were for the use of every traveller and merchant regardless of race and creed. They were a kind of hotel and very cheap at that. Now, many of these, like many of the 180-odd that remain in the city, are used as stores, shops, workrooms, counting-houses and so on. A number harbour the looms and paper presses and in those quarters a thunderous noise fills the air and the ground and the walls shudder and throb to the powerful rhythms of piston and rod. It is like being in the engine room of a great liner.

The bazaars proper are reminiscent of an improbably large cathedral or the cisterns, though built fairly low. Long colonnades and cloisters lead off the main nave, as it were. They are made of stone and are vaulted, arched and pillared. The windows are high and through their dusty and sometimes coloured panes the sun diffuses rainbowed arcs and beams, stippling the stone-flagged floors and glorifying the artificial foliages of brocades and silks and cottons festooned on all sides. The shops and stalls and cafés have accumulated in blocks among the concentration of pillars and fill in the spaces down the colonnades.

Many dozens of jewellers' shops lie near the main northern entrance. There is an almost disgusting profusion of wealth here ranging from the tinsel to the genuine, from mass-produced bracelets to rare gems. There are argosies of silver, ruby, diamond, onyx and amethyst,

> wedges of gold . . . heaps of pearl,
> Inestimable stones, unvalu'd jewels.

The ransoms of a hundred kings propound and glitter themselves in tiers and stacks. Clarence saw nothing like it wooing the slimy seabed.

There is something desirable as well as repellent about a quite barbarous excess of wealth. The purified and frigid senses of the ascetic, and the would-be ascetic, are easily stung, brutalized again. The saints who sought the solitudes of Egypt and Asia came face to face with the Tempter. He knew his business. Desire for worldly things became acute and sudden. Temptation found its source in the imperfectly subdued energies of the physical organism. Every excursion of the mind could be turned to evil account. The nearer they drew to God the more urgent became the efforts of the adversary. They prayed for sleeplessness that they might not be outwitted by dreams. St Hilarion, faint with fasting, was confronted with magnificent banquets. Before St Pelagia, who had once been an actress at Antioch, the Devil paraded rings and necklaces and bracelets to awaken the old desires. Again and again he performed the most fabulous conjuring tricks to undo them. We, the rank and file of sinners, are not so entertained.

The Harpagons and Sir Epicure Mammons and Eugénie Grandets are despised and condemned but it is easy to see what a delicious debauchery it must be to have bag upon bag of nuggets and ingots and bars, to have sack upon sack of gems, to have a room hung with crystal chandeliers and to have hundredweights of gold and silver poured out like cataracts upon ebony tables, to watch the light drenching the metal, quivering on sovereigns and nobles, crowns and Napoleons, to watch it lying in long deep lagoons on the black polished wood. What a base pleasure to bury one's arms to the elbows in hoards of jewels, to see them cascading from opening palms, to dally with pistoles and revel among doubloons.

It is not so difficult to understand why Caligula, according to Suetonius, developed such a passion for the feel of money that he liked to walk over heaps of gold pieces or else lie down and wallow in them. And it is no wonder that the most persuasive speech of all in the Council of Pandemonium was that of Mammon whose gaze, even in Heaven, was always cast down to admire the pavements of beaten gold.

In the bazaars among these arrays the merchants perch on stools and squat on chairs and move about from shop to shop swapping the international tittle-tattle of dealers, big money and 'rocks'. They hover at the entrances to lure in customers and mingle among the crowds to spot and waylay the likely client and draw him to their pile. They are no longer the 'withered and one-eyed waiters on Providence and a good bargain' as Warner described them at the end of the last century. They are no longer suave and gracious, 'patient, gowned and turbaned, sitting cross-legged behind their trays and show-cases'. Not at all. They are brisk, importunate and tenacious. There are no more of those long rituals interspersed with coffee and sweetmeats, sherbet and *tchibouques*; no more preambling and gambiting in the chivalrous game of polite swindling, each advance and rejection following certain prescribed laws. Business is business. The tills clock up their scores. Time and patience are enemies, not allies.

After all this it is something of a relief to stroll among the quieter and more sombre aisles and apses where the rugs and carpets hang in walls of dull crimson and peacock blues, spread invitingly across the grey pavings, lying in thick rolls and banks: carpets brought from all parts of Turkey, Arabia, Persia and Syria. The men, however, are as persistent as ever, and once you are in you are on the end of some high-powered salesmanship. One rug after another is speedily unfurled and in a few minutes you are standing shin-deep in hundreds of pounds' worth wondering how you can possibly get away and making absurd calculations with money that you do not possess. A hard and indifferent front is the only resource.

Most things can be bought in the bazaars and a great many valuable items pass through them in the course of a year on their way to the greater museums of the world and into the collections of the rich and the connoisseurs. Antiquities are plentiful if you have the time and inclination to search. Roman and Byzantine coins abound though I have yet to see anything especially rare through my untutored eyes. There is a wide variety of pottery of all ages. Modern Turkish ceramics bear traditional designs and colouring: usually subtle combinations of turquoise, beryl and madder. Many of the plates carry in Arabic script the names of Allah and verses from the Koran: bold, black writing on white backgrounds. I have bought a number of these and it was some time before I realized that I would not dream of buying a plate inscribed with the names of God or Christ and extracts from the Testaments. Some kinds of ignorance are bliss after all.

There is one quiet and small *han* which I used to visit often. The building was high and the courtyard narrow. Some trees grew in it and a fountain trickled in the centre. Masonry and statuary lay about in neglect. A small shop lay behind one of the pointed arches. It was kept by a little man from Azerbaijan; a sad little wiry man with loose false teeth and a bony, hairless head that was too big for his body. It was painfully bald. Veins stood out beneath the fine skin which was the colour and texture of parchment. I always wanted to put my hand on it to feel how dry and cold and fragile it was, and whenever I saw it exposed and defenceless immediately beneath me as he bent over a case I thought with what ease it would crack—like a piece of blue-veined porcelain. He used to make jokes about it and I regretted making one in very bad taste by telling him how Victor Hugo used to write verses to Sarah Bernhardt on the top of a skull. 'Didn't the ink run?' he asked. I didn't know.

He was something of a connoisseur and retained an old-world gentleness and indifference to quick profits that was very refreshing after the brash forwardness of other dealers. He would peer about through steel-framed glasses which hung on his nose in a delicate balance like that of a baiting arm on a poised mouse-trap. He reminded me of a mouse. He was nimble and furtive and he would hold things up close to his eyes between slim finger-tips. Wistfully he would lay out jewels and coins, of which he had a valuable hoard, and keep up a curious running commentary. He wanted to sell them and at the same time he did not want to. He had some ivory and amber pieces as well and some beautiful Byzantine rings: plain gold with jasper and cornelian stones.

In his way he was as much of a sensualist as Caligula but it was a fastidious hedonism; the circumspect pleasure of the scholar. He would not roll and trample in piles of moidores. He balanced and revolved things on his finger-ends, sucking his old lips and whistling. His mellow skin enjoyed their hardness and brittleness and his cool grey eyes assessed them with deliberation.

In the end I bought two Roman tear-bottles from him. They always look as if they are difficult to fill until you see somebody really weeping.

In adjoining streets the bazaars have overflowed, and, as in the bazaar, the products of the various trades are grouped in more or less definite regions, so, outside it, the workshops and crafts have roughly allotted quarters and streets. There is one of particular note near Beyazit Square and the mosque. It is a long street and is devoted largely to the workshops of coppersmiths and workers in brass, iron, tin and pewter.

The work is done in cramped surroundings and, it seems, with ancient and inadequate equipment. But the craftsmanship is excellent and the products are cheap. There is an ever-diminishing number of places where it is possible to see the raw material pass through all the various stages of its transformation into the finished article. And there is nothing quite like watching men at such work, to see the actual coalescence of form and matter, to observe the relationship of eye and hand and material.

The street is a study in begrimed faces and dusty, sweating torsos, rippling muscles and dexterous fingers, metals being twisted and shaped and hammered, twirled in tongs, tossed to and fro, plunged sizzling and steaming in and out of cold water, the clang and clatter of fashioning and tempering. Much of this is becoming a novelty. We have to go far afield now to see the farrier, the wheelwright and the bowl-turner. The blacksmith, he of an ancient and venerable profession, is fast becoming a figure of legendary proportions and achievement—at any rate in England: one who, the bearer of massive shoulders and arms and hands like knotted, seasoned oak, opens village bowling with an improbable speed, and who is reputed to perform feats of strength with crowbars that would make a professional weight-lifter look like a child. All the blacksmiths I have known have been slight, sinewy men, and three of them were slow bowlers of only average guile.

The slave market, of course, no longer exists; in fact it was defunct at the beginning of the century, though even early in the 1900's traffic in white slaves was still carried on in secret in a modified form by Circassians and a diminishing number of black slaves were brought annually from Africa. The slave market for women was at the south end of the Grand Bazaar, somewhere near the Burnt Column.

The Caucasian tribes, especially the Circassians, had always done a very lucrative trade in slaves with neighbouring lands. There was a regular demand for handsome girls and boys in Istanbul and Persia. The Ottoman government collected a purchase tax on them which brought in a substantial revenue. Because of frequent wars slaves were plentiful and prices were low. In Evliya Efendi's day there were two thousand slave-dealers and these lodged in the great market which had three hundred rooms. On certain days the slaves were clad in their finest clothes and paraded before the Sultan who would take his pick. Rules, it seems, were strict in the market and the slaves were quite well cared for. They had to be to bring good prices. There was also a decorous procedure in buying. Sir Adolphus Slade, who spent some time in the city in the nineteenth century, refers to it with Victorian propriety: 'The would-be purchaser may fix his eyes on the lady's face, and his hands may receive evidence of her bust.'[1]

✳

Some wag once observed that most women can be divided into three categories: the pretty, the intelligent, and the majority. Turkish women are divisible into the beautiful, the middle-aged and the old.

Within half-a-century a number of startling reforms have taken place in Turkey and one of the most important of these has been the emancipation of women. The abolition of the veil has enabled everybody to judge for themselves of those attributes which before were only suggested. But suggestion is a powerful aid and in the course of centuries Turkish women, who, originally, before they came to the city, appear to have led fairly open and unrestricted lives, became very skilled in the arts of partial revelation. They always had a reputation for beauty, and a deserved one. Beyond that a good deal of ignorance about them and their way of life prevailed.

It is alleged that it was a common belief among Turks for hundreds of years that women have no souls. True or not, the Koran, which has a great deal to say about women, stresses their subservient position. 'Women are your tillage', it says. The main object of marriage was procreation and partly for this reason a Muslim was and is allowed four wives and as many concubines as he can support. In Turkey monogamy is now the general rule, though I have seen older men with two or three wives in tow.

In the Mohammedan Paradise the worldly order is reproduced—
and once again women are in a state of servitude. A whole multitude of the men of old, says the Koran, but only a few from later generations, will be brought near to their Lord in the gardens of delight.
There they will be able to recline on jewelled couches face to face,
while they are waited upon by immortal youths with bowls and
ewers and a cup of purest wine which, adds the Holy Book, 'will
neither pain their heads nor take away their reason'. There will also
be abundant fruit of their own choice and the flesh of whatever
fowl they choose. And, best of all, 'theirs shall be the dark-eyed
houris, chaste as hidden pearls: a guerdon for their deeds'. In fact,
a combination of the harem and the Sweet Waters of Asia—and no
hangovers, a home from home. This may seem a rather gross form of
spiritual life and it also raises the awkward question of sexual re-
lationships—Milton's stumbling-block. Nevertheless it seems as satis-
factory a conception of heaven as most.

During the empire large houses were built in two parts: the
haremlik for the women, the *selamlik* for the men. In the former
were all the domestic quarters for wives, odalisques and servants.
The less wealthy and the poor did not have such a division and
when men came to the house women either withdrew or veiled
themselves heavily. The rules about veiling were strict. Normally a
woman might bare her face before her father, husband, brother and
son. The Koran is as comprehensive about this as Polonius is about
the varieties of drama. Believing women are enjoined to turn their
eyes away from temptation and to preserve their chastity. They are
advised to cover their adornments except those normally displayed;
and to draw their veils over their bosoms, not to stamp their feet in
walking in order to reveal hidden trinkets and not to reveal their
finery except to their husbands, their fathers, their husbands' fathers,
their sons, their stepsons, their brothers' sons, their sisters' sons, their
women servants and their slave girls, male attendants 'lacking in
natural vigour' and children without carnal knowledge of women.
There seems to be enough licence here to allow of some hope. Eunuchs
though sterile were often not impotent, and children, with or without carnal knowledge, are notoriously unreliable. Consanguinity is
seldom a deterrent. Infidelity, however, was a serious offence, as the
floors of the Bosphorus still witness. John Sanderson, who was in the
city about 1600, refers to the method of disposal: 'Thier usuall
punishment for adulterouse women is bindinge in a sack and so

throwe them into the sea.' 'Seven', he adds laconically, 'I have seene so used one morninge.' It was either that or decapitation. It was no uncommon sight to see a floating basket containing a head.

In the days of the *harem* system no woman went out in public with a man—not even her husband. If husband and wife were bound for the same place—and always when a woman went out by herself—the wife was unrecognizably swathed in veils and was escorted by a female relative or shadowed and guarded by a manservant at a distance. Otherwise she went in a carriage with drawn blinds. At the destination husband and wife went to their respective apartments.

Despite the many obstacles to any kind of accuracy travellers formed various opinions of Turkish women: most of them more or less favourable. At the beginning of the seventeenth century Lithgow, who took a rather gloomy view of life in his *Rare Adventures and Painefull Peregrinations*, reported them to be of a low 'stature, thicke and round of growth . . . lascivious within doores, and pleasing in matters of incontinency'. Eighty-odd years later Thévenot described them as being usually beautiful, straight and well-shaped. He comments on their veils, their black eyebrows and their reddish-brown fingernails. He adds that they were 'cleanly and neat, from their bathing twice a week. . . .'[2]

Somewhat later still that rather turgid and understandably neglected writer Aaron Hill devoted a good deal of attention to them. He remarks favourably upon their beauty, their complexions and their eyebrows. He goes on: 'I can hardly speak of their *Shapes*, with so large *Ecomiums* as I have done of their *Beauty*, since the Looseness of their *Dress*, denies them that *forc'd Slenderness* of *Wast*, so much admired by our *European Ladies;* but tho' they boast not that *one Excellency*, Nature has adorn'd 'em with a *Thousand others*, which sufficiently supply its want, for their Bodies have somewhat of an *agreeable* turn, and their Motions carry a *Peculiar Grace* in an *Easy* and *unaffected* Freedom of behaviour, the Native Cha[r]ms of an *Amorous Softness* appear unfeignedly in *every look*, while *every Step* bears somewhat of an Air not altogether free from a *Majestic Gravity*, and yet entirely Govern'd by an *Uncommon Easiness.*'[3]

From this ramble one concludes that their carriage was supple and graceful, and from these and from the comments of other

travellers one also concludes that the reputation of the Turkish
woman for beauty is long-lived.

Close surveillance and limited activities plus competition and a
certain lack of security tended to propagate jealousy and selfishness.
Every wife tried to get as much of her husband's property as she
could. In the case of divorce her possessions would be her own and
the property rights of married women were strictly regarded by
Ottoman and Koranic law. In this respect they were better off than
in other countries. In England, under common law, a wife had no
right to her property and earnings until late in the nineteenth
century. In the 1930's in America there were still twenty-five states
in which a woman could not make a contract of her own and six
in which she was not the possessor of her earnings. In France a
woman still cannot sell her property without her husband's consent.

The Prophet had provided a legal means of divorce but it was not
often used. Instead was substituted the method of repudiation: a
nefarious arrangement which entailed merely the pronunciation of
a simple formula three times. What easier magic could be devised
for the removal of a spell?

Divorce on false pretexts was a serious matter—in theory; and
the Koran made the situation clear with some naïvety. 'Those of
you who divorce their wives', it says, 'by declaring them to be
their mothers should know that they are not their mothers. Their
mothers are only those who gave birth to them. The words they
utter are unjust and false: but Allah is forgiving and merciful.' How
fortunate that he is. It would be a grave state of affairs were we
able to get rid of our wives by alleging them to be our mothers. But
how delightfully convenient, and, conversely, our mothers could be
dealt with more easily by discovering them to be our wives. But, says
the Koran, those that 'divorce their wives by so saying and afterwards retract their words shall free a slave before they touch one
another'. This you are enjoined to do because, like Big Brother,
Allah is 'cognizant of all your actions'. On the other hand 'he that
has no slave shall fast for two successive months before they touch
one another. If he cannot do this he shall feed sixty of the poor.'

When repudiation took place the wife had the right of keeping
the girls of the marriage but the boys only until the age of seven,
when the father could reclaim them. But, of course, the birth of a
boy was a matter for rejoicing; that of a girl the signal for explicit
regret and condolence.

It was also possible to have temporary wives. If you came to stay in a city for a time and wanted a regular bed-fellow all you had to do was to see the local *Imam*. He found the wife, certified her for a period and a contract was drawn up.

It may easily be imagined then how strange everything must have been when Atatürk's reforms were introduced, when many of the embargoes and inequalities were eradicated and men were able to see women publicly. In the past it had given great offence when unveiled women were seen in the streets and European women were always getting into trouble. When Lady Neave was in Constantinople at the end of the nineteenth century it was not safe for a European woman to appear on the streets unattended by a man. It infuriated soldiers, among others, to see them uncovered. She recalls the pleasure they took in 'pushing us off the pavement, pinching our arms and kissing those who took their fancy, especially if they were buxom'. There were compensations for being offended.

Now the position is comparable with that in England. Women take an active part in the running of the country. They are to be found in every profession. They wear copies of the latest fashions from Paris and Italy and the main street in Pera on a summer's evening is like the *corso* in an Italian town. The cosmopolitan nature of the city is very noticeable in the women, but there are common denominators. They have fine figures; elegant legs and lustrous eyes. Corsets are a problem, so are cosmetics. But natural grace and good complexions tend to offset these disadvantages. They are inclined to blossom early, mature young and grow old soon. After the initial shock of seeing many pneumatic and nubile women it is the middle-aged whom one tends to notice. Some of their mannerisms are historical footnotes. They have the habitual gesture of drawing something across the lower part of their face, and as you wander among the back streets you can just see them sitting behind half-shuttered windows observing but scarcely observed, prying through the *jalousie*. Except in the Europeanized quarters you seldom see a man with his wife or a woman or a boy with a girl in the streets and restaurants, etc. Many marriages are still arranged but divorce entails modern court procedure. The divorce rate increases but against that no heads are to be seen in baskets floating on the Bosphorus. Considering the rapidity of the reforms during this century one can have nothing but praise for the way in which women have adopted the new ways of life. Once I visited a lady who belonged to both worlds.

★

Beneath the grey ruin of her partially visible features it was sometimes possible to detect momentarily the lineaments of a beauty that
had flourished at the turn of the century. Veiled and swathed in
black she crouched on a divan: '*povre, seiche, maigre, menue*'.
Above her hung a faded portrait of Sultan Abdul Hamid II: the
heavily lidded eyes, the hooked nose and black moustache. Canaries
twittered in a cage by the half-shuttered window. Near them a gaudy
and restless parrot shifted from side to side on its perch. Periodically
it uttered one of its sentences in rasping Turkish. A sweet smell of
stale roses pervaded the room. Below, from the street, I could hear
the reiterated cry of a water-seller and the rattle of his glass and
saucer. It was three o'clock in the afternoon in an old wooden *yali*
on the banks of the Bosphorus.

'I don't remember,' she was saying. 'It was such a long time ago.'

'It must be nearly fifty years since you left ——'

'Very nearly fifty years.' She put out a frail hand and soothed
the arching back of a Persian cat.

It was difficult to believe that this bent and antique woman had
once been an odalisque clad in luxurious silks; had attended parties
in the Garden of Tulips in the Sultan's palace; had reclined in
sumptuous *kiosques*; had walked beneath The Gate of Felicity and
been tended and guarded by black eunuchs—one of the pampered
and imprisoned elect of the Sultan's stud. She seemed to epitomize
the regrets of '*la belle Héaulmière jà parvenue à vieillesse*'. Villon
seldom wrote more sadly than when he lamented the decay of the
beautiful face, the golden hair, the arched brows and the crimson
lips.

We drank some coffee, that rarest of drinks in Turkey—and
smoked. She rummaged in her memory for something to say. I did
the same. It was very difficult to think of anything sensible. Another
cat poured itself in through the window. I ventured a direct question.

'Did you like living in the Seraglio?'

Her cracked lips moved a little. 'Yes. It was very comfortable.'

'But boring sometimes?'

The water-seller's cry died away. In a house opposite a wireless
was switched on. The doleful keening of a woman singing a Turkish lament came through the window.

'Yes. Yes. Boring. Quite often it was boring.' She looked over in my direction, fingering her necklace.

But there was competition and jealousy and make-up; intrigue and gossip—both under the most favourable circumstances, if sometimes dangerous. There was the occasional trip into the city or up the Bosphorus by *caïque*; excursions to the Sweet Waters of Europe and Asia; fêtes in the palace gardens, and amidst all this otiose industry the hope that one day she might fall under the Sultan's eye and become 'gözde'. Then would come the long and skilled process of preparing her to share the bed of the Shadow of God on Earth. The complicated ritual of bathing, manicuring, coiffuring, perfuming and, ultimately, dressing, would involve the art and assistance of many experts. No pains were spared to make them delectable for their great master. Who was to know—she might bear a future Sultan. On the other hand, if she offended, she might be thrust into a sack and drowned in the Bosphorus: that graveyard of thousands.

But from 1850 the old Seraglio fell into disuse and the Sultans lived at Domabahçe Palace and then at Yildiz, both on the European shore of the Bosphorus. A reduced establishment was retained and they waited hopefully for the return of their lord. Once Abdül Hamit went back to the old Seraglio and saw the survivors of three reigns.

For a few brief hours the crones, matrons and still nubile virgins tricked themselves out in their paint and finery and with that art matured in centuries of usage. It was a truly ephemeral blossoming. Then the frost of neglect descended again. From then on and until the final dispersal in 1909, when Abdül Hamit's *harem* at Yildiz was also disbanded, they frittered away their lives.

In the end thirty-one laden carriages took away the working contingent from Yildiz back to the old Seraglio. The government advertised for their next-of-kin and from distant villages in the plains and mountains of Anatolia manly Circassian warriors came to the city to claim their relations. Extraordinary scenes of jubilation and reunion took place. Two hundred and thirteen women were freed. But for some no one came. These who were unredeemed lingered on:

> Still round and round the ghosts of beauty glide,
> And haunt the places where their honour died.

I wanted to ask her if the Sultan had ever summoned her to his bed: it is not everyone who may sleep with the 'Shadow of God';

and how she got on with the eunuchs—those extraordinarily power-ful and influential people; whether Lesbianism was common . . . Dozens of questions were possible. Perhaps she would have been will-ing to answer some of them.

But instead we talked about her cats, the danger of fires in wooden houses, the difficulties of living. The parrot rasped, the singer's dirge wavered through protracted vowels, the big clock ticked away the minutes of a golden afternoon in Istanbul, and she went on talking quietly and urbanely of the trivialities which composed a life which seemed to have been so wasted but which she had always managed to make worthwhile in her own estimation. I could not bring myself to intrude brashly and practically upon the frail and dusty privacies of her aged memory.

So I missed my chance which, like her beauty that bloomed when Queen Victoria was celebrating her Diamond Jubilee, will not come again.

★

The city is full of open-air cafés and one of the pleasantest of these lies under a huge plane-tree on the north side of the mosque of Beyazit II on the third hill. It is near the big roundabout and within sight of the university. The Sultan was well known for his piety and his simple tastes: in fact, a rarity. His mosque was built by Hayred-din at the very beginning of the sixteenth century. Near by is a small creeper- and trellis-covered street, leading into the bazaars, where there are many bookshops: the Parkers, Blackwells and Heffers of the city.

It is known as the 'mosque of pigeons', and certainly there are thousands there: more, if that were possible, than at Eyüp. They are reputed to be the descendants of a pair given to Beyazit himself. The mosque has a magnificent courtyard before it with an octagonal fountain in the centre. The columns of the cloisters which run round the yard are of granite and porphyry and jasper. Its arches are of black and white marble.

There used to be a permanent market in it and every Friday there was a distribution of food to the dogs of the quarter. Now only one or two cripples sell beads and souvenirs, and children and old women peddle seed for the sacred fowl. In the garden at the back by the bookshops lies the tomb of the Sultan—and two others. His catafalque—he was a large man in estimation if not in fact—is more than thirteen feet long. Railings encrusted with mother-of-pearl fence him off. During his campaigns the dust which came from his garments was always preserved and when he died it was made into a brick upon which his right arm now rests.

Evliya, who always finds it difficult to omit a good story, believes that he died twice. In the last seven years of his reign he ate nothing which had blood and life in it. One day, wishing very much to eat calves' or sheep's feet, he had a long struggle with his conscience and his soul. At last a dish of well-seasoned feet was put in front of him. He said to his soul: 'See, my soul, the feet are before thee; if thou wishest to enjoy them, leave the body and feed on them.'

At that moment a living creature was seen to come out of his mouth, which drank up the juice in the dish. Having satisfied its appetite it tried to return but the Sultan prevented it and ordered his pages to destroy it. This was done and the *Mufti* decided that as the soul was an essential part of man, this dead one should be buried. Prayers were said over it and it was interred in a small tomb. 'After this murder of his own soul,' writes Evliya, 'the Sultan remained melancholy in the corner of retirement, taking no part or interest in the affairs of government.'[4] All but the soul emerge with credit from this episode.

The rickety chairs and tables of the café lay at random. Many habitués seem to spend all day and every day there: the pigeons waddling importunately among their legs, the boot-blacks hovering in search of clients, waiters passing to and fro with tea and lemonade and nargiles. It is a perfect place to rest in the heat of late afternoon and enjoy one of those prolonged and contemplative smokes which only the nargile can provide.

It is not known who first brought tobacco to Turkey, but certainly it was being used in the latter half of the sixteenth century. George Sandys who visited Constantinople in 1611 says quite definitely that the English introduced the habit, 'I doubt not but lately taught them.' But smoking was prohibited about this time in the reign of Ahmet I. Greater privation was to follow in the time of Murat IV. An imaginary prophecy by Mohammed against tobacco was aired and when much of the city was burnt down in 1633 the Sultan took his chance. Tobacco and coffee houses were destroyed and the consumption of tobacco, opium and coffee made a capital offence. The drinking of wine was already punishable by death. Fortunately this

Sultan died before he had reached thirty but not before he had executed a hundred thousand people. James I of England was almost as foolish though less barbarous. Later Mehmet IV rescinded these ridiculous legislations.

One of the most frequent clients at this café was a remarkable old woman. She had the face of a seer and the gaze of a sleep-walker. Strands of irrevocable grey hair floated away from her balding head and long Roman brow. Her fine nose and jaw and her slender predatory hands were those of a man. Her eyes were ash-grey and uncomprehending. She sat alone and soliloquized incoherently. I always found her rather a frightening figure, but nobody paid attention to her, though the insane are often identified by the more superstitious Muslims as sainted. 'Madmen and *Fools*', wrote Aaron Hill early in the eighteenth century, 'are by the Turks esteem'd the Favorites of *Heaven*: They think 'em taken *from their Tenement of Clay*, to talk with *Angels*, in the upper Regions, and will therefore beg the blessing of an *Ideot*, when they meet him in the Streets, and bending forward, *kiss his Garment*, with the most *profound* and *humble* Veneration.'[5] But no one knew anything about this woman. And, as is often the case, many did not wish to. I was content to think of her as one of those ancestral voices that Kubla Khan heard prophesying war. A safe prophecy.

One day I was sitting there having my shoes cleaned and watching the bubbles rise in the bowl of the nargile. It is always pleasant to idle for an hour or two, thinking of nothing in particular, observing the shifting pattern of movement about, following the dissolutions and precipitations of activity, to lapse into a kind of grey and aquarial lassitude, to be an octopus or a sea anemone, to be 'drawn down,' as Henry James put it in a splendid simile, 'as by a siren's hand, to where, in the dim underworld of fiction, the great glazed tank of art, strange silent subjects float'.

A little spry man materialized, a quick, volatile little man who moved like a water-spider. He emerged and sat down opposite. His glance enjoined conversation. I discovered that he was translating the *Odyssey* into Turkish: a formidable task, but he thought lightly of it. For a time we discussed the problems of translations in general terms.

In the course of this I was happy to discover that he shared my dislike for Odysseus. Making all allowances for epic scale I find few heroes so tedious and unpleasant: perhaps it is a gross heresy.

Occasionally, if we are unlucky, we meet his kind at a public school.
They get their 'colours' for everything, even discus-throwing and
swimming. They keep well in with the authorities—all except one
master with whom there is a feud. They possess brawn, charm when
necesary, and a good deal of guile which enables them to do the right
thing and to behave like gentlemen when others expect them to.
They wind up their school career by spending two years grazing
magnificently in the luxuriant pastures of the 'Sixth', scoring a certain number of runs and tries in the process. Later they go abroad.

Their wives become grass widows. They have the occasional affair
to preserve their sense of manhood. Eventually they come back with
a number of tall stories which they save up for people who will be
impressed and on which they dine out for the rest of their lives.
They create a tremendous fuss because they find that eligible young
men have been chasing their wives. At last, if we are fortunate, they
die. But then it is too late. We are too old to enjoy their absence. I
cannot believe that the example of Odysseus is one which many
would like to emulate. How poorly he compares with Aeneas—
despite the unfortunate 'pious'—Beowulf and Roland, and other
heroes of that kidney.

'But you must remember,' said the little translator smiling, 'that
Odysseus was a Greek.' Then he was joined by a fellow poet and
they both ran off to the local book-shops. They bought me copies
of their works which they signed and presented to me with much
humility and deprecation.

They were very keen to learn about literary activity in western
Europe and England. One can well understand why. For long, now,
Turkey has looked to the West but only recently has the West tended
to take her seriously as a democracy and to interest herself in her
literature and art and so on. Turkey is relatively remote, intellectually
in arrears. The Turks have, of course, produced some fine writers in
this century, novelists, essayists and short-story tellers especially, but
the people have been separated in varying degrees of severity from
European culture for the best part of five hundred years. The fact
is that Turkish literature is hardly known in the West; and a number
of writers use French rather than Turkish. To a certain extent
writers and their kin have adopted the café life of Paris and its
parody in London: the kind of existence which, for the bogus, has
the double advantage of involving no work and at the same time
giving an illusion of intelligence. Fortunately the illusion is not

normally shared by the onlooker. Bohemia always lies at the frontiers
of Parnassus. Let us hope it remains there. Like the 'Remove' it is
a transit camp. The blessed part about it is that few of its company
are ever drafted for operations. Sooner or later they tire of their
peripheral loitering, their anxious forays into Wittgenstein, their
outings with Camus, their stabs after Bratby or Chadwick. They get
lucrative jobs instead. But the Turk has not been and is not so lucky.
The Sultan and the *Ulema* banned printing-presses long after
Europe used them lest they might affect the art of writing in the
script of the Koran, and also for political reasons. Illiteracy was
widespread. The representation of the human form was forbidden.
Now it is not so difficult for a writer to publish, though paper is
scarce and critical standards low. But there are few lucrative posts.

There is a desire to forget the past of Turkey and concentrate on
the present and future. The modern is always extolled at the expense
of the ancient. A visit to the new bathing-beaches at Florya on the
Marmara are invariably recommended before the Seraglio. But then,
of course, some people would encourage a trip to Butlin's rather
than Windsor Castle.

The translator of Homer was no exception and one day I was
persuaded to go with him to the famed Florya. A swift electric train
bore us some miles to the west of the city, through straggling suburbs
out into Thrace. Soon we were at the shores of the Marmara. An
artificial beach has been created. Cafés, shower-baths and changing-
rooms were in profusion. Everything has been done on a large scale,
and few places on a hot afternoon could be more tedious. The
Riviera, the Costa Brava, the South Coast—it might have been
almost anywhere. There is a depressing uniformity about bathing-
beaches. The women parade, the men exhibit. The littered sands
look like the tableaux of some gaudy massacre, a carnival of sun-
worship and sand-wooing. The human being who would not dare to
reveal his deformities in his own house to his most intimate friends
does not hesitate to display them on a crowded beach. There, in the
common cause and purpose of sport and ablution, wasted muscles,
bow legs, sagging abdomens and round shoulders are all forgiven
him—and her. It is not fair to expect it to be otherwise. In the end
I dissembled well enough to convince the poet that Florya was the
best resort I had ever seen: a verdict which had the advantage of
being complimentary without being honest. They are all the same.

Probably the better place to bathe is in a quiet bay on the Bos-

phorus provided that one does not go out too far and into the grasp
of the dangerous currents. Better still are the Princes' Islands. But
the best of all is the Turkish bath (the *hamam*).

Half a century ago there were as many as a hundred and thirty
of these in the city. Now there are about six. One I know lies in a
little cobbled street in Sirkeci near the main station.

The Turkish bath still seems to be the best remedy for a hangover
of any kind—though this is a minor recommendation—and there is
nothing to equal the gradual and enveloping voluptuousness which
the complete treatment induces. The masseur kneads, thumps and
pummels the flesh. For a time you are treated like dough, like clay,
like—there is no doubt about it—mud. This process can border on
the painful but it forms a desired contrast. Then you are immersed
in boiling water, water that seems, and probably is, so hot that no
lobster would tolerate it and in which an egg would disintegrate
instantly. You wash. Then you rinse and go on to more but less
boiling water and steam. There are a number of variations. A lot of
people know what a Turkish bath is like without ever visiting one.
It is not possible. It is virtually impossible to communicate how the
stiffness, the aches, the pains, the soreness, all the thousand shocks
and inconveniences the flesh is heir to, are gently drawn out, dissipated, dissolved. A calorific magic regenerates the cells, a delicious
weariness steals along the limbs, a 'drowsy numbness pains the
sense'. Then thick rough towels abrase and tingle the skin. They
operate like very fine wire gauze or rubber grafters. The fainting
nerves are recharged with messages. Then you are swathed in more
thick warm towelling—and recline. No hedonist could wish for a
more exquisite excursion into the ease and indolence which that
repose provides and that effortless sleep:

> that gentlier on the spirit lies
> than tired eye-lids upon tired eyes.

In the old days you were served with coffee and a *tchiboque*
while a menial dried your flesh by pressing his fingers lightly into the
towels—a species of magnetism. Then iced sherbet revived you.
Now you have tea and a cigarette, but the results are much the
same. You feel as if you have been gently flattened by a hot rubber
steamroller. You feel ten years younger and as if you are wearing a
brand-new issue of bone and muscle. Above all, you feel almost unnaturally clean.

For the uninitiated they are curious places: the aquatic equivalent of an opium-den. Figures sprawl languidly, mummified by towels, lost in drowsy forgetfulness—like the Lotus Eaters that labour no more. Shapes float forward through mists of steam, revolve and vanish like wraiths. Form is blurred, eyes grow dim, bodies move in the trance of slow motion. All is chiaroscuro, like some bizarre cauldron in a Nordic underworld. Better this by far than the brash revelations of over-brief costumes and all the vulgar gambolling and uproar of Floryas.

Lying in stupefaction I used to visualize analogies: some crevice in a circle of the Inferno where the delights of the sybaritic and the slothful are parodied grotesquely, where steam turns to smoke, water to ice, strigils and loofas to whips and scorns, the masseurs into torturing demons. And always the baths drew up for me the recollections of damp afternoons at Richmond and Twickenham and Iffley Road, the more robust smells of sweat and linament and vaseline in the dressing-rooms, 'pep talks' that never worked, and the comparable relief of sliding into one of those great baths after a tiring game and the curious and rather unpleasant sensation of other peoples' naked flesh under the water against one's own.

The history of bathing and baths is an entertaining subject. On the whole, water has been used, but there have been a number of other substances—milk, of course, blood, human blood, guano, sand, earth, broth, peat and dung. In the West we have been very tardy about plumbing and hygiene. Louis XIV bathed once a year and hardly ever washed his face. Marie Antoinette washed once a week. The feet of Henry IV smelt so strongly that people felt sick within six feet of him.

When Bath became a meeting-place for the aristocracy of England, Russian vapour-baths, which had degenerated into brothels, were 'out' and sweating-baths were 'in'. One of the most famous was a medicated sweating-bath which an Italian mountebank opened in Cheyne Walk. It was a luxurious place and became extremely fashionable. Dr Johnson, who, as we know, had no great love for clean linen, thought the whole idea ridiculous. 'There is nothing in this boasted system,' he said. 'No, sir, medicated baths can be no better than warm water: their only effect can be that of tepid moisture.' Nevertheless, everybody who was anybody went to them, including masochists, nudists, exhibitionists and homosexuals. Nothing could have been more suitable for the exercise of various sexual aberrations. Boswell thoroughly approved of them and as a result earned one of the great Doctor's most vigorous rebukes: 'Well, sir, go to Dominicetti and get yourself fumigated, but be sure that the steam is directed to your head, for that is the peccant part.' But he was wrong. It was not Boswell's 'head' that was the 'peccant part'.

The first Turkish bath available to the general public was, curiously enough, at St Ann's, County Cork, in 1856. And they became extremely popular during the latter half of the nineteenth century. In May 1861 the *Builder* recorded that they were springing up everywhere. Once again the aristocracy of England flocked to them. The sick, the hypochondriac, the neurotic were all to be found at them; plus all those suffering from the various forms of sexual maladjustment. The baths were reputed to cure many afflictions: cholera, diabetes, hydrophobia, syphilis, bronchitis, consumption and asthma. They were said to deter disease and to prolong virility. They were advertised as cures for drunkenness and extolled as fertilizer for bald heads.

So great became the popularity that Turkish-bath cabinets were installed cheaply in people's homes. The whole body except the head was enclosed in these contraptions which were heated by a small spirit lamp. As is so often the case, credulity and hope had collaborated to deceive. By the end of the nineteenth century the fashion had waned. Many had enjoyed themselves; some had made a great deal of money; others had lost a lot of weight, but none had put forth the crisp shoots of a new spring and youth upon their wintered and deforested brows.

Like a number of things in Turkey, Turkish baths are not Turkish in origin. They were adapted or rebuilt from Byzantine models and these themselves had developed from Greek and Roman originals.

In Constantinople public baths as club-houses and places of popular resort were less important than in Rome. They were smaller but very elegant and luxurious, decorated with many valuable objects. The greatest of all were the baths of Zeuxippus which lay at the northern end of the Hippodrome. Tradition held that the bath marked the very spot where Hercules tamed and yoked the steeds of Diomed. They were first erected by the Emperor Severus in reparation for some massacres for which he had been responsible. Nowadays it is not so easy to get away with a massacre. Their final remains were used by Mehmet II to build his mosque.

The Spanish traveller Pero Tafur who was at the city between

1435 and 1439 relates a curious custom about them. There were
doors on either side of the bath opposite each other, and any woman
accused of adultery was ordered by the judges to be brought there.
They made her go in by one door and come out by the other. If
she was innocent she passed through without shame. But if she was
guilty her skirts and chemise 'raised themselves on high without her
perceiving it' so that from her waist downwards everything could be
seen. Tafur adds, 'This ... it may be no sin to doubt.'[6] It would
seem to be a matter largely of the weather and underclothes.

Water has always played a great part in the life of the Turkish
people and so has the bath. They are, and always have been, a very
clean race. Few changes have taken place in the composition of the
baths and the rituals performed in them. Bassano da Zara in his
work on *I costumi e i modi particolari de la vita de Turchi*—he was
in the city about 1520—gives an account which differs little from
our experiences today and those of intervening travellers. He observes that middle-class women went three or four times a week and
always once. Cleanliness was necessary on religious as well as sani-
tary grounds. You had to wash before visiting the mosque—as everybody still does. Lithgow, writing about 1611, says, rather quaintly,
that the women 'are wont to go to bathe themselves in Stoves twice a
weeke, as well as men'.[7] Later Evilya Efendi records that there were
as many as three hundred public baths in the city and over four
thousand private ones.[8] Of course, Lesbianism and homosexuality
were not uncommon. Grelot, at the end of the seventeenth century,
observed that the 'women are allowed to take their turns, though
more out of wantonness than necessity; it being the chief place
where the Gossips meet and spend the afternoon in tattling and
junketing, according to that of Ovid, "Condunt furtivos balnea
multa jocos." '[9] It can hardly be doubted that the baths were responsible for many 'furtive pranks'; and as the removal of pubic
hair was de rigueur the various depilatory operations gave scope for
that 'junketing' which Grelot mentions.

One of the best accounts of the women's baths comes from the
witty pen of the formidable Lady Mary Wortley Montagu who
enjoyed a long stay in the city early in the eighteenth century. 'It is
built of stone,' she writes, 'in the shape of a dome, with no windows
but in the roof, which gives light enough. There were five of these
domes joined together, the outmost being less than the rest, and
serving only as a hall, where the Portress stood at the door. Ladies

of quality generally gave this woman a crown or ten shillings,—(this seems a great deal to me)—and I did not forget that ceremony. The next room is a very large one, paved with marble, and all round it are two raised Sofas of marble, one above another. There were four fountains of cold water in this room, falling first into marble basons, and then running on the floor in little channels made for that purpose, which carried the streams into the next room, something less than this, with the same sort of marble sofas, but so hot with streams of sulphur proceeding from the baths joining it, it was impossible to stay there with one's cloaths on. The two other domes were the hot baths, one of which had cocks of cold water turning into it to temper it to what degree of warmth the bathers pleased to have.'

She was received very civilly among about two hundred women and observed that there were no 'disdainful smiles' and 'satyrical whispers' that were usual in assemblies at home when anyone appeared who was not dressed exactly in the fashion. She saw 'Many fine women naked, in different postures, some in conversation, some working, others drinking coffee or sherbet, and many negligently lying on their cushions, while their slaves (generally pretty girls of seventeen, or eighteen) were employed in braiding their hair in several pretty fancies.' In short, 'tis the women's cofee-house, where all the news of the town is told, scandal invented, &c.—They generally take this diversion once a week, and stay there at least 4 or 5 hours, without getting cold by immediate coming out of the hot bath into the cool room, which was very surprising to me.'[10]

One dare not imagine how much scandal two hundred naked women might generate in the course of four or five hours. It is no wonder that the Prophet himself regarded baths as the resorts of evil spirits. 'Whatever woman enters a bath,' he said, 'the devil is with her.' He forbade mixed bathing and believed that the whole earth might be regarded as a place of prayer and as pure except the burial ground and the bath.

Despite Lady Mary's account it seems likely that the women wore some kind of garment, however transparent, when at the baths. The French writer Flachat records the ruse of a prurient Sultan—Mahmut I—whose habit it was to ensconce himself at a window overlooking the baths and wait for the women. They came dressed in chemises but the Sultan had had all the stitches removed and the material glued together. The doors were locked and gradually the heat of the atmosphere melted the glue.

★

The University of Istanbul, a few minutes' walk from the Beyazit mosque, was founded as long ago as 1453, the year of the conquest. Originally it was a *medrese* though not an altogether typical one since it offered courses in science and mathematics in addition to the main theological studies. Then in 1900 it was reorganized with new science and literature departments and theology again. In 1908 there began a school of law and a school of medicine, both formerly independent institutions. Now it has all the usual faculties and twelve thousand students, two thousand five hundred of whom are women. It may be judged from this last figure how fast reform has moved during recent years. The buildings themselves are undistinguished but functional and are surrounded by beautiful gardens. Before the main entrance is a huge and hideous symbolic sculpted group: a stolid, solid boy and girl sheltering beneath Atatürk. It is a 'Going Forward to the Future' study—phlegmatic optimism in uninspired bronze.

But obviously the intentions are good and it must be remembered that education for the masses on Western lines is quite new. The progress already made is something to be proud of. Until the middle of the nineteenth century the only education available for the majority of the people was in the religious schools. Here people learnt the Koran by heart in Arabic and recited it. In the middle of the nineteenth century some attempt was made to establish secondary schools. In 1859 the Sultan ordered compulsory education, but with little result. The system of capitulations enabled foreign schools to be started and the Christian minorities sent their children to British, French and American establishments. Few Muslims attended. Later, in the regin of Abdül Hamit II, practically all education was suppressed. The foreign schools survived. Even as late as 1935 the situation was extremely serious. Now, tremendous advances have been made and it is reckoned that sixty or more per cent of the people are literate. There is now a comprehensive system of elementary, secondary, vocational and, of course, university education. There is a technical university at Istanbul as well as the main one, and a further ordinary university at Ankara which, though only twelve years old, has already a reputation and eight thousand students. Two others are growing at Izmir and Erzurum.

People of middle and old age still tend to use the old alphabet and script but all printed matter is in Roman lettering. Atatürk was ruthless about this reform and while publishers changed over to the new type all printing was halted. Then all standard works and literary classics were reprinted. During this period all government employees were given three months to learn the Roman letters or lose their jobs. Atatürk himself went round the country, chalk in hand, and taught the script on blackboards in towns and villages. As a result of this it is now easier for Turkish people to learn foreign languages and, conversely, for foreigners to learn Turkish. The re-form also simplified and standardized the language, for previously many among the educated classes had developed and used an ornate and intricate language which was laden with expressions from Arabic and Persian and which was in large part incomprehensible to the man in the street. All these upheavals, of course, have retarded the growth of literature. If, in the course of the next few months, we were obliged to re-learn our tongue in Greek characters it may be imagined how long it would be before we were able to write it with any ease, let alone express ourselves in an original manner.

★

The massive grey bulk of the mosque of Süleyman the Magnificent —one of the greatest of the Sultans, who flourished in the six-teenth century—lies on the third hill. It is huge and almost squats, or so it seems at a distance; but it is too beautiful for that verb. The grey hump of its dome, like an immense tureen-lid, is flanked by many little domes, and at the four corners of the courtyard, like candlesticks, stand the minarets—the western pair a little shorter than the eastern. It is the greatest work of that remarkable architect Sinan and was built between 1550 and 1557. It dominates a sky-line that would still be incomparable without it.

I went to it first through the fruit market which stretches all the way along at the foot of the hill between the edges of the bazaar and the warehouses on the Horn. Many buildings are being pulled down here and new roads built. Billows of dust hang over collapsing walls and the wind blows it in swirling gusts over the exposed waste-lands.

In the fruit market you may see millions of melons: melons on a scale quite unparalleled. There are many large stalls, rather like small hay-barns, roofed over, open in front and filled with straw.

The men sleep on their pitches week in, week out. In mounds and pyramids and stacks and tiers are their livelihood: water-melons and honey-melons and musk-melons. There are melons as big as green medicine-balls, like yellow cannon-balls and lemon-coloured foot-balls, melons speckled like thrushes' breasts, mottled like frogs and mackerel, marbled like porphyry and verd antique, streaked like tiger lilies, striped like orchids, flecked with orange and black like adders' backs; big saffron orbs, lozenge-shaped melons glow-ing like Chinese lanterns and the dark green of starlings, oval ones as pale as eucalyptus leaves and as dark as cedar fronds, melons turnip-shaped and plover-coloured, solid globes the colour of fading carp, and many smaller ones, not much bigger than grapefruit, the hue of dandelions and drakes' necks and leopard skins—millions and millions of melons. Among these multitudes many are laid open and the raw sweet flesh keeps the attentions of wasps and flies.

And what can one say of the peaches—surely nowhere are there such peaches—and the pomegranates and the mulberries, the milky figs, the black and white grapes, the cherries, the purple aubergines, the tomatoes, the bundles and garlands of paprikas, bright green, scarlet and orange like harlequins' caps? The eyes become a little unhinged before such profusion, such magnificence.

Amidst all this donkeys with wicker panniers laden with fruit go by in files; carts and lorries piled high with it rattle to and fro; *hamals*, bent almost double, hands hanging to their ankles, trudge by with box upon box of fruit roped in white towers upon their backs.

From here the road to Süleyman lies up very steep, twisting, cobbled streets overhung by wooden and balconied houses. They bulge out and lean at such acute angles that they are almost quaint, like those illustrated in nursery books.

There is a forecourt to the mosque and a garden behind and a large court all the way round planted with trees. The forecourt, adorned by twenty-four small domes, is cloistered, resting upon columns of porphyry, granite and white marble. It is paved also with white marble and in the centre is the customary fountain for washing. There is calm here, calm and dignity. The doves warble and dander importantly over the flagstones; the wind rifles the tops of the huge plane-trees surreptitiously. Peace and proportion after the superabundance of fruit, the labour and sweat of men, the rickety houses and the irregular streets. As soon as I had entered the courtyard I realized yet again how much one needs this kind of peace and proportion, how often they induce each other. So many of us city-bound, desk-bound, forget what the sky looks like—especially at night, scarcely hear the wind and pigeons, are deprived of or are not presented with order.

Here, men, under the direction of an original mind and a superbly disciplined creative force, had made something for the glory of God and for their own satisfaction and use, and they had done it supremely well. To look at such a thing, to become familiar with it, is almost bound to settle the turbid motions, the shifting quantities of restless sediment, the laying waste of power which obstruct so much of the time the worthwhile courses. In the mosque of Süleyman all this settles. Direction become clear. Perception balances and is balanced. The harmonies of stone reflect themselves in the now still and pellucid surfaces of apprehension.

I took off my shoes and entered. Carpets, crimson, dark blue and russet, were spread across the vast floor space. Rich stained-glass windows dispersed deep and even richer light:

> Innumerable of stains and splendid dyes.

Arcs of ruby lay across casements and vaults. Beams of bronze struck and stippled green brocades and draperies. Marble was flecked and fretted with blood-coloured patterns. Leaves and drops of blue light were spilt and scattered on stone. Light fragmented on silver and gold, and lay in beads and globules on clusters of jewels. The eye was glutted with the wealth of it all.

Four enormous piers rose up and supported the main structure. Aisles and galleries blended in the ascent. But the profusion of light and colour was disciplined and combined, subservient to the grace and power of the main shape, the energy and strength of stone and marble. Here, in verbal and poetical terms, were joined the luxuriance of Keats and the strictness of Pope. It was a place fit for admiration and worship.

The term 'mosque' means 'place of prostration' and here it is no hardship to make a bow to Sinan and his masons as well as to Mecca.

From the dome hung long chains suspending lights fixed on circular frames. There are hundreds of them and at night when they burn the flame creates a sombre splendour of truly Miltonic proportions. The Pandemonium devised by Mammon could hardly have been much more magnificent.

I strolled about enjoying the great silence. A hundred and fifty feet above, the pigeons clapped their wings and flirted by the lunette windows. In an aisle one of the mosque servants, legs akimbo, swayed forwards and backwards before his Koran. He cried out and began his recitation. His high-pitched, nasal, but melodious voice sang. Many of the men and boys who repeat the Koran regularly do not really understand what they are singing but the chanting of the Holy Book is highly esteemed by Allah. There have been those who committed all of it to memory—a stupendous achievement. Though it meant great spiritual advancement it also meant that their minds were fit for little else. But if by such a task the hinges of the paradisal gates can be oiled who can complain of a memory that has seized up?

The mosque was well equipped with the usual dependences of soup-kitchen, hospital, *medreses* and schools. These were also built by Sinan and to these humbler but no less useful undertakings he brought as much skill and sense of proportion and beauty. The soup-kitchen, the *imaret*, is now a museum of Turkish art. It lies a little to the west of the mosque and consists of a garden in a courtyard surrounded on three sides by cloisters with pointed arches. The garden is full of trees and flowers and has a running fountain. It is exquisitely cool and quiet and elegant. In the rooms is to be found a superb collection of rugs, some of which are eight hundred years old. There are also Persian miniatures, porcelain and some illuminated Korans. Some of the volumes are written in Cufic characters and date from the seventh century.

At one time the city was full of courtyards and gardens like this, urbane oases designed for whiling away a lifetime in comfort and prosperity. In such matters the Ottomans showed the most admirable taste—as they still do, though usually on more modest scales.

Few people visit this museum and I often used to spend whole afternoons reading in the garden, listening to the the limpid disquisitions of the fountain and dawdling in the purlieus of that '*aula ingenti memoriae*', as St Augustine put it, the huge court of memory.

★

Below and beyond to the west the aqueduct of Valens strides colossally between the third and fourth hills. I was walking up the side of it one day when, outside an undertaker's, I found a mobile restaurant.

The coffins, about fifty or sixty of them in stock sizes, were stacked against a wall. Within the yard I could hear more being hammered together. They might have been preparing for an epidemic. Anyway, in the course of half an hour, three hearses called and took off a brace each. I often wonder why more people do not go in for undertaking. There can be few professions more certain of custom and profit.

The restaurant, or rather the kitchen unit of the restaurant, consisted of a large green box-shaped affair with a tall tin chimney set on a frame and supported by three old bicycle wheels. A collapsible table had been erected under one of the arches. It was laid with newspapers and round it, on folding stools, three soldiers ate their *kebab* and salad. Private enterprise.

I was with an Arab schoolmaster from Nasriyah at the time and as it was about midday he suggested we stopped. Absent-mindedly I agreed. A few minutes later two hunks of bread and two whole sheep's heads appeared, complete with eyes. I was the Arab's guest and thought I had better go through with it. At any rate I discovered that I would never eat sheep's head again. It tastes quite pleasant but the gradual baring of the head and face to bone vitiates the pleasure. It takes an effort to strip off the upper lip in a long strand. The eyes were beyond me. The Arab popped his down with relish and I watched him do it, half-expecting something to happen. I suppose they feel rather like *ly-chees*, which always remind me of peeled eyes. Mine, blue and glazed, were left staring incongruously out of the bare bone.

The soldiers were pleasant, robust and well-muscled. They were clean-shaven and their heads were also cropped. Hygiene again; and, of course, it is cooler thus. According to other travellers there were other reasons. Gainsford observed in 1618 that they shaved all their heads 'saving one tuft on the crown, superstitiously imagining to bee pull'd up to heaven thereby'.[11] Seventy years later Thévenot gave another reason, and perhaps more practical. He reported their heads were shaven because they believed the Devil nestled in long hair.[12] In the Middle Ages such infestation happened regularly and preachers and homilists were always warning people—especially women—about the dangers of elaborate coiffures. One woman from Eynsham arrived late for Mass because she had spent so much time on dressing and the Devil clambered into her hair in the shape of a spider, '*ita caput pedibus constringens*'. The consternation may be imagined. The usual antidotes of exorcism and holy water proved useless and the fiend was not removed until a local abbot had held the Sacrament before her. The perils of long hair were no different under Islam.

The Turkish Army has been improving steadily over a long period and there is now a large reserve. There are half a million men under arms, but, of course, Turkey is still very dependent upon foreign air and sea power. Istanbul is full of troops and in an unspectacular fashion they are very impressive. No attempt is made to turn out the rank and file in smart uniforms; on the contrary, they are clad in the simplests and drabbest mode, but they are an exceptionally fit and strong body of young men.

After lunch we went down the other side of the aqueduct to the north and on the slope of the hill eventually found the church of St Saviour Pantocrator tucked away among back streets and a huddle of houses. It was founded in the middle of the twelfth century and has now been converted into a mosque. In the square outside was a big green sarcophagus fouled by refuse. An empress, Irene, is supposed to have once occupied it. A couple of goats, well guarded from the evil eye by blue beads, cropped seedy grass busily. Children scampered about barefooted.

The church is now sadly disfigured and the mosaics have long since gone. Laundry hung in the narthex and a woman in black silk spun on her distaff under a portico.

It used to be the home of many relics, among which was a slab of porphyry brought from Ephesus on which the body of Christ was said to have been laid and anointed after being taken down from the Cross. There was also a picture of the Virgin ascribed to St Luke, an icon of great power which was used regularly to repel enemies during sieges and invasion. It was eventually destroyed by the Turks at the conquest in the church of St Saviour in Chora. Pero Tafur, the Spanish traveller who was in Constantinople shortly before, saw these and tells us of them, though he seems to be slightly confused.

He describes a picture painted on stone with a frame and stand all of which weighed several hundredweight and was too heavy for six men. On the other side of the stone was a second picture. They represented the figures of Christ and the Virgin, that drawn by St Luke.

'Every Tuesday,' he says, 'some twenty men come there, clad in long red linen draperies which cover the head like a stalking dress.'

These men, he explains, were of a special lineage and by them alone could the following rituals be perfomed. There was a procession and the men went towards the picture one by one. If the picture was favourable to a man he could pick it up as easily as if it 'weighed only an ounce'. The bearer then put it on his shoulder and the whole company went out of the church singing and down to a large square where the man carrying the picture walked with it from one end to the other and fifty times round it.

'By fixing one's eyes', Tafur goes on, 'upon the picture, it appears to be raised high above the ground and completely transfigured. When it is set down again, another comes and takes it up and puts it likewise on his shoulder, and then another, and in that manner some four or five of them pass the day.'[13] For this function an enormous crowd always assembled in the square and there were priests who touched the picture with cottonwool and then distributed this among the people. At the end of the day they processed back to the church.

The Arab and I pottered about but he found it difficult to concentrate on ruins and sarcophagi. He kept on thinking about the battles he was fighting *in absentia*. He wanted to get rid of his wife whom he did not love but who loved him. He was young and handsome and soft-hearted, and he was very sad. The emotional crises had been too much for him and he was defeated. His eyes were brown and damp and cornered. And his whole attitude, his postures, his speech, were full of helplessness and hopelessness and self-pity. He knew he was being a coward because he had given up and was retreating steadily before his inability to meet his conscience: completely flabby and dispirited and dejected. It is sad to see a man whose morale has become limp and futile like a wrung-out rag.

He was taking a holiday alone and periodically he would turn and make a stand, as it were, and then retreat again. He kept on buying things to take home to his wife and children as if he hoped to atone for his cowardice with presents and placate his conscience with material reparations.

About every three days he got a letter from his wife: long, lachrymose, pleading letters, and after reading them his shoulders drooped more than ever and his brown eyes were damper than ever. I could see that soon, if he were not careful, all his pride would go and he would turn to treachery. Every time he yielded up a yard of self-respect, every time the encirclement of his cowardice inched inwards, he would, as it were, take courage from money, from self-bribery, from self-justification, from deceit.

I never discovered how it ended. Perhaps he never discovered himself. He was killed a few weeks later in an accident.

★

It was a day in March borrowed a month in advance from April, the kind of day that E. V. Lucas once described as 'a promissory note issued by spring'.

A week before it had snowed. Brown lumps of it remained, like dirty Demerara sugar. Sheltered roofs were streaked with white, and in some places it lay like blobs of foam. The Judas-trees were blossoming, clusters of purple and pink. Pink and purple against grey and white walls and lead-coloured domes. Leaves were prising open tight-jacketed buds, miniature pale emerald frills and flounces.

> Diffugere nives, redeunt iam gramina campis
> Arboribusque comae.

It is vain to compete with Horace. Like the snow, Ramadan was over, the new moon had risen. The cannons had boomed and the fast had concluded.

In his tomb, a plain, octagonal building with a porch and two rows of windows, Mehmet II ('The Conqueror') lay alone, behind the fence of mother-of-pearl railings and beneath an enormous turban. In another *türbe* nearby lay his wife. I strolled through the garden and met the aged custodian of both of them. He had the skinny hands of an ancient mariner and the stoop of a man who had devoted his life to sweeping and dusting. He was proud of his post and they survive in families for generations. Padding soft-footed and reverent, these guardians haunt the death-chambers of the great and infamous, erasing the silent spells of dust and suffering the poor benefits of the bewildering minute.

He assured me that Mehmet was a noble man and, in fact, he was. After securing his throne by having his small half-brother strangled he began a reign which lasted for thirty years (1451–81) and which was, on the whole, glorious. He was a civilized and talented man and an able soldier, also a poet. His reign was marred by one piece of legislation stemming from his own ruthless prudence. He laid it down that the sons of Sultans who ascended the throne were allowed to destroy their brothers in order to ensure their position and the succession against rivalry. It was a Machiavellian device which was eventually responsible for much decadence and corruption.

Between 1463 and 1469 he had a mosque built to commemorate himself, near which lies his tomb. A Greek architect, Christodoulos, was responsible for it. Unfortunately it suffered several times from severe earthquakes and in the middle of the eighteenth century had to be rebuilt in great part. The result within is disappointing. More interesting is the story attached to the building of the original.

The Greek, apparently, shortened two of the principal columns of the mosque because he did not want any of the pillars to be larger than those in St Sophia. The Sultan was angered by this and ordered the Greek's hands to be cut off. This was done, but the Greek complained to the *Cadi* and accused the Sultan of depriving him of means of support: the right of everyone. The Sultan and the Greek were ordered to appear for trial.

The Sultan came and was about to sit down when the *Cadi* commanded him to stand as he was accused of a serious crime. The Sultan thereupon confessed his guilt and was condemned to the severest penalty. The *Cadi* then prostrated himself before the Sultan and kissed his feet. At this crucial moment a tame viper slid from his sleeve. The Sultan asked the meaning of it and the *Cadi* told him that it was there to kill the Sultan had he not obeyed the law.

'Righteous judge,' replied the Sultan, and revealed an axe hidden beneath his cloak. 'I would have crushed your head with this,' he went on, 'if you had acquitted me and thus dealt unjustly.'

For building the mosque the Greek was given a curious payment, namely the whole of an adjoining street. Now Turkish law and justice are less haphazard and less rough. There are higher and lower civil and criminal courts and there is a supreme court of appeal in the capital. Each region has its own public prosecutor and there is a national public prosecutor. However, there is no jury system and cases are tried by judges in both grades of court. Comment by the press during a case is forbidden.

Crime consists largely of theft and violence, and the commonest examples of juvenile delinquency are theft again and gambling. Much of the theft springs from mere necessity. Organized 'rackets' are rare, and so are bank robberies. Vendettas used to be responsible for as much as a fifth of criminal convictions, but feuds are less common now. Experimental penal reform has produced many advances including an island prison in the Marmara—Imrali. Here there is a self-supporting community of convicts, including a number of murderers, guarded by very few warders. It has been a most successful venture, as have been open prisons. Many of the prisons are still bad but not worse than in many other countries.

Punishment is now more often designed to reform and thereby heal, and not to injure. In the old days the chances were that if, as an Istanbul merchant, you were detected in giving false measure you would be nailed to your shop-front by the ears. A bad judge, on the other hand, was pounded to pulp in a stone mortar. A false witness was sat upon an ass facing the tail which he was obliged to hold in his hands. The entrails of a bullock were then poured over him and he had to ride through the city advertising his ignominy. Even more ingenious was the punishment meted out to officials convicted of theft. They were bound to the mouth of a cannon and shot into the sea. In 1600 Sanderson found that the commonest death for men was 'gauchinge': which is to be 'stripped into their linnen breches, with thier hands and feete bound all four together at thier backs, and so drawne up with a rope by a pullie uppon the gallowes and lett faule uppon a great iron hooke fastened to the lower crosse barr of the gallowes'. Usually it pierced their sides and then their thighs. 'There they hange,' adds Sanderson laconically, 'sometim[e]s talkinge a day or two together.'[14]

What terrible, despairing, suffering dialogues they must have been. What must it be like to eavesdrop upon men racked with agony who, each minute, leave the world a little further behind them? One is irresistibly reminded of the three figures hanging on the crosses on Good Friday and the few words they exchanged. One is glad not to have lived when such spectacles were common, and yet whenever a man is hanged a crowd, usually of women, always gathers outside the prison gates to participate, however vicariously, in the last moments of the victim. And if Harringay were booked for a public execution would not the touts be selling tickets for five and ten pounds apiece and, what is more, getting their money? As La Rochefoucauld put it: *'Nous avons tous assez de force pour supporter les maux d'autrui.'* It is one of the more peculiar forms of pleasure.

★

In the north-west corner of the city, near what was called the Koilio-meni Gate (The Rolling Gate) and now called the Ayvan Saray, there used to lie the imperial wharf for the great Palace of Blacher-nae. Near it is a church which once held the robe of Our Lady. In the fifth century in the reign of Leo I, two senators went to Caper-naum and stole the robe and left a substitute. They brought the gar-ment back to the church of SS Peter and Mark from where it was later transferred to the church of St Mary of Blachernae.

I came upon the church by chance one winter afternoon as I was rambling about. A green iron gate in a wall leant open and I walked through it into a garden carefully and richly cultivated. A decrepit and ageing Greek shuffled out of a building jangling his keys. He looked like some Terisias, but his sight was good despite his pink and rheumy eyes. The church, ramshackle and without symmetry and made of a variety of materials, backed on to rising ground. It was little more than a shelter for the sacred pool in which the emperors frequently purified themselves, especially on the Feast of the Assumption. The water was supposed to come from a marble statue of the Virgin, through the hands.

The rickety church is now full of icons and pictures and the walls are damp and peeling. A big marble trough has iron railings in front of it and a dark passage leads away behind. The old man offered me a tin cup of the holy water. It was thick and tepid. But I drank it down. One cannot tell what such things may achieve. Then the old man quite unnecessarily slew a small frog on the grating over the trough and pushed it into it. It was a senseless deed and I told him so. He was indifferent. How futile to hold out a cup of holy water and the next minute slay a harmless creature. The Muslim has more respect for life—and I told him that as well. He did not like it.

A couple of minutes' walk away was the church of SS Peter and Mark, now a little mosque. Opposite, a small and primitive public lavatory exhaled richly. A child squatted in the gutter disdaining the provision. The mosque was securely locked but I hovered about hoping to find somebody. Eventually a young Turk, the servant of the mosque, wearing a little white skull-cap and clogs, let me in. He had bright, fanatical eyes in a lean face. He was clearly a very devout Muslim and he spoke with a passionate intensity. A pleasing contrast to the sloppy fool who was left to look after what was once the most holy place in the whole of the 'God-defended city'.

At one side of the mosque, which had been disfigured by clumsy woodwork and pale-green paint, in a recess shielded by green curtains, lay the mortal remains of Djaber, son of Abdullah, companion of the Prophet, who was killed at Blachernae during the siege of Constantinople in 668.

The servant edged the curtains apart very cautiously. He did it with such care that it was as if he did not wish to disturb the son of the companion of the Prophet; as if he expected to see him sitting up in his coffin, the lipless mouth reciting soundlessly verse after verse of the Koran. Having gazed reverently within he allowed me a momentary glimpse; then drew the curtains again softly. Then he began to speak: the history of the son of the companion of the Prophet, his piety, his nobility, his courage. Soon my exiguous Turkish was exhausted. On he went, for a quarter of an hour, for half an hour, for three-quarters of an hour. Periodically he drew apart the curtains and dutifully I looked again and again and again, repeating after him key words and phrases to show that I was following his discourse. I felt it was the least I could do. The big grandfather clock ticked away ponderously; the sun moved downwards; the curtains were parted and closed. At last, at the risk of discourtesy, I could stand it no longer; but, as I made to leave, the *muezzin's* summons came as a blessed reprieve and as a cue for exit.

★

Ahmet, whom I first met when I saw a rather bad bust of him in the art gallery by the Dolmabahçe Palace, was a poet and a scholar. He was fat and short and volatile and acted and thought with bewildering rapidity. I met him in the flesh in the university library late one afternoon. He was tinkering with a translation of one of his poems into French. With the characteristic courtesy of the Turk to the stranger he had soon supplied me with drinks and books and many opinions. He was, he assured me, famous; and he produced scrapbook after scrapbook to prove it. He also had a weak heart, a passion for coffee, which he would go to any lengths to obtain, and the remains of the filthiest and most rotten teeth imaginable.

One day he propelled me into a taxi and took me to the Palace of Blachernae which lies quite near the church of SS Peter and Mark. From outside the land-walls the galleries are visible high above the fosse, but the only way to get to them was from above and inside the walls.

We clambered up the hill. Everything had been built over and filled in, but imperfectly. Caverns gaped in the earth, arched chambers appeared at the roadside. Houses and shacks had been built at random. Lopsided tombstones stuck out. All was chaos. We went down some steep steps and then plunged into the intense darkness of the now subterranean palace. Most of the flooring had collapsed and every step was perilous. Rats scurried among the galleries. Once I snapped on my cigarette-lighter and found I was just about to tread on forty feet of air. I held up the lighter and the flame leapt and wavered, the shadows wagging across the vaulted ceilings. Clusters of bats were hanging up like bundles of black rags. In the wobbling flame of the Ronson I could distinguish slender pillars and domes, marble pediments and the remains of mosaic and fresco. Once this palace was as fabulous and rich as the imperial one the other end of the city. A sad end to such magnificence; all sinister and decayed, damp, gloom, vermin, bats. The only thing that relieved that discordant evidence of ruin was the gentle quibbling of the doves.

The palace is ascribed to the emperor Anastasius (491–518), and it is believed that a villa or *kiosque* was built there to start with for the convenience of the emperor when going for purification to the sacred pool and for hunting expeditions to the west and north of the land walls. In the ninth century its size and importance grew. It was here that Peter the Hermit and Godfrey de Bouillon conferred with the emperor and where many interviews with the early crusaders took place. In the end it became the habitual abode of the court and remained the imperial residence probably until the thirteenth century. But it had fallen into disuse well before the Turkish conquest, as Pero Tafur discovered at the beginning of the fifteenth century.

The thick, grey, machicolated walls bulge out to the north before reaching the Golden Horn. They are the result of several hands and developments but they are usually known as the work of Manuel I, Comnenus (1143–80), and they are fortified with nine immense towers. From one of them the emperor Constantine XI, Dragases, and the historian Phrantzes heard and watched the Turkish preparations for the final assault on the city on May 29th just over five hundred years ago. It is strange to stand there and participate for a few moments in the imagination and echo of such a momentous event. Between the sixth and seventh of these towers is the 'Crooked Gate' or ancient Porta Caligaria, so named because there was a factory nearby where military boots were made. One of the towers is named after the luckless Michael Anemas who was imprisoned for conspiracy against the emperor and horribly tortured. The Christian empire of the Byzantines has a long and sombre record of murders, tortures and abominations.

Ahmet and I walked back away from the Horn, going approximately south, following so far as possible the line of the walls. It was a cold day and we walked briskly. It had snowed and the cypresses in the cemeteries beyond the walls stood up like cone-shaped white brushes flecked with black. The summer's dusts on the roads were turning to ooze. We went up a narrow street of wooden houses in good repair. An *hamal* came by bowed under four coffins roped together. I asked Ahmet how the people kept warm through the winter. 'They don't,' he said, 'but they are used to it.' We passed a mosque, the domes bulging irregularly under the snow. The minarets rose slim and knife-sharp against the pale sky. We came out on a small plateau on the top of the walls and there before us was the Palace of Porphyrogenitus. Very near here, Tekfur Saray, there was a talisman which Evliya mentions— a solid bust of black stone on which was placed the brazen figure of a demon. It spat out fire and flames once a year. Whoever caught a spark kept it in his kitchen and so long as his health was good the fire never went out. There was also a cavern somewhere, which he mentions, dedicated to St John, in which, in the winter, demons hid themselves.

The palace is a magnificent rectangular shell with an open gallery at the bottom and two rows of arches above. Outside there is a rich polychromatic decoration of brick and stone. It was built in the twelfth century and was one of the dependences of the main palace of Blachernae. A number of small boys were playing football in front of it and regarded the palace as their domain which, with the usual courtesy and cheerfulness of Turkish children, they were very happy to show us round. Three of them practised their English with me which, considering they were thirteen-year-old urchins, was remarkably good. They hopped about the ruin like mountain goats and dragged Ahmed, protesting and clasping his uncertain heart, and myself up a most dangerous piece of stone-work. They knew all about the palace; when it was built and by whom. When they had exhausted their repertoire they gave me some fragments of pottery and pieces of mosaic as a parting gift.

Where emperors have dined off gold and envoys chatted of the affairs of an empire a gaggle of street-arabs now rules. Yet another salutary lesson. But John Sanderson wrote its epitaph as long ago as 1594. 'On the first hill,' he says, 'is to be seene, beginninge frome the west towards the port of Adrianople, a fragment, standinge memory of the ould emperiall pallas, with certayne gallaries, waist romes, and pillors within itselfe, doth well shewe the great power of Time the distroyer and overthrower of all, that a prince of the wourld his pallas is nowe become a lodge for oliphants, panthars, and other beasts.'[14]

From the topmost point of the palace it was possible to see a considerable distance. To our right unfolded Thrace: near at hand the fields, the cypresses, the cemeteries, white sheets of land mottled and splashed with dark strokes, and the burial grounds printed, to adapt Stephen Spender's phrase, with the heavy pages of death. In front of us stretched the land-walls.

The original walls were built by Theodosius II in 413: in fact there were three parallel and concentric walls fortified by towers and protected by a deep moat. They extended from the Marmara to the Golden Horn, over four miles. Apart from the very extremities they still do so. They were virtually impregnable if properly guarded, but not proof against everything. In 447 a terrific earthquake brought down fifty-seven of the towers. These were rebuilt in three months— an achievement which must rank high among such records. For a thousand years they protected the city and were repaired, reinforced and extended again and again. Now, as Grosvenor put it, they are 'venerable ruins, sublime and awful in their unutterable desolation and decay'. This sounds a good deal worse than the reality. 'Desolation and decay' there is in plenty, but nothing when compared to the walls on the Marmara side. The amazing part is that so much of these land-walls is still in excellent repair: a tribute to the skill of their conception and execution. The long line of stone, grey and pale red and buff-coloured, punctuated by towers and bastions and crenellated ramparts, stretches on and on, far out of sight, rising and falling to the contours of the ground. Many of the towers are jagged and broken. Huge black fissures, like strokes of still lightning, zigzag down them. Clefts gape open. Weed and grass and small trees cling in their crevices. In some places they have fallen completely, in others they have been tilted by the shuddering of the earth. And in yet more they look as if they have been built only fifty or a hundred years ago. And whereas the walls on the Horn are mere vestiges embedded in later construction, and those on the Marmara a sad and squalid ruin, the walls of the land still have a noble strength, a tragic beauty.

The moat beneath them has been filled in some parts, but much of it has been left and taken for cultivation of vegetables, fruit and olives. One day, where the new arterial dual carriageway ends and where a breach has been made in the walls, I watched some bull-dozers clearing the filled moat. The walls had been exposed to a further depth of about fifteen feet. Roaring, the dozers heaved and lurched at the base of a small cliff of earth. An avalanche fell. Then the powerful grabs swung down, jaws gaping, and gobbled up hundredweights of soil and rubble. There was a gleam of white in the red earth—bones: some long-inhumed skeleton, of Arab, Crusader or Turk. A skull toppled and rolled down the red slope, then was scooped up, devoured, as the steel teeth plunged into the soil.

NOTES

1. Sir Adolphus Slade, op. cit.
2 Thévenot, *Travels in the Levant*. London, 1874.
3. Aaron Hill, *An Account of the Present State of the Ottoman Empire*. London, 1709.
4. Evliya Efendi, op. cit.
5. Aaron Hill, op. cit.
6. Pero Tafur, *Travels and Adventures*. Broadway Travellers Series. London, 1926.
7. Lithgow, op. cit.
8. Evliya Efendi, op. cit.
9. Grelot, op. cit.
10. Lady Mary Wortley Montagu, *Letters*. Dublin, 1763.
11. Gainsford, *The Glory of England*. London, 1618.
12. Thévenot, op. cit.
13. Pero Tafur, op. cit.
14. John Sanderson, *Travels*. Hakluyt Society. 2nd Series vol 67

CHAPTER FIVE

Pera and Galata

'LET us then proceed to view this City in her modern Dress, *perhaps*, not less illustrious tho' more enslav'd, than when she shon the *Empress* of the gazing Universe; her Situation . . . has open'd all the Gates of Plenty and Command to her unbounded *Sway* and *Traffick*, and the unexampled Beauties of the Prospects she affords, are such as render her the Seat of Pleasure, and the Paradise of Nature.'

AARON HILL, *The Present State of the Ottoman Empire*. London, 1709

On a broad island in front of the station in Sirkeci long and amorphous queues for taxis were formed. There are more taxis than any other kind of vehicle in Istanbul: mostly large and well-sprung German and American cars. Their size and their springs are very necessary since many wish to travel and the roads are steep, tortuous and rough. With the possible exceptions of the Italian, the Yugoslavian and the Corsican there is nothing quite like a Turkish taxi-driver. He is a born road-pirate—daring, temperamental and ruthless. Wherever you are going and whether you have all day or five minutes to get there he always drives as if you were to catch the last plane or the last train for an indefinite period. Every journey is a race against nothing, a mere contest of wits and dexterity.

He is also a good deal less skilful than the Italian, the Yugoslavian and the Corsican. His audacity is too often reckless without the inspiration which can ensure it against disaster. They spend a lot of their time drinking *raki*—a sure and cunning saboteur of reflexes—and accidents are frequent. Fully loaded taxis have been known to plunge into the deep waters of the Golden Horn and the even deeper and swifter waters of the Bosphorus. From such mishaps there is little chance of survival.

But despite these dangers, and in part because of them, there is something very exhilarating about Turkish taxis. The majority of the drivers are, as might be expected, young, and they seem to spend their days in a fictional world. They are like children in a nursery with a real gun. They seem to be imagining the enaction of bold exploits, exciting raids and getaways, as if they are stand-ins for some film of robbery, a splendid contrast to their dull and often rude London counterpart who, eye cocked on the meter, stops sanctimoniously at 'zebras' and plots an interrupted course through the hazards of traffic lights. The Turk is a freebooter; the cabby a phlegmatic mariner. It is probably just as well.

They have a sensible and useful institution called a *dolmuş* literally a 'stuffed' taxi, which fills with people at a fixed tariff for specific destinations. They coast along the streets and at regular points load and unload.

I joined a queue—a mere formality. The powerful and raffish machines wearing chequered bands along the sides swept in, the drivers shouting their districts—Taksim, Karaköy, Bayazit, Eyüp. The queue disintegrated and each car was boarded without ceremony and often by force.

We swung away through Sirkeci, over the Galata Bridge and the Golden Horn. In front, the massed lights of Galata and Pera were stacked and spread across the hill. Buildings were coroneted with bright lights. The Horn was full of a hundred different kinds of vessels, their innumerable lights threading the dark water with needles of gold. Away to the north and west the sky was pale primrose and green and against it, in a great sweep, clear and black, carved, as it seemed, in ebony, stretched the line of the old city: domes, towers, pinnacles and minarets.

It is a view worth travelling a long way to see. It is a view which one would like to look at every evening. It is something which, once seen, is ever remembered.

Then, in a moment, the silhouette was obliterated and we swung up the long hill into Pera.

There are parts of Istanbul which are strongly reminiscent of Liverpool, and Pera is one of them. The drab, cobbled streets, the heavy, dark buildings of banks, offices and merchant houses, the clanging, ringing trams, the crowded pavements, the whole garish paraphernalia of modernity—all these immediately transport the mind to the big cities of the north. But, of course, Pera is the European quarter.

The taxi dashed along Istiklâl Caddesi—the main street, the Oxford Street (it is like it)—of Istanbul, dodging the ponderous trams and elephantine buses, cutting in, intercepting, braking. The driver, one hand nonchalantly on the wheel, threw out laconic comments over his shoulder at the ineptitude of other drivers. Hundreds of faces floated up in the lights and swam past the windows. The gleaming shoals of bright chequered taxis surged, hooting. Limousines, grey, red and black, slid among them, skimmed like enormous sleek fish, and through half-closed eyes it was the bizarre vision of a drunken, drowning sailor grouping in the phosphorescent, flourescent chaos of a tropical, submarine highway.

Batteries of thousands of exploding, bickering, jigging, bobbing lights bounced off the pupils like coloured ping-pong balls in a nightmare contest. Neon signs flickered, advertisements contracted and expanded, unrolled and re-rolled. Glasses were constantly replenished with bubbling green and red lights. Light was scooped up in shop windows, flashed and was flung back from windscreens. It scampered up and down the sides of doorways and, garrulous, repeated itself in a hundred different announcements. It exploded on jewellery and silver, became pink and amber, green and yellow, breaking and snapping. On the pavements and overlapping into the road, thousands of people shuffled, sidled, dawdled or just stood; Piccadilly, Helsinki, New York, Istanbul—it was all the same in the lighting.

The taxi jerked to a dramatic halt and emptied in a second. We might have been doing a smash-and-grab.

I paid my fifty kuruş and walked across Taksim Square, pausing for a moment to look at the news: a 'ticker-tape' in big coloured lights, like an enormous bracelet, running in a band across the top of a building. 'Tension grows on Syrian frontier...' The lights nudged their way over like a horizontal rope of fixed stars, a stellar bulletin. 'Russians make accusations...'

In the centre of the square is a large grey monument to the dead of the war of independence. Can there ever be another century when more monuments to more dead will be erected? Sculptors must have made a large amount of money out of them during the last fifty years. The Socialist Republics are littered with them. Every township has its bronze soldier, more or less defiant, standing on bones or cannon-balls or empty cartridge-cases.

The big open-air café under awnings which overlooks the square was full. There were mostly Arabs and Syrians and a few Greeks, tourist Turks, the occasional European and Persian. I walked in and Mahmoud, an old Turk with a bulbous nose and a bald knobbly head and little spinneys of hair sprouting out of his face, greeted me. I ordered a glass of tea.

Away to the west the sky was still aquamarine, dissolving into violet. One star, keenly, almost painfully bright, stood high above; below, the incomparable carbon silhouette of the sky-line, St Sophia, and the mosques of Süleyman, Beyazit, Fatih, Selim, and many more stretching away to the edge of sight and into the darkness where night lay already over Europe.

★

Beyond Taksim to the north lay gardens, the municipal casino, the tennis club and the radio station. Garlands of coloured lights hung among the trees. Couples sat and made love surreptitiously on the benches. Shadows moved up and down the walks. In the distance I could hear dance music drifting from the big hotels which lay along the broad Cumhuriyet Caddesi. The road went on north, smooth and brightly lighted, lined by big blocks of apartments, airline offices and garages, into the suburbs and then into the rolling country of Thrace. All this was America up here—and its imitations. I felt, no doubt quite wrongly, that it had far less to offer me. I was happier among the back streets, the cheap night-clubs and the shabby and shady cafés; or pottering among the crumbling court-yards of mosques and the narrow cobbled streets overhung by decaying wooden houses in the Turkish quarter.

Beyond and below the Hilton Hotel lay the suburb of Maçka. There was the military museum, interesting as such museums go, big white houses with balconies and shutters mixed with the new packing-case architecture of flats. There were large, desolate open spaces in many directions like the hinterland of Milan and Turin. The roads were made up so far and then moved by degrees to rubble and dust, everything gradually petering out like plans and money. Isolated houses and shacks lay at the end of paths and tracks. In a few minutes you could move from tarmac and large motor-cars to stones and donkeys.

To the east of the square a steep, broad road wound downwards to the Bosphorus, past more offices and blocks and hotels, finishing near a fine football stadium built in the Roman manner. I used to watch 'futbol' there sometimes. To a rugby player the Turks appeared to have a high standard though fights broke out periodically.

To the west were what I called Wigan and Warrington, a mixture of harsh cobbled streets, dingy nineteenth-century buildings of more or less confused pedigree, bars, cafés and workshops. You would be back there in Lancashire when suddenly a mosque rose up out of the ground, fig-trees transformed a bare garden and bougainvillea cascaded purple over old walls. Or you would turn a corner and there see the great sky-line like a mirage on the other side of the Horn, another Xanadu glimpsed between the chimneys and rotting roofs. Amidst the babble of half a dozen languages I heard a strong north country accent go past one day. I remembered the little Lancastrian who went to Heaven and who, before he had been there very long, grew intolerably bored. St Peter found him looking especially dejected one morning. He asked him what was the matter. 'Ee,' he said, ''alo worn't fit, I've bust string of 'arp, I dorn't knaw a sorl 'ere, an' I wish I were back in Accrington int foost place.'

But Accrington was there, and Heaven, and Hell. As Satan put it in *Paradise Lost*:

> The mind is its own place and in itself
> Can make a Heav'n of Hell, a Hell of Heav'n.

★

I used to go to the big café at Taksim to meet people and to hear the news. It was one of the principal lungs of the city. It inhaled and exhaled all the gossip. It was almost exclusively the resort of men. If you took a woman in there you felt as if you were taking one into the Long Room at Lords. The men sat there and talked and smoked and played with their coloured beads and gambled.

It was also a useful place to change money. One of the local magicians of black-market currency was always shuffling to and fro among the customers like a discreet master of ceremonies, changing a cheque here, lira there, dinars somewhere else. It was all done gently, courteously, by sleight of hand. You never actually saw the money. He might have been passing a benediction upon the glasses of tea but for the occasional testimony of a chink and a crackle.

It was also a place to shake off and banish the apathy that, sooner or later, tends to overtake one in Istanbul. I used to blame it on the city, and in a way it was always induced by it. But . . . *mon semblable . . . mon frère.* The ghosts of unfulfilled intentions are always haunting the emptying mind, dogging the slowing paces of the heart.

I was reading there one night, reading *The Scale of Perfection* by Walter Hilton. It is a fine book and its calm, sane counsel lasts well over six centuries. 'Your enemies may begin by troubling your mind with doubts, hinting that your confessions have been invalid; that some old sin lies unremembered and unconfessed in your heart; that you must give up your desire, go back to the beginning, and make a full confession. But do not believe their lies. . . .'

I looked over the edge of the balcony. There was a man coming along the pavement on his hands. He moved easily, pliantly, his arms swinging his body over the ground with long—with the equivalent of long strides. His legs had been cut off a few inches below the groin, and he sat in a kind of shallow leather bucket strapped round him. His shoes were on his hands—an old brown and white pair.

I watched him coming, smoothly, powerfully; a comfortable rhythm. His leather bucket scraped on the pavement as his muscular shoulders and arms levered and propelled him. He did not beg but of the five people that passed him in the course of fifty yards four stopped and dropped some kuruş into his hand. He went past me at about half a mile an hour; a little more perhaps. He was quite young, about forty. I watched him going beyond me, a grotesque contrast slithering between the trousered legs and brisk feet. Then he turned to cross the road, eased himself off the pavement. The traffic stopped.

He accelerated a little over the road. I was reminded of some animal that is dangerous, that is protected by taboo, for which everyone must make way. I thought how terrible it would be to run down a legless man.

He reached a small café, slipped his shoes and quickly, dexterously pulled himself up on a chair and sat, almost normal again, the burly stumps of his thighs protruding a little over the edge of his chair. He leant forward and drew his hand across his face.

There are a number of men like this in the city and one woman, a wizened, knotted creature, like an old lopped branch clad in rags, who haunts the bazaars and the streets nearby. She drags herself about the crowded alleys and plucks people by their coats and trousers with a tabid hand. But people are generous and she is quite cheerful.

Quite often, especially in Pera and near the approaches to the big hotels, women sit on the kerbstones with children in their arms and beg openly. But open beggary is rare. The giving of alms is obligatory for the Muslim and in any case Turks are openhanded people.

Sir Adolphus Slade once saw a man in the city who had had his feet cut off as a punishment for some crime. He became a beggar and 'enforced his arguments by carrying in his hand the skeletons of his poor feet'.

When William Lithgow was in Constantinople in 1610 he reckoned that there were as many as 40,000 brothels in the city and added to this remarkable figure by warning that, if any Christian were apprehended in one, he was obliged to become either a Turk (meaning a Muslim) or a slave.[1]

At the end of the previous century another traveller, Sanderson, stated that in 1594 there were a thousand whores 'of all sorts at least', not to mention three hundred falconers, dwarfs and dumb men.[2] This also is a pleasantly round but arbitrary figure; and he was probably referring to the Sultan's concubines rather than to the public and professional harlot.

Now such needs are catered for on a more modest scale and there is no such awkward choice as Lithgow's for the erring and captured Christian.

There is one street in Pera, not far from the main street, where the majority of the brothels are concentrated: perhaps twenty or more. Outwardly there is nothing remarkable about the street, except, of course, the extraordinary number of men in it day and night—but fewest in the mornings.

The houses are large and can be entered through one solid door from the street. In each of these doors, roughly at eye level, there is a small grill. Prospective clients crowd round taking it in turns to see if there is anything which appeals to them: a flesh and blood peep-show; what the butler saw but could not have hoped for.

Being curious, I explored one evening. I felt very self-conscious, nervous even. At last I plucked up enough courage to join a queue and eventually arrived at its head. Beyond the grill lay a salon: a spacious apartment full of sofas, divans and easy-chairs upholstered in more or less gaudy fashion. The boudoirs of lust are always tricked out in some finery.

About the furniture, pneumatic, lolling, sprawling, strolling, were the women. They were usually nine-tenths naked and tended to be large, heavily built, powerful almost; strapping succubae with ponderous, pendulant breasts, hurdler's thighs and discus-thrower's shoulders. Some wore chintz pants: the smallest and most absurd of concessions to modesty. Others were partly draped in transparent negligées; others still minced on high-heeled shoes. They lounged there basking in the harsh electric light and the contracting pupils of the desiring. I was vaguely reminded of alligators on a sandbank. There was a bored and animal lassitude about them and their heavily shadowed eyes were vigilant.

By the door, seated at a desk, was the manager, the pimp: the box-office. Periodically one of the women would throw out a casual remark, light a cigarette or stroll languidly and provocatively across the room, rolling her flaccid buttocks for the benefit of the craning audience which she knew were goggling at her through the grill. I was reminded of something else. It was like looking into a cage full of indolent panthers.

Sooner or later such a voluptuous display of curved and alabaster flesh would be too much for one of the men. There followed a sharp tap at the door. The ready and dexterous hand of the pimp opened it quickly. The man passed in. For a moment or two there was a mild disturbance of choice and transaction. Then the lens cleared and the tableau was as before—but with one fewer in it.

One evening I was persuaded to show the street to a lady who insisted, with the curiosity of the sex, on finding out what happened there. We had scarcely arrived when a bystander came up anxiously and, recognizing us as foreigners, said in English: 'Sir, sir, you must not go further. It is not for the lady to see the street of shame.' To have ignored such courtesy would have been very rude. I was relieved, she disappointed.

Sexual immorality stands high on the list of those things which tend to excite those periodic fits of morality when indignation and self-righteousness make a vigorous and futile excursion from the museum of public rectitudes. Swindling, robbery, manslaughter, blackmail, suicide and a dozen more the public take daily in their stride. The press ensures that the evenings are not dull. But suggest that prostitution is out of hand, that the government is concerned

about it, that foreign visitors are disgusted by the streets, suggest that
sexual vice is gripping society, that homosexuality is on the increase,
that Lesbianism is up compared with before the war, and the wind
of scandal and alarm hustles through people's houses. The puritans
put away their whips and take up their pens. There is a cry for
inquiry, for the law, for victims, for increased penalties. The in-
violable castle of public chastity is threatened once again and, hey
presto, we have the *Wolfenden Report*. 'The Game', as the prostitutes call it, goes on. The *Report* gathers dust on the public-library
shelves, the borrowing dates grow further and further apart. It was,
in the end, something of a failure, and moral uproar gently subsides
once again into emotional lassitude.

Society, it is fairly clear, is genuinely afraid of the prostitute. It
has always been. Gladys Mary Hall summed the matter up in 1933.
'Throughout history,' she wrote, 'the existence of prostitution has
produced repeated waves of uneasiness quite inconsistent with its
complete acceptance as a social necessity. To study the history of
prostitution itself is to discover that the custom has been continually
assailed by attempts at repression, and the prostitute herself the
object of variable and inconsistent social treatment. She has been
offered as a luxury to visiting potentates, treated as a criminal, sub-
jected to extremities of severity, or accorded a sort of semi-recogni-
tion. But under whatever conditions, she has survived.'

It is also an historical fact that for centuries in western Asia and
in Europe forms of prostitution were obligatory and it was an honourable profession. Lydian girls earned a dowry by prostitution. So
did the Armenians and Etruscans. In some quarters the practice was
a solemn religious duty. At Babylon, every woman, rich and poor,
once in her life had to yield to the embraces of a stranger at the
temple of Mylitta, that is of Ishtar or Astarte, and to dedicate to the
goddess the wages earned by this deed. The sacred precinct was
crowded with women waiting to observe the rite. Some of them,
according to Herodotus, queued for years. At Heliopolis or Baalbec
in Syria every maiden had to do the same. In Phoenician temples
virgins prostituted themselves for hire in the service of religion, thus
propitiating the goddess and gaining her good-will. In Cyprus all
women before marriage were obliged to do likewise. Frazer tells us
that in Camul, formerly a province of the Chinese empire, men
placed their wives at the disposal of any foreigners who came to
lodge with them and thought it an honour if the guests made use of

the amenity. Apparently the emperor forbade this practice and for three years the people obeyed. Then their lands grew sterile and their crops failed. They begged the emperor to raise the embargo. He did so and soon the corn grew.

We have progressed since those days perhaps. Unlike the crops of Camul, prostitution, like religion, has flourished under persecution and there is no social class in which prostitution for gain is unknown. Except in parts of southern India and parts of Africa prostitution in religious and fertility rites is now obsolete, but other forms are vigorous. In many ways nothing new has been done to stop it or regulate it. As long ago as the seventh century B.C. Solon established the first licensed brothel in Athens—a precedent later to be followed by the Church and the State in order to provide extra revenue. The Greeks' system recognized three classes of prostitutes: the *hetaerae*, who were civilized and sophisticated women; the *auletrides*, a superior kind of entertainer and dancing-girl; and the *dicteriades* who were the common prostitutes and were confined to definite quarters and obliged to wear distinctive clothes. Things have not changed much. There are still a good many professional mistresses of the *hetaerae* kind, though less learned and less witty. There are call-girls and dancing-girls and 'hostesses' (a new snobbery) in clubs —often the products of good schools and with semi-blue blood. And there are the rank and file of Soho and Paddington and Mayfair. The Romans were stricter and less successful in these matters. Their prostitutes were licensed and taxed and were obliged, like the Greeks, to wear noticeable clothes, to dye their hair or wear wigs. Nominally, in those days, once a prostitute always a prostitute. There were laws forbidding the daughters of equestrians to become whores. There were also brothels and some equivalents of the *hetaerae*.

The spread of Christianity brought new policies, greater humaneness and efforts at reclamation. It was in Constantinople itself that Theodora, a retired prostitute and the consort of the emperor, established a home for whores; and Justinian carried out a vigorous campaign against pimps and brothel-keepers. Later, however, throughout Europe, prostitution increased rapidly. Royalty had private brothels and public bath-houses served a variety of purposes. In the twelfth century the only state-licensed brothels that England has ever had were established. They were the 'stews' at Southwark which provided a handsome revenue for the bishops of Winchester.

Later, venereal disease on an enormous scale in the fifteenth and

sixteenth centuries proved in the end a stronger incentive to chastity
than religious teaching and the idea of chastity.

In Greece the *hetaerae* enjoyed a position of influential intimacy
with the most distinguished and eminent men. The names of the
hetaerae, who were often cultured, intelligent and versatile, still
survive—Aspasia, for instance, and the fourth-century Phryne who
began life by gathering capers and finished it by cutting them with
many lovers, during which she amassed a fortune. But not so the
names of the wives of those men. In fact the history of mistresses
proves the lamentable point that legitimacy and fidelity are uninter-
esting. Most people prefer the *News of the World* to the *Lives of the
Saints*. And there is another reason. In the *Laws of Sex* Houghton
Hooker suggests it. 'Prostitutes', he writes, 'everywhere report that
their trade is in large measure financed by married men, who, weary
of the indifference or antagonism of their wives, turn to public
women for sympathy and gratification.' Unfortunately, married
women, wearied for the same reasons, have not a similar outlet—or
not on any scale. Perhaps in a predominantly polyandrous society
the situation would be reversed. The prostitute thus serves a useful
purpose. She absorbs the surplus biological urges which far exceed
the procreative ends to which they can be put. She is a kind of
emotional and physical shock-absorber. She is bound to continue
and, as Mr Wayland Young has recently pointed out in an excellent
article in *Encounter*, before we can possibly hope to understand the
causes we must learn to treat 'that pleasant, beautiful, interesting,
and useful faculty all men and women have for sex in the same way
that we treat our other important faculties, like learning, work, and
prayer; by welcoming it, enjoying it, studying it, and talking about
it without constraint, without "reverence", without botanizing, and
in English'.

My main regret when seeing those magnificent Amazonian women
in the Istanbul brothels was that they should be immured day after
day and only seen in the less than favourable circumstances of an
artificial and pimp-ruled domain.

★

Night life in Pera is rather limited. There are a number of clubs of
one kind—and another. They tend to be cheap, noisy and tedious.
Indifferent cabarets are performed amidst tawdry surroundings, that

particular kind of pretension which turns the simple and perhaps naïve into the vulgar. There are also a couple of very pleasant and enormous open-air restaurants, at Tepebaşi and Taksim, which are popular and a little expensive. There is usually a cabaret and variety show, both of which are of a high standard. The performers are international, if not of international repute. One man who appears regularly at both is worth going a long way to see. He is Celal Sahin, a comedian and imitator of remarkable ability. He has the rare gift of satirical humour which Turkish people appreciate. His ridicule is against universal characteristics and faults so that much of his performance can be enjoyed without understanding the tongue. He can imitate anything from a poodle to an Istanbouli tram; and always acts with an irrepressible verve.

The movies are popular and consist largely of foreign films. The cinemas are cramped and frequently intolerably hot.

Progress in the theatre is slow. In the past non-Muslim Turks, usually Armenians, Greeks and Italians, were the actors. Muslim women were not allowed to appear on the stage and official disapproval prevented most men. No doubt the Koranic interdict on the representation of human forms was in part responsible. The theatre before the Republic usually performed Shakespeare and Molière and Greek comedy and others of that kind. But in 1939 Carl Ebert was engaged to lead the drama and opera group of the Ankara State Conservatory and interest was promoted. In 1945 *Our Town* was produced. But still the open-air theatre below the Hilton Hotel sticks to traditional material. The playwrights of the republic used patriotic themes but achieved little success. But after all, drama is an art which burgeons and grows very slowly indeed.

Periodically I used to visit an Armenian gentleman, a retired chemist. He was a charming man, civilized and droll, and with the easy, gentle manners of an older generation. He spoke perfect English with a grave, soft voice. He had kept up the language all his life by reading newspapers and by making the best of what conversation came his way. It is always a salutary pleasure to hear one's own language spoken clearly and eloquently by a foreigner.

The first time I met him he was playing patience. 'You find me bored to death,' were his opening words. 'Like Napoleon on Elba.' I used to play chess with him quite often and drink too much Turkish brandy—which is really excellent. He was an amiable opponent, placid and courteous, and a good player. But chess in itself is a wonderfully soothing game, even more so than billiards. The pieces have fine movements. They make contrasts which are especially pleasing: the long raking diagonal moves of the bishops; the powerful rooks quartering the board, the curious sideways prances of the knights. How appropriate it is that the queen should be so mobile and functional, the king so restricted, barriered by protocol.

I told him the story of the saint who played chess with the Devil. The saint's soul was the stake. The game lasted many days and gradually their forces dwindled. But the saint won in the end because he so manœuvred the game that the Devil was left with only two moves. If he made one he allowed himself to be checkmated. If he made the other his pieces formed a cross. He resigned the game and the soul and vanished in a flash of lightning. 'There was nothing else he could do,' said the chemist.

One of the centres of evening activity, one mentioned with particular pride by the Turks, is the Istanbul Hilton, a monstrous building of three hundred rooms: fashionable and opulent. Occasionally I used to go there to meet a friend or read a newspaper I could not get elsewhere, and as soon as the swing doors had given their rubbery gasp behind me I was in the cosmos—the scented and padded luxury of the international circuit. Sitting on a high stool in the cocktail bar, where were you? London, Rio de Janeiro, Johannesburg, Paris, Berlin. It was difficult to tell and sometimes I forgot. The coiffured barmen spoke fluent American and in the dining-rooms coveys of elegant waiters glided, bowed and flourished as they performed their obsequies and put upon the tables food you could buy outside for a quarter of the price. And all day long droves of travellers, many Turkish included, passed in and out in their motley. The taxis and the Pullman coaches emptied and filled, smart feet sank in the thick beige lawns of pile, and the tourist and sightseeing agencies boomed. The 'mozaicks' of 'Sanda Sophiar' were extolled, the mosques adjudged as 'cute'.

For a time, one winter, I lived in a pension in a tall, solid house just off the main street of Pera. The street was rough and pitted, and littered with refuse.

On the ground floor there was a hall and one small room with a kind of passage beside it—a large cubby-hole. There was the equivalent of a concierge, a dumb peasant woman with a masculine face and lustreless eyes, her features wasted and lined by poverty and ill-health and child-bearing. There was a bed in the hall and another in the small room; and here, in this minimum accommodation, lived the woman, her husband, her daughter of about seventeen and five small children. It seemed that they slept in relays and two or three in a bed.

The woman who ran the pension was Greek—Madame Mioneder —an ex-actress and almost a comic-opera figure. She spoke French volubly with a strong accent. Everything was always 'terrible'. Fortunately she didn't sing, but she had the explosive temper of her race and a weak heart to boot. Both were liabilities. One of her favourite stories recalled how her heart had given way and how she lay supine for three months, not recognizing anybody. At this she would lean back and roll up the whites of her eyes to simulate one struck immobile and sightless.

Despite these defects she was full of vitality and humour, a good 'ham' actress of the melodramatic school. A situation or a 'scene' brought forth her best, and in a long linen gown, not unlike a toga (and she looked like Nero), she would move about with great speed and alacrity. Her obese body wobbled and undulated frightfully. Her eyes flashed. Her arms flailed. She would clasp her balding head with heavily ringed fingers while her voice discovered unknown notes in the diapason. It was all quite ludicrous and the only thing to do was to get out of the way as quickly as possible.

She always needed somebody as a scapegoat, a butt for her temper and a whetstone for her wit. This was usually her maid, a bovine but shrewd peasant girl who was given her notice regularly two or three times a month. But she was always reclaimed in time for she was essential as a stalking-horse if not as a servant.

She found an ordinary Englishman exasperating and inexplicable. For weeks, unknown to me, I had a mounting reputation for piety, for I rose early in the morning and went for a walk; she thought to church. Her occasional outbursts at my expense fell heavily in the end on phlegm—usually because I lost the track.

One morning a flood was discovered. I heard screams, went out of my room and saw a small tide spreading down the corridor. The bodies of some cockroaches rode upon it. At the other end of the corridor stood madame—shrieking. She was not actually shrieking but I have been unable to find a verb in Roget's *Thesaurus* which describes the noise she made. It was generated from some source of sound entirely peculiar. It was a kind of broken ululation. Arrêtez-la! Arrêtez-la! she cried and her voice rambled down the scale like the protest of a wounded camel. She said the water would not run away and the tap could not be turned off: a strange conspiracy in the plumbing.

Then she dashed forward holding up her toga. The water spurted about her fat ankles. She went into the bathroom and I followed. Somebody from downstairs began to hammer on the door. She flung out her arms. I dodged backwards. 'Hélas! Hélas!' Then she rushed out into the passage. I bent over the bath. The explanation was simple. The plug had been left in. I told her and she was furious. 'You imbecile,' she shouted. 'Why didn't you tell me?'

The day before I left she had a heart attack. While she lay prostrate in her bed we wrangled for two hours over the bill. I held each set of calculations horizontally over her face so that she could read them without moving. From time to time she gave me her opinions of all the doctors she knew. If a tenth of what she said about them were true it seems to me that she was extraordinarily lucky to be alive. But she was a good and kind woman, despite everything, and I was sorry to go.

★

It was a comfortable place and cheap and central for transport but otherwise it did not have many advantages. Pera is the shopping and residential area and the site of the majority of the embassies, many of them great and ostentatious buildings and many of them now only a quarter or a half used. It is not a misleading commentary on the history of Turkish relations with other countries that the British embassy stands upon ground given by the Ottomans in gratitude for British aid against the French in 1801, while the French embassy stands upon ground given by the Ottomans to France in return for aid against the British.

Pera is cosmopolitan but dull. It has always been cosmopolitan. When Lady Mary Wortley Montagu was there she reported hearing people speak Turkish, Greek, Hebrew, Armenian, Arabic, Persian, Russian, Slavonian, Walachian, German, Dutch, French, English, Italian and Hungarian. With the exceptions of Slavonian and Walachian all these may still be heard frequently.

There used to be a Dervish monastery there. The Prophet said that there were to be no monks, but as early as A.D. 657 the Ouveis sect was founded. They were like the 'Sleepless Monks' in that their worship was ceaseless. Eventually, at least a hundred and fifty orders grew up with a large membership. They were allowed to marry and each sect rallied round a central idea and had its own ritual. They carried rosaries bearing thirty-three or sixty-six or ninety-nine beads, the last bead being much larger than the others. Allah had ninety-nine beautiful names.

The Whirling Dervishes, whose devotions Lady Mary Montagu found 'as whimsical as any at Rome', used to perform their rites every Tuesday and Friday. All the countless details of behaviour and posture were prescribed and symbolic. They began a session by filing in before their Sheik who blessed each one with a strange gesture of the hand.

The leader made a final salutation to the Sheik and then began to revolve on his bare right heel. His eyes were half-closed and his head was bent over his right shoulder. Both arms were extended: the right one raised aloft, palm upwards, to signify petition for and reception of divine boons; the left was depressed, palm downwards, indicating that the blessings had been received and had been bestowed on others.

The procedure was reminiscent of starting the propeller shafts of an aeroplane. As soon as the first Dervish was well under way, another would begin to turn; then another, then another and so on until the room was filled with spinning forms. As each one revolved so he circled others and each wheeled within a wheel. Their long white robes which hung to their feet began to spread until they stood out almost at right angles to their bodies. Faint and melodious music accompanied them. They went faster and faster, until gradually their features became fixed and they passed into a kind of trance. It continued for an hour or more but, as Lady Mary Montagu observed, they did not become giddy. 'Which is not to be wondered at,' she wrote, 'when it is considered, they are all used to it from their infancy; most of them being devoted to this way of life from their birth.' She also saw a number of little Dervishes about six or seven years old, 'who seemed no more disordered by that exercise than the others'.[3]

In times of emergency and distress the Sheik took part himself. He occupied a central position, the sun, as it were, round which his satellites revolved.

At the end of the ceremony they all shouted out 'There is no God but God.' Then they kissed the Sheik's hand and retired. The whole thing was performed with, to quote Lady Mary again, 'the most solemn gravity'.

The Dervishes apparently have never agreed as to the exact meaning of the ritual. In moments of great excitement the Prophet was suppose to leap up and gyrate many times. It is possible that the Dervishes imitated him. The dance, after all, is a fundamental part of religious and cosmological belief. One thing seems to be fairly certain and that is that the circle represents the traditional emblem of perfection and in their motions the Dervishes symbolized, as Grosvenor put it, 'the concordant and revolving stellar system'.

★

Nowadays there are not so many mosques in Pera, but the other religions have the majority of their churches there. In the days of religious tourism and relic-mongering Pera was as fruitful a place as anywhere. When Gonzales de Clavijo visited the city at the beginning of the fifteenth century he went to the monasteries of St Francis and St Paul and saw dozens of relics in priceless reliquaries. He saw the bones of St Andrew and those of St Nicholas. He found the habit of St Francis, a hip-bone belonging to St Catherine, the bones of St Louis King of France and those of St Sí of Genoa. He was shown the long bones from the arms of St Pantaleone and St Mary Magdalen, not to mention that of St Luke the Evangelist. He saw the right arm of St Stephen the protomartyr encased in silver and ornamented with pearls, and the right arm and hand of St Anne. The latter was minus its little finger because the then Emperor Emanuel had cut it off to keep it among his private relics. There was also a bone belonging to St Lawrence and another owned by St Basil. Chief among the collection were three skulls from among the eleven thousand heads of the Virgins, a bone of the body of St Ignatius and 'a very holy relic of the Blessed Virgin Mary'.[4]

Most of these relics later became bones of contention and many were lost at the sack of Constantinople, while those that survived were pillaged at the conquest. But long before that many similar ones had found their way into the satchels of itinerant Pardoners, or so they alleged, and where they did not exist they were invented.

Now relics are in much shorter supply and as the Muslim contents himself with one of the Prophet's numerous hairs, so the Catholic relies upon the properties of pieces of the True Cross. Because they are fewer and probably also because less trust is put in them, relics are now not often used, as, for instance, during the Crusades, to invoke divine aid and to disperse crises brought on by incompetent generals and insufficient supplies.

Now more attention is paid to practical religion though it is always difficult to withstand the temptation to revere something which purports to be a relic. When I bend to kiss a piece of the True Cross every Good Friday I am amazed to think that it is possible that it was actually touched by the Redeemer.

Lacking the diversions available to Clavijo I had to be content with the routines of religion. I used to go to Mass in a small church off Istiklâl where there was usually a handful of people, mostly women. The priest was an old Italian Franciscan. It was always a pleasure to hear him speak Latin. Naturally enough, Italians give it a roundness and sonority of their own, but this man was born for singing. When he preached a sermon it grew, it flourished, like something alive. You could see him fashioning it, breathing life into it, launching it.

Once I went to confession to him. It was one of those days when one does not feel like doing so at all. It is easy to say the words, to run through the inventory of futile offences against God. The priest has heard it all before, hundreds of times. There is an old story about the murderer of no religion who, filled with remorse for his crime, travelled from clergyman to clergyman asking for succour and forgiveness. From door after door he was turned away. Then, at last, in despair, as a final and hopeless resort, he went to the confessional. He knelt down and said: 'Father, I have committed murder.'

There was a momentary pause and then the tired, gentle voice of an old priest came through the wire: 'How many times, my son?' Murder, sodomy, bestiality, pride, adultery, avarice, hundredweights of spiritual filth have been filtered through the mesh of the confessional. That the priest has heard it all before does not matter. It is his profession; and he will not tell anyone what he has heard. There is not so much difficulty in telling the priest. The task begins after that. The labour is being sorry, genuinely sorry and—the sting in the tail of sorrow—with a firm purpose of amendment.

Somehow the act inhibited and I could not get the Italian words sorted out. I had to fall back on Latin—a useful language. 'Peccavi.' It sounded absurd, for more reasons than one. Of course, why else was I there? I went on, stumbling badly, creating ludicrous constructions. The church was very quiet. The woodwork cracked loudly from time to time. A grandfather clock boomed pontifically. My Latin must have pained the priest almost as much as the catalogue of error.

Absolved, I left with a lighter heart. It is not comfortable to carry about the weight of one's sins for long; to feel the slow famine and decay, the stealthy corruption in the stagnating spirit.

★

Once, when I had returned to Istanbul from the south, I spent the first night in the Hotel Konak on Istiklâl. I had never been there before and never will again for it has ceased to be a hotel. There can be no regret for that. It was a large, sombre, palatial building with lofty rooms and heavy furniture, furniture that looked as if it had spent half the year huddled in a corner under dust-sheets. The *salon* was like a waiting-room on one of the big Midland stations, or those cafés in Russian comedies where the sad aproned waiter shuttles to and fro with vodka and tea, weaving among elegiac dialogues bulging with unpronounceable patronymics.

In summer it was stuffy; in winter, cold. The matting in the corridors lifted uneasily in the draughts. Prices were high. Cisterns never worked. Taps were stiff, basins and baths stained brown. It was like a mausoleum, a shabby relic of faded comfort, and every day you expected to see the auctioneers walk in and put everything under the hammer.

But I was glad I went, otherwise I would never have met Mrs Tarpin. Imagine a heron with a poodle's head. She was like some bizarre bird from an early bestiary, a stray from Bosch's *Garden of Delights*.

She was old but deceptively spry. She looked English but I could not be sure. There was some betrayal in her clothes or the way she walked. She sat at my table and her eyes, lizard-like, did not blink. She had been abroad so long that she spoke English with a foreign accent, but of no particular kind. Her French was near perfect; Serbian, Turkish, Greek and so on very competent. She was one of those resilient and, in a way, quite formidable ageing English ladies whom you meet all over the world and in the most unlikely places. They have long since come to terms with life and many of them have buried their husbands. As she had lived in Istanbul for twenty years she was worth listening to. Of course, I had to ask her why she had elected to live there—she called it Constantinople—for so long.

The climate? The people? But the climate is not ideal; the people not exceptional. It was a good base for her travelling. Periodically she returned to England for a holiday. It was difficult, she said, sometimes, to think of a better way of spending a holiday, except of course, when you live there.

It was she who introduced me to Nasreddin Hoca. He is believed to have lived in the thirteenth or possibly the fourteenth century. He is supposed to have been a native of Anatolia and to have spent much of his life at Akşehir. He was an *Imam,* a sort of country parson. He is buried in a marble mausoleum in which, at his request, a small hole was left in the masonry, so that he could continue to look out on the world. Over his grave hang the ball with which he played and the lock of his house which he refused to entrust to his wife.

As a wit and a humorist he was without equal in his own line. It was an odd mixture of buffoonery and astuteness. He was often called upon to settle disputes. For instance, one day three men were quarrelling about their shares in a bag of walnuts and one of them asked Hoca to make the division. 'Divide with absolute justice,' said the second. 'Justice is not enough,' said the third. 'Divide as Allah would divide.' 'Yes. As Allah would divide,' they all said.

So Hoca gave one walnut to the third man, a handful to the second and the rest to the first. They protested that it was not an equal division.

'Fool!' said Hoca. 'Since when did Allah divide anything equally among men? As Allah would have divided, so have I divided.'

He began his career as a wit when a child and certainly he must have been a formidable pupil. One day he and his form were rebuked for some joke. To make the punishment fit, the master asked each boy what part he had taken. 'What did you do?' he asked Nasreddin. 'Nothing,' he replied. 'I just watched and laughed.' The master happened upon a quick answer. 'In that case,' he said, 'as long as the world exists people shall laugh at you.'

The prediction was correct. He has been described as Turkey's chief jester and as Turkey's chief justice, since, for five centuries, so many disputes have been settled by his particular kind of logic.

Conversation with Mrs Tarpin ambled pleasantly, digressed, picked up, stood still. 'You must come and have dinner,' she said. It

would be a pleasure, and she loped away through the gaunt *salon,*
a scraggy, tufted figure, independent and happy.

I lingered over some more tea, enjoying the prospect of discovery;
then went out down Istiklâl and down the long steep, winding,
cobbled street which leads past the Galata Tower and on to the
bridge. Half-way down a crowd had assembled. A fight perhaps? I
joined the throng. It proved to be a funeral, that of a Jewish merchant. There are always funerals going on in Istanbul and every
day I passed two or three doors which had pasted on them notice
of death edged with black or purple: a brief eulogy and a pious
exhortation to prayers.

There was a mass of magnificent circular wreaths on long sticks
and hung with purple and silver bows flanking the approaches to
the synagogue. Some men began to stack them on a small lorry. The
curious and cheerful crowd shuffled about, thinned and clogged
again. A young Jew came up and spoke to me. He had the suitable
name of Israel. He spoke eight languages and in no time at all I
underwent a thorough interrogation.

Soon the flowers and the body went off down the hill, bumping
and jolting over the cobbles. Music blared out of a café. The crowd
dispersed, laughing, chattering. A child squatted in the gutter. How
casual it all is, living, dying. Everybody was walking about, shopping, breathing, sweating, and there was the stiff body and the pale
face, features already sagging, jerking away over the cobblestones.
A Jewish merchant.

★

There was a drunk lying in a trough of the Tophane fountain. He
was sound asleep and his feet were protruding over the edge. This
fountain, marble and rococo, is one of the most beautiful in the city.
But it is not used now—except by the drunks. Ahead stretched a
steep, dark cobbled street which led up into Pera. Men were hanging
about in twos and threes and on the site of a demolished building a
meeting was being held. There was an air of stealthy uneasiness
abroad. Two policemen in blue breeches and jackboots, well armed,
leant against a wall and kept an eye on the meeting. One of them
swung his truncheon idly. Through the drifting knots of men the
taxis swung, gaining speed for the long climb to Taksim.

Nearby, alongside the Galata Quay on the Bosphorus, were the big stark buildings of the shipping offices, customs and warehouses. One of the small cruising liners of the Turkish Lines, cheap and very comfortable ships, had just docked from a trip up the Black Sea coast. Hawsers were rattling and the sirens of tugs shrieked and bellowed across the waters.

Passengers were spilling out of the customs and shipping offices, spreading across the roads and the Tophane square, loaded with everything from chickens to portmanteaux. Three *hamals* wove their way among them buckled under enormous bales. A woman's voice was moaning across the square from a radio—'There are two things I want in life.' They were anybody's guess.

This was a combination of China Town and Soho: dingy streets and lofty, dark buildings, roomy, gaunt cafés, cheap lodging-houses, a brothel or two for merchant sailors.

Docklands are very similar wherever you may be. Things are always going on not far below the surface of the apparently casual rhythm of life. People are lazily vigilant. An American had been murdered here a week previously. He had disputed a fare with a taxi-driver and struck him. It was believed that he was drunk. The driver retaliated and some others joined in. They beat his head against the wall and before they knew what they had done he was dead at their feet, some of his brains adhering to a warehouse wall at two o'clock in the morning.

There was a sudden burst of laughter from one of the cafés. 'Another bottle of *raki*,' said a man. Four men were playing cards and becoming merry. A man had been murdered—but life goes on.

In his day Evliya Efendi formed a low opinion of Galata. He saw hundreds lying drunk in the streets—bareheaded and barefooted. Drink was cheaper in those days. Evliya was a Muslim and Galata was principally a Christian quarter. There were about three thousand shops in his time and two hundred taverns, and a lot of private houses as well, many of which had their own baths. Most of the inhabitants were sailors and merchants and handicraftsmen. It is not so very different today. The Greeks kept the taverns and the Armenians were the merchants and bankers. The Jews dealt with love and did all the negotiations. 'Their youths,' wrote Evliya, 'were the worst of all the devotees of debauchery.'

As he wandered among the Hogarthian scenes of profligacy and excess men sang and cried out, boasting of their drunkenness. Every city has its *Gin Lane*. A little piously, Evliya assures us that he drank only 'a syrup made with Athenian honey'.[5]

Galata, known in the Byzantine period as Sykae (the fig-trees), was a walled city and was the thirteenth ward of Constantinople. The name Galata appears in the ninth century, the word probably deriving from the Galatians who had a settlement there and not, as Evliya says, from the word 'gala' meaning milk. It is dominated by the enormous tower which rises a hundred and fifty feet from very near the end of Istiklâl and the long 'Step Street' up the hill. The present tower was built in about 1348 on the foundations of an earlier Byzantine tower of the early fifth century. From the top of it one can enjoy an almost uninterrupted view of nearly the whole city. It is now used as a fire-watch station; like the Serasker tower on the Stamboul side, near the university.

In a city composed of so much wood extra precautions were essential, as they still are, but the methods and organization for extinguishing fires—especially the organization—were remarkable by any standards. They illustrate the dangers of unintelligent capitalism and private enterprise.

When a fire was observed a signal was hoisted and cannon let off, the number of discharges revealing the quarter in which the fire was. 'Deputies', young and active men and lightly clad, then set off from the tower in the direction of the main streets shouting appropriately. The 'street-watchers' then sallied forth adding their voices and naming the area. Soldiers situated in special guard-houses and armed with axes and long hooked poles and leather buckets then joined the throng. By this time the firemen themselves, with portable pumps, and water-carriers, would also be travelling towards the blaze. The fire 'engines' were small boxes carried on the shoulders of four men. When the firemen arrived at the scene they stood about waiting to be hired by those people whose houses were in danger. When the tariffs had been settled the task was undertaken. One may easily imagine the results.

Charles White, writing of the city in the early part of the last century, says that no regular force of firemen existed but a number of porters and boatmen and suchlike were enrolled in each quarter and were given various privileges provided they performed their duties. A reward, he says, was paid to those who arrived first, and 'punishment is not lacking to those who are neglectful'.[6]

★

For a time I lived in one of the small hotels in the dock area of Galata. It was a tiny room but there was a looking-glass, a basin and running water—both rarities. Across the landing there was the usual lavatory: a hole in the floor, a faulty cistern and no paper. In the mornings I used to be woken up by the flies running over my face and feet. At night I could hear the uneasy stirring of the bed in the next room as a man made love to his wife. They seemed to be permanent residents. For a week a baby on the floor above woke every few hours and howled because it had a skin disease. Each day a woman cleaned after a fashion and twice a week I had a long argument with her about the price of my laundry. She always won in the end because she would think of some emotional ruse like her starving children or her ragged clothes. She had three fingers missing from one hand and when all else failed she would look mournfully at these and then reproachfully at me.

I came in at about four o'clock one morning and woke up Ali, the half-idiot boy who acted as porter and who slept on the tables in the *salon*. A few minutes later, without warning and as I was looking at it, the glass fell from the wall and landed in the basin. There was a terrific crash and the bottom fell out of the basin. By some extraordinary chance the glass was not even chipped.

Silence fell, a profound silence. Then the baby upstairs began to cry. Then I heard doors opening all over the hotel. Then they shut again. I knew it would be awkward in the morning.

The proprietor was an idle and good-natured man who really could not be bothered. It was his son of seventeen who ran the establishment, and with a strict hand. He was a thin, dark boy and was always immaculately dressed in a black suit with a white collar. He had ambition and knew how to make other people work while he gave the appearance of being important. He would have made a good civil servant.

He said I had to pay for the basin and the full cost of repairs— about seven pounds. We argued for an hour. The other guests assembled and threw in their advice. Soon there were about a dozen people listening. All were very impartial. It became embarrassing. I went on explaining that the fixture was loose. In the background Ali grinned. I knew what he was thinking. I offered to go to court.

I left to get a lawyer and eventually found one in the law courts. I then went round to the police station and an hour later arrived back at the hotel with a senior police officer and a constable in a police jeep.

The audience had thinned in my absence. With the arrival of the police it quadrupled in a few minutes. We began all over again. I took them on a tour of the hotel and showed them all the other loose fixtures. It was a solemn procedure. We returned to the *salon* and wrangled and wrangled. The affair became more and more ludicrous but Ali was the only one who enjoyed it. At the end of two hours we were at a standstill. The police, who had shown the most admirable coolness and impartiality, were at a loss: divided between the wish to see fair play and the need to be about more important business. I persisted, though becoming a little disgusted at my own tenacity which was beginning to look parsimonious. But that was their intention. About every quarter of an hour I reduced the bill by about ten shillings. Eventually we settled for three pounds ten. It was after lunch-time.

The incident was, I thought, a good example of Turkish dogged-ness—for which I admired the manager's son. But I was wrong. He was Greek. There is an old proverb that it takes ten Turks to defeat a Jew in a bargain, but that it takes ten Jews to defeat one Greek. What was an Englishman against so many?

Below and about the hotel, steep, heavily cobbled streets were full of tradesmen's shops and houses; and among these labyrinths it was possible to discover fine relics of Venetian and Genoese structures, as de Clavijo found right at the beginning of the fifteenth century. Near the bazaar on the Horn shore is one of the few churches that survive. Now it is a mosque, the Arab mosque—the name perpetuat-ing an old tradition that there was a mosque built there when the Arabs were besieging Constantinople in 715. The church was erected in the thirteenth century. It has a square tower and a spire; and inside beautiful galleries and carved woodwork. The courtyard is a playground for children, a drying-room for laundry and a lavatory for dogs. It is surrounded by dingily picturesque streets and houses: dark, dusty and decaying. It is probable that soon all this part will be razed.

A great many travellers have recorded their keen disappointment at finding beyond the 'fair, outward show' of the city what may be summarized as squalor and gloom. This is how Thomas Gainsford put it when writing of Galata in 1618: 'a city over against it, (Stamboul) divided only by sea, no broader heere than our Tamisis, of great antiquity, walled about, and retaining a particular name and renowne, for holding out a yeere and better, after Constantinople was surprized: it standeth likewise up a hill, and equals it both for beastlinesse, confusion and uncomely streets and houses: heere live Greekes and the Franckes, as they terme the Papists (of what nation soever), have a Church by permission; the Courtezan likewise liveth at some liberty; yet is it death for any Christian to lie with a Turkish woman or Jew.'[7]

Pera, on the other hand, he describes as a place of 'quiet dwelling, good aire, and pleasant gardens'. Times change—but perhaps it is more a matter of opinion.

★

Near the gigantic grey column of the Galata Tower is the entrance to the funicular railway which runs from the top to the bottom of the hill. It is reputed to be the oldest underground train in the world. It was built as long ago as 1873 by a French engineer and is known among old Periotes as the 'Mouse's Hole'. Near the top entrance lived a Greek friend whom I used to visit regularly. His company had the advantage of ensuring Turkish coffee. He was a lawyer and worked in a large, shabbily comfortable room in a block of old houses: a desk, armchairs, a sofa and an ancient iron stove made the principal furnishings.

I was on my way to him walking down the main street one morning when suddenly, a few yards in front, a mouse sprang from beneath a building and capered across the pavement, dodging the moving pillars of legs. What a terrible plunge into light and noise that was. It evaded one blow of a boot and for a moment I thought it would run beneath a tram. But it did not. It crouched in the gutter, its little black eyes distended with terror. With a swift movement I managed to scoop it up and popped it into my pocket. I could feel its tiny body scrambling about amongst envelopes and cigarettes. I came to an open space and took it out to set it free. But it was dead. Its heart must have failed in fear. A mouse is a small thing and the death of one a minor affair, but it was a poor way to begin another day.

Many Greeks, like the lawyer, work; and they have a well-developed knack of making money. This some Turks tend not to like. They are not great workers and they want the knack. The

lawyer frequently complained of the lack of organization and indolence of the Turkish people. He was fond of referring to the adage
that 'The Devil tempts all, but the idle man tempts the Devil.' As
against that there is an equally good Arabic proverb which says that
'Haste is from Satan, and leisure from the Merciful One.' The first
implies that God will give reward for labour, the second that He will
punish speedy or ill-considered action. Both are flimsy notions, but
labour is more often used to serve ignoble ends than is leisure. Sin
is active, not passive, and it is less easy to sin when doing nothing.

The Turkish people, among others and those further east, have
always been great practitioners of leisure. It will be said that it has
got them nowhere or not far, and if success is to be measured
economically, as most success now is, this is in part true. Many
Turkish people, if one may risk a generalization, are not really
materialistic; they tend to be spendthrift and liberal, and they are a
great deal more honest than many are willing to admit. Many
Greeks, on the other hand, to hazard again, and by comparison with
Turks, are materialistic and are a good deal less honest than many are
prepared to admit. They are not a success either—if we measure it
economically. But there is no great advantage in judging people by
their material success. Both Greek and Turkish people spend much
time in this particular pursuit.

The majority of travellers in Turkey during the past five hundred
years have remarked the probity of the people, probity often coupled
with generosity and courtesy. They are usually more prepared to
give than to take. This has certainly been my lot, especially in the
country. But this is a tentative record of personal experience.

Over a considerable period it has been my misfortune to meet a
preponderance of Greeks who have turned out to be greedy, under-
hand, unreliable, ill-tempered and vain. On the other hand it has
been my good fortune to meet a number of Turks who have turned
out to be openhanded, candid, dependable, equable and modest. At
one time I found myself drawing unfavourable and favourable conclusions from this evidence and foolishly went on doing so until I
was told by an African priest that it was my duty always to search
out the good in other people and let God take care of their vices.

Perhaps there will come a time when all the absurd importance
attached to nationality and nationalism and national characteristics
will be dissipated and people will be regarded first and foremost as
people, without regard for language and pigment. It will hardly

matter then whether the human race is pale grey or piebald, whether it speaks Chinese or Virginian (the advantages of superficial uniformity will be enormous), provided that its members live more peacefully.

The idea of purity of race, like that of purity of language, is extremely dangerous. The former is one of the bases of the power-pride complex and a sure mounting-block for political crooks. The latter means fossilization and, ultimately, death. 'Words', said Johnson, in that marvellous preface to his dictionary, 'are too subtle and volatile for legal restraint. To enchain syllables and lash the wind are equally the undertakings of pride unwilling to measure its desires by its strength.' The same is true of people. It was De Stogumber who illustrated very clearly the stupidity of such purities and conceptions: the idea of France for the French, England for the English and so on. He paid a harsh penalty and rightly so.

Language, as Johnson realized and as the French Academy did not, lives and, necessarily, dies; or parts of it die. The pages of the *N.E.D.*, like the various layers of society, are full of the obsolete, the obsolescent, the archaic and, it is inevitable, the dead. But wastage is slow, death gradual. Language, by its very nature, is constantly changing: every day a word acquires a new meaning or a new shade of meaning. Any attempt to interfere with this natural growth and life is bound to be harmful. From time to time we realize that a word or phrase has fallen out of use, but for every one that dies a dozen replace it: a replacement of quantity, not of meaning.

The language of a primitive society is limited in vocabulary, especially for the expression of abstract ideas, and, like the users of it, restricted in development so long as it is self-supporting and separate. As groups commingle they become more civilized, as they become more civilized they commingle. Their languages gain from each other.

The English language, astoundingly copious and heterogeneous as it is, has benefited by the importation and loan of tens of thousands of words from other tongues. So, I believe, by the introduction of foreign influences, have the people. The processes of intermingling bloods and words have ensured both a remarkable degree of freedom and peace among people and a language ever rich, ever young, a language with a huge potential. There is probably no other country which has enjoyed such a measure of internal peace for so long.

There is probably no other language which is so flexible and so
widely spoken.

Nationalism, of a kind, is quite strong in Turkey—especially in
Ankara, the new city. But it is a more liberal form than that which
prevailed between the wars. Periodically it leads to trouble.

Most of the Greeks in Istanbul are in the Pera quarter, and most
of them seem likely to remain there. They are, after all, Turkish
citizens. They are not, by all accounts, wanted back in Greece; and
as they have been brought up in Turkey, as all their roots, families,
businesses, connections and so on are in Turkey, they not unnaturally want to remain there. But they are afraid, or some of them are.
From time to time, so they say, the 'squeeze' is put on. The Turkish,
of course, deny it. It is one of those everlasting problems. Dislike
and suspicion move uneasily beneath the surfaces of outward appearances. The ice is always cracking. Sometimes there is a complete
break—as in September 1955.

There are also a number of Greeks living on the Princes Islands:
that beautiful group which lies in the Sea of Marmara a few miles
from the city. A small pine-covered cluster with exquisite bays and
clear healthy air, they still belong to an unhurried world of elegance
and peace.

During the Byzantine period they were a favourite summer resort
of the emperors; also a place of exile for deposed sovereigns and
intransigent noblemen. Monasteries and convents abounded there,
and some survive.

There is something altogether idyllic about these islands. Motor
traffic is barred and you must travel either by donkey or by the little
one-horse carriages; phaetons with frilly awnings. Fine villas and
magnificent gardens are scattered about them, and the little town-
ships themselves are no less delightful. All travellers have extolled
their beauties and Grelot, who was there at the end of the seventeenth century, tells us that the Turks were fond of going there to
escape the embargo on drinking in the city. 'Away they go to these
Islands,' he says 'with a design to bouze it about briskly.' For, as he
explains, they loved to take their 'full swinge when they can get a
private convenience, not believing they have so much as tasted it,
unless they can feel the effects of it in their heads or their Stomachs
three days after'.[8]

In the middle of the following century Bishop Pococke remarked
upon their popularity. He spent some time at Büyük Ada where the

French used to have country houses for retiring as the Greeks do
now. He found the remains of iron-mines on the island and a well
near the town 'esteemed good in venereal cases'.[9]

NOTES

1. Sir Adolphus Slade, op. cit.
2. Sanderson, op. cit.
3. Lady Mary Wortley Montagu, op. cit.
4. Gonzalez de Clavijo, *Embassy to Tamerlane.* Broadway Travellers Series,
London, 1928.
5. Evliya Efendi, op. cit.
6. Charles White, *Three Years in Constantinople.* London, 1845.
7. Thomas Gainsford, op. cit.
8. Grelot, op. cit.
9. Richard Pococke, *Voyages and Travels.* Pinkerton, vol. 10. London,
1811.

CHAPTER SIX

The Seraglio

'THE *Seraglio* is rather a Collection of Palaces and Apartments added to one another, according to the Caprice of several
Emperors, than one single Palace. It is justly called the Great,
since perhaps 'tis the largest in the Universe, and it lodges him
who is call'd by way of Excellence the *Grand Seignior, Emperor
of Emperors, King of Kings, Distributor of Kingdoms and
Principalities, and Lord of the White, Black and Red Seas,* &c.
Nothing can be richer than the Materials of it; 'tis a pity they
are not employ'd more agreeably, or put into better Order.'

A. DE LA MOTRAYE, *Travels through Europe, Asia and
into part of Africa.* 3 vols, London, 1723

Just beyond St Sophia is the spot where they still erect a gallows,
and even now the early wanderer may see, as the Bosphorus is
silvered and then turns to gold and the minarets and turrets are
looped and caught by the sudden lariats of light, the body of a hanging man silhouetted against the rose and amethyst sky. Not far away
is the outer wall of the Seraglio Topkapí Sarayí, about thirty feet
high, and in it is set the Imperial Gate the *Bab-i Hümayun.*

It used to have a guard of anything up to fifty, reinforced at
night by the Janissaries who, as a Venetian diplomat Bon observed
at the beginning of the seventeenth century, travelled about in little
wooden houses on wheels.

Going through the great double-arched portal for the first time
was both a surprise and a disappointment.

I entered an enormous court of irregular proportions, much of it
sparsely populated with trees. This was the outer court, once known
as the court of the Janissaries. In the days of the Sultanate anybody
might enter it, but once they had done so they had to behave

themselves. Above all they had to be silent. A traveller of the sixteenth century, Nicolas de Nicolay, remarked that the silence was
so intense that visitors neither spat nor coughed.[1] Another, Tournefort, in 1700, mentions how he thought that even the horses had
been taught to tread more softly lest the slumber and meditation of
princes should be injured. Anyone who forgot where they were
would be evicted or punished—perhaps by bastinado.[2]

It is still quite silent but occasionally a car or a lorry races through,
churning up a wake. The lawns are decayed and flurries of dust
mingle with leaves and refuse. Away to the left the wonderful Byzantine church of St Irene, having been used in turn as an arsenal and
a museum, stands empty and crumbling, inhabited by pigeons. Outside is a miscellaneous collection of ancient bronze cannon usually
guarded by two soldiers who live in a wooden hut and who repel
inquisitive intruders. One supposes that they are afraid that some
globe-trotting collector of armouries and arsenals will filch one. A
powerful tractor or a team of horses would be required for the task.
The cannon have been assembled to form part of a museum but
already they have lain there for over three years.

And here, in the first court, among the trees and the straggling
bushes, even quite late in the morning, or, for that matter, in the
afternoon and evening, you may see bedless and perhaps homeless
Turkish men, lagged with newspapers, stretched out in sleep.

Of the four principal extant churches St Irene seems to me to be
by some way the most beautiful. It is much bigger than St Saviour in
Chora and SS Sergius and Bacchus but much smaller than St Sophia
(Haghia Sophia). It has never been turned into a mosque. The floor
is below ground level and a stone ramp goes downwards for several
feet through the entrance and leads to the superb narthex. The nave
is straight and flanked by seemingly slender pillars. The galleries
above the aisles are broad and arcaded. The great dome is unbeliev-
ably light and graceful. There is no ornament at all in the church, so
that its perfect proportions are evident. The components are joined
and rest upon each other like the gracile and unobtrusive structure
of an Horatian ode. They prove themselves, as it were, with the ease
and satisfying certainty of an Euclidian theorem. Little recovery of
mosaic has been done and the plain grey and buff of stone and
marble add a simplicity which is in accord with the clean lines of
columns and arches. All is pure and calm and the only sound within
is the gentle warbling of pigeons.

The custodian is a character: a grey old satyr, burly, with blue eyes like a jay and all that bird's mischief and many of its mannerisms. He is lazy and lascivious, and his lopsided wicked smile, his gammy leg and the stumps of fingers on his mutilated hands make him a thoroughly depraved and attractive scoundrel. He lolls about waiting and hoping for women. These he pursues relentlessly, and I believe, given the slightest chance, would try to seduce any presentable woman in any place—on the roof if need be. Indeed it very nearly happened thus on two occasions.

There is a small colonnaded courtyard overgrown with grass at the rear of the church. In it are two magnificent sarcophagi of dark-red porphyry. They are supposed to be those of Constantine and his wife. They are unadorned except for the Cross and the Monogram of Christ. That of Constantine still has its lid. That of his wife, which lies beneath a luxuriant fig-tree, brims with water. Near by is a very old car indeed—about 1905—in which a Turkish general is supposed to have been assassinated. True or not, it is certainly sieved with bullet-holes.

Over all this peaceful, tumbledown, beautiful domain the satyr rules: a Pagan survivor, a descendant of Pan guarding the ruins of a Christian temple.

Tranquil now it may be, but many remarkable things have happened in and about it. According to the ecclesiastical historian Socrates it was one of the Christian sanctuaries founded by Constantine. Socrates also says that in a more modest form it had been a church in the old town of Byzantium. The biographer of the Patriarch Paul confirms this. Until St Sophia was opened for public worship it appears to have been the cathedral of the city. It became prominent during the dispute between the adherents of the Nicene creed and the Arians. Constantine attemped to suppress the controversy and commanded the patriarch Alexander to admit Arius to the Communion. He refused and the followers of Arius opted for violence. Alexander prayed in the church for many days and nights for a solution. He begged that if the opinions of Arius were true then he, Alexander, should die; that if not Arius should be tried and judged. His supplication brought rapid results. Arius collapsed in the Forum and died almost at once.

When Alexander died in 343 there was another dispute over his successor. The Arians favoured Macedonius; the Orthodox, Paul. They won the election and Paul was installed. Then Constantius, a vigorous Arian, vetoed and rejected the election and appointed Eusebius. But he died three years later. Then the Orthodox recalled Paul and the Arians consecrated Macedonius. Thereupon the emperor banished Paul who very sensibly departed and secured the support of the Pope. On his return to the city the emperor ordered the prefect to expel him and recognize Macedonius. Paul was removed but Macedonius had still to be installed. He went with the prefect by chariot to St Irene and there the troops cut a path with their swords through the immense crowd in order to get Macedonius into the church. Over three thousand people are believed to have died in this appalling episode. These three thousand people died because the Arians believed that Christ was created inferior to God the Father and that the Holy Ghost was created by the Son, and was not God.

This seems a particularly futile shedding of blood, but those people happened to be in the way. That is how it is these days—people happen to be in the way. Perhaps they could have got out of the way. They did not. They died instead but they were not martyrs —not officially anyway. They were all anonymous. Every day someone dies for a similar reason but few hear of it. Being murdered for your money is news. Being murdered for your religion is not—or very seldom.

The Arians held the church until 381 when the second General Council adopted the Nicene Creed. It is as if the Protestants settled in Westminster Cathedral and the Catholics entrenched themselves in St Paul's.

A number of other notable fortunes and misfortunes befell the church. In 427 the remains of the great John Chrysostom lay in it. The usurper Basiliseus is alleged to have taken refuge in it with his wife and children when he was overthrown and Zeno recovered the city. In 532, during the Nika riots, the whole building was burnt down. Then Justinian rebuilt it. In 740 it was damaged by a very severe earthquake in which much of Constantinople collapsed. In 857 it harboured another opposition faction. Since then eleven centuries have passed. Eleven centuries! It does one good to think of that. Now it is only disturbed by the debate of doves and the discussions of archaeologists; and, perhaps, the occasional protest of an unsuspecting female tourist.

★

Hard by the church stood the imperial mint and the water-works and near them the famous plane-tree of the Janissaries under which those troops overturned their kettles as a signal of revolt. At other times they were hanged from its branches.

It is not altogether clear when this body was first formed but it seems to have been some time during the latter part of the fourteenth century. The corps was composed of levied Christian youths and prisoners of war and was designed to fight for the Muslim power. They received a thorough and arduous military training and the elect were given a complete education. They were then used to command garrisons on the frontiers and in the provinces. Discipline was strict. To start with they were not allowed to marry. Their obedience was total; luxury forbidden. They grew long moustaches, wore dark-blue coats and plumes of feathers which cascaded nearly to their knees, and red, yellow or black boots according to rank. Food was important and their titles evolved from the language of the kitchen. The corps were called the *ocak* (or hearth); a battalion was known as the *orta* (the middle) and a barracks became known as the *oda* (a room. The officer commanding an *orta* was known as the *çorbaci-başi* or chief soup-maker. His next subordinates were the *aci-başi* or head cook and the *sakaci-başi* or head water-carrier. The sign on their standard was a huge kettle or cauldron and much of their ceremonial life revolved round these vessels.

According to tradition the first kettles to be issued were based on those used by a class of Dervishes and were supposed to have been presented by Mohammed II before the capture of the city. Prior to that each man provided his own rations. After that each *oda* had its own messing officer. Also, each *oda* had one large kettle and smaller kettles were divided among the troops in a ratio of one to twenty. The loss of any of these kettles was a grave disgrace which could only be atoned for by some outstanding deed. If the Janissaries were dissatisfied and intended to revolt the formal declaration of war was to overturn their kettles; and many Sultans had their hands full when this happened. In fact, the Janissaries acquired much power during the seventeenth century and at least two Sultans were murdered by them.

As the Sultanate became indolent and corrupt so the morale and discipline of the troops deteriorated. And for a long time they did much as they pleased. They expanded and they married. They recruited their own children for the force and also Ottomans. When they grew short of money for food or became bored they burnt, massacred, plundered at will. They are even supposed to have practised arson in order to make looting easier. They eventually became a disorganized but extremely dangerous body full of rogues and criminals, and it was not until Mahmut II (1803–39) developed a full-scale plan to exterminate them that they were got under control. In 1826 they revolted for the last time. The Sultan was ready for them and many thousands were butchered in a final blood-bath in the city. Now, even their tree does not exist.

★

On the right-hand side of the first court the infirmary used to stand: a place presided over by the Chief White Eunuch who had many lesser white eunuchs beneath him. It was here that the pages of the Seraglio went when ill, and there was a good deal of competition to get in since they could listen to music there and, much more important, drink wine.

Passing through this desolate open-air ante-chamber tenanted by tramps and desultory winds you eventually reach the fountain of execution, where the Sultan's executioner, who was also the head gardener, and his subordinates, washed their hands. The usual method was decapitation but royal clients were strangled with a silken cord—a compliment, no doubt, to the nobility of their necks. The bodies were then either thrown into the sea or given to relatives. Their heads I shall come to in a moment.

Just beyond the fountain is the *Orta-kapi* or central gate which, since it was the threshold to the Grand Seigneur, had to be approached with the greatest humility. Here the real kow-towing began, and those who were wise obeyed the old Chinese proverb which says that if you bow at all, bow low. Beyond this gate, for centuries, none but the privileged and those who belonged to the establishment were allowed to pass.

One time when I arrived the gates had not been opened and a group of visitors had accumulated, wearing their various badges and impedimenta, sprayed with sun-lotions and insecticides, shielded by hats and shades and seeing all the world through glasses darkly, a world threatened by an apparently continuous thunder-storm. Two of them, Bostonians, I think, shifted uneasily, resenting the twenty minutes wasted, their cameras primed, their faces resolute. They had allotted three days for Istanbul and time was nagging them urgently. It is necessary to be lazy and poor to enjoy indifference to time.

They wanted to know how long I had been in the city. I told them three months. They gasped, incredulous. 'You must be almost Turkish,' replied the woman.

In the end the doors were opened and a surly janitor claimed a shilling entrance fee and removed all cameras. The Bostonians were furious. They did their best but they would not have uttered a word had they known how difficult it is to move a determined Turk once he has made up his mind. He dismissed their protests with a long, upward motion of the head—'*Yok.*' A powerful word.

It had after all been a rapid entry. Where, in days gone by, the most illustrious were kept in suspense for hours or even days in order to impress upon them the dignity and might of the Sultan, we had passed in a few moments.

Adjoining this gate were the rooms of the executioner; above them cells; below, dungeons. Those condemned spent their last days here, and their severed heads, if above the rank of *Pasha*, were impaled on the iron spikes which used to rise above the gate. Those below that rank were exposed on the *Bab-i Hümayun*, in the niches provided for the purpose. When there were too many heads, ears and noses only were put up, in much the same way as gamekeepers adorn their larders with vermin and hunt kennels display foxes' masks and pads. The heads were accompanied by a scroll bearing the name and the crime. After the eyes had provided delicacies for observant birds the heads and the epitaphs rotted together.

We passed through the gate. Beyond was a smaller courtyard. Paths zigzagged among balding lawns and carious flower-beds. Across them, cypresses, sentinel straight, cast the broad, black blades of their shadows. The sun cut into my face. It was very quiet. It has always been so. At the very beginning of the seventeenth century Sandys wrote: 'Had you but onely eares you might suppose . . . that men were folded in sleepe, and the world in midnight.'[3]

The scene, also, has hardly changed since those days. A few years after Sandys the Italian Pietro Della Valle visited the Seraglio and described the second court almost as it stands today. But on the lawns, which were better then, he observed tame birds, gazelles and other animals.

Away to the right lay the former kitchens. There were ten in all, arranged in line and overlooking the Marmara. They were rebuilt by the great Sinan after a fire in 1574 and they have survived because of the immense thickness of their walls—proof against fire and earthquake. Now the kitchens have been converted into the showrooms of a museum.

Early in the sixteenth century there were between 150 and 200 cooks employed in these palatial quarters providing for most of the Seraglio. The Venetian traveller Bon reports how the food was brought from all parts: dates, plums and prunes were transported from Egypt; honey, which was consumed in great quantities, came from Romania and Hungary; oil from Greece; butter from Moldavia; cheese from Italy; fruit from Broussa. Great quantities of wood were used and these came from the forests on the shores of the Black Sea.

Refrigeration was ensured by bringing snow all the way from the Bithynian Mount Olympus (Ulu Dağ). It was packed in felt sacks and carried down on mules to the port of Mudania and then shipped to Istanbul where it was stored in pits. I have climbed up the mountain and down it. There are eight thousand feet of it and it is no easy journey. By road it is twenty miles.

Evliya Efendi also went up Mount Olympus and when he came near the top he found a 'delightful spot with a spring of water so cold that a man cannot take out of it three stones in succession'. Even on the hottest days the water of these streams and springs is so cold that it numbs the mouth and hands. For the shepherds who live up there it is the only drink. After this extremely neat illustration Evliya goes on to say that there was there a large mass of rock 'the size of the cupola of a bath, which vibrates on being touched, and also many rivulets containing trout'. He then explains the gathering of the ice. When the brooks are frozen in the winter 'the head ice-man ... sends two or three hundred persons to cut the ice, which, transparent as crystal and brilliant as diamonds, is used in summer to cool their sherbert by the inhabitants of Constantinople and Brussa'.

It is of this region that Evliya tells what seems to be one of the tallest of all his tall stories, and yet he is so factual that he makes you wonder whether or not there may be something in it. Not long ago there was a concerted search by mountaineers and scientists for the Snowman. Evliya's creature is an ice-worm. This is to be found in the midst of ice and snow as old as the creation, but, he adds, it is difficult to find. 'It has forty feet, and forty black spots on its back, with two eyes as red as rubies, all ice, without a tongue, and

its interior filled with an icy fluid; it shines like a diamond but melts
quickly away, because it is all ice. In size it is like those cucumbers
which are sold for seed in Langabestan, sometimes larger, sometimes
smaller.' He himself took one to Sultan Ibrahim which was smaller
than a cucumber. It has a number of properties: it is an aphrodisiac,
it sharpens the sight, and makes a man as vigorous as a new-born
child. 'It is rarely found,' says Evliya, 'and falls but to the lot of
kings!' He goes on to tell us that on the Caucasus they are the size
of dogs with four feet. 'Faith be upon the teller!' he adds. 'I have
not seen them.'[4]

When it snowed in Constantinople the principal officer in charge
of snow ordered out his men with shovels and they collected it on the
Ok Meydan where it was pressed into the pits. On the processional
days the men wore turbans made entirely of frozen snow.

The kitchens in the Seraglio are now in part reproduced and some
rooms contain an astonishing array of utensils and vessels. There are
spoons, ladles and various other implements three or four feet in
length. Jars big enough to conceal a man; cauldrons of a size to take
two or three sheep. A dummy clad as the head cook dominates the
scene. In wealth and weight his robes seem to equal those of an
emperor on a state occasion. But, of course, his duties were considerable. In the early seventeenth century as many as two hundred sheep
were consumed daily, a hundred head of lamb or kid, forty of veal,
fifty brace of geese, and hundreds of pigeons, chickens and guinea-
fowl. A century later De la Motraye referred to the prodigious
quantity of provisions consumed in a year: thirty thousand oxen,
twenty thousand calves, sixty thousand sheep, sixteen thousand
lambs, ten thousand kids, a hundred thousand turkeys and so on.[5]
And all the time the enormous staff devoted their labour and in-
genuity to the device of novel and bizarre confections and to the
creation of rare and delicate dishes to titillate the royal palate and
satiate its stomach.

Now the other rooms of the kitchens harbour priceless collections
of porcelain and china and everywhere the ornaments and impedimenta of a thousand gorgeous and barbaric banquets lie splendid
and useless, guarded by spruce attendants in dark suits and white
shirts. Outside the cicadas perennially strum an empire's epitaph
and a notice forbids one to smoke.

★

In this court the most important item was the Divan, and to there I usually made my way after the kitchens. It was here that the state council met four times a week to administer justice, to receive envoys and to attend to the business of state and religion. It is a large, rectangular room panelled and ornamented in Louis Quinze style. Low sofas run round the sides. Opposite the door and high above the Grand Vizier's seat is a grilled window which bulges from the wall. From this window from the time of Süleyman onwards the Sultan was able to observe everything that went on beneath without anyone knowing whether or not he was there. It was an ingenious idea but also foolish, for obvious reasons.

Here no pains were spared to impress upon the visitor the dignity and power of the Sultan. An elaborate ritual was accompanied by lavish clothes and luxurious entertainment. Ambassadors practically crawled to kiss the emperor's robe. De la Motraye described the Divan as the '*Ne plus Ultra* of Strangers,' where 'the *Grand Seignior's* Throne is erected ... almost entirely incrusted or cover'd over with Mother of Pearl and precious Stones. One must approach it to receive Audience without Arms, and make three low Bows almost to the Ground; to which two Officers of the Porte ... contribute the most, by holding each of them the Ambassador ... under one Arm, to conduct him to the Foot of the Throne, and laying at the same time one Hand upon his Neck, first at the Door, secondly in the Middle, and thirdly at the Foot of the Throne, and as often when he retires backwards, that he may not turn his Back upon the *Sultan* after having had Audience.'[6]

Near by was the treasury, now the Arms Museum which contains a formidable collection of weapons and armour—as cumbrous as they are ornate. Out of the second court, in one corner, leads the Gate of the Dead—a gate used a great deal. And near this was the court of the Halberdiers, a body of servants who served the *harem* as well as the *selâmlik*. Those appointed to the *harem* wore two false curls hanging from tall hats so that their view of the women should be obscured.

From the second court one passes to the third, through a gate dignified pleasingly by the title The Gate of Felicity, the *Bab-us Saadet*, also known as the Gate of the White Eunuchs or the King's Gate. This was the entrance to the sanctorum. It was used for a variety of purposes. Here each new Sultan was proclaimed, and anyone entering bowed to kiss its threshold. When the Janissaries revolted, as so often happened, the bodies of scapegoated officials were flung to the mob through it. This was the entrance to the most secret enclave of all. Beyond it was the throne-room and no one might pass it except at the Emperor's bidding. It used to be guarded by as many as thirty White Eunuchs who presided jealously over the privacy of their master. Now it is held by one Turkish fireman, a Gilbertian figure in ill-fitting clothes with a head-dress reminiscent of a Household Cavalryman's helmet. One day I forgot the 'no smoking' rule and he shouted at me and abused me vigorously. Aldous Huxley's axiom that 'official dignity tends to increase in inverse ratio to the importance of the country in which the office is held' was proved once again. Days of fruitless fire-watching seemed to have pent up his feelings and the sight of a tourist with a cigarette was too good a chance to be missed. Eventually, feeling guilty, I obeyed. We parted firm enemies.

★

The White Eunuchs, of course, played a most important part in the organization of the *selâmlik*, while the Black Eunuchs were joined to the *harem*. In the sixteenth and seventeenth centuries there were four Chief White Eunuchs, the first of whom, the *Kapi Agha*, was a personal counsellor and underling to the Sultan and was in charge of the palace school. Like Pooh-Ba he had many other offices, Master of Ceremonies, Head Gate-keeper and Head of the Infirmary. He had a say in many matters of state and was one of the very few who was actually allowed to speak with the Sultan. His three immediate subordinates had various posts of importance and the rank and file were likewise busily engaged. Prisoners of many nationalities formed this body.

Eunuchs, 'that pernicious vermin of the East' as Gibbon described them, 'those effeminate slaves' that gradually rose with the decline of the empire, are a neglected subject.

Etymologically, 'eunuch' means 'chamberlain', a guard of the bedchamber. Some hold that the creation of the *semivir* or *apocopus* began as a punishment in Egypt, and elsewhere under the Roman rule amputation was frequent. Others trace the Greek 'invalid', that is an impotent man, to marital jealousy, and some to the wife who wanted to use neuter creatures to work in the house so that the honour of slave girls would not be jeopardized.

The custom spread westwards from the Middle East. Ammianus Marcellinus refers to Semiramis, an ancient queen of uncertain date, as the first person to castrate men. There are a number of references in the Old Testament. Potiphar was *castrato*. Herodotus tells us that Periander, the tyrant of Corinth, sent three hundred Corcyrean boys to Alyattes king of Lydia for castration and that Panionos of Chios sold caponized boys for good prices. He observes that eunuchs of 'the sun, of Heaven, of the hand of God' were looked upon as honourable men among the Persians. Ctesias also states that the Persian kings were under the influence of eunuchs.

According to Xenophon, when Cyrus captured Babylon in 538 B.C. he came to the conclusion that eunuchs were ideal servants because they possessed no families and would only serve their employers. He reasoned that a eunuch might well be superior to all others in fidelity and that as horses and bulls and dogs are made more tractable by gelding so men become gentler. He found them to be brave and faithful in war and accordingly selected eunuchs for every post 'of personal service to him, from the door-keepers up'.[7]

Eunuchism was also closely connected with religious practice. The goddesses Artemis and Astarte of Hierapolis were ministered by eunuch priests, and these resembled those of Cybele. The manner in which they dedicated themselves to the religious life was also similar. The greatest festival of the year came at the beginning of spring and many people assembled from a wide area for it. To the playing of flutes and the beating of drums the eunuch priests lacerated themselves with knives. The frenzy soon spread among the onlookers and many men, wild with excitement, ripped off their clothes and joined the *élite* of the sexless. Many also repented at leisure for their rashness.

In the Christian Church this barbarous practice was continued, and eunuchs were used at the altar as well as at the bedside. There is a curious passage in the nineteenth chapter of St Matthew's gospel which says: 'For there are eunuchs, which are born so from their mother's womb: and there are eunuchs, which were made eunuchs by men: and there are eunuchs, which made themselves eunuchs for the kingdom of heaven's sake.'

Absolute chastity was greatly prized by the early fathers and Tertullian declared, no doubt on the strength of St Matthew, that the kingdom of Heaven was thrown open to eunuchs. Valesius created a sect in Arabia and maintained that no one could be a priest unless he were castrated. Origen was one of many who became castrated. Some great saints condemned it, notably St Augustine and St Basil. The latter thought eunuchs an abominable tribe, past the sense of honour, being neither men nor women, and made mad by the love of women. He described them as jealous, despicable, fierce, effeminate, gluttonous, covetous, cruel, inconstant, suspicious and insatiable.

Nevertheless many men made themselves eunuchs in the spirit of devotion. Others were made eunuchs as a punishment for adultery. There was no end to the inconsistency. Hottentots were as logical who cut off the left testicle in order to prevent the begetting of twins.

In the religious world the practice was maintained in order to preserve voices for the Papal Choir until as late as 1878 when Leo XIII stopped it. Many famous *castrati* also sang in Italian opera. The audiences used to applaud, shouting, '*Viva il coltello!*'

There was one survival of religious eunuchry—a Russian sect which had the strange belief that our original parents were sexless and that after the 'Fall' the halves of the forbidden apple were grafted on to them in the shape of breasts and testicles. So, they argued, it was necessary to restore themselves to the original and pristine condition. By now the Party has probably suppressed them.

Castration was performed in a number of different fashions and in the classical period there were approximately three varieties of eunuch: *Castrati, Spadones* and *Thlibiae*. The *Castrati* had their genitals completely removed. The *Spadones* lost only the testicles by a method of prolonged dragging; rather, it seems, on the same lines as straightening a tail by weighing it down with a stone. The *Thlibiae*, who were usually mutilated when young, had their testicles bruised and squeezed. Similar to these were the *Thlasiae*.

In the East there were also three kinds of eunuchs. Firstly, the *Sandali* or the clean cut—the classical *apocopus*. Their parts were removed by a razor. A tube was put in the urethra and the wound was cauterized with boiling oil. The patient was then planted in a fresh dung-hill and passed his water through a tube. Secondly, there was the kind whose penis was removed. They retained the power of copulation and procreation without the instrument. Thirdly, there were those whose testicles were removed by bruising, twisting, searing or bandaging them. The priests of Cybele were castrated with a stone knife.

According to Sir Richard Burton a more humane process was later introduced: a horsehair was tied round the neck of the scrotum and was gradually tightened until the circulation was stopped. Eventually the parts dropped off. This method was also used by Indian irregular cavalry regiments on their horses.

Early in the eighteenth century a curious work on eunuchs by one Comte d'Ollincan was published. It was translated into English under the title *Eunuchism displayed, describing all the Different Sorts of Eunuchs . . . with several Observations on Modern Eunuchs*. Ollincan distinguishes four kinds. First, those born so. Second those castrated because of some distemper—Pasqualini was supposed to have been an example. The third class is of those whose testicles 'by a detestable Art have been made so frigid, as at last quite to disappear and vanish, this is done by cutting the Vein that conveyed their proper Aliment and Support, which makes them grow lank and flabby, till at last they actually dry up and come to nothing'. He describes another method which was to remove the testicles at one fell swoop and this operation was commonly done 'by putting the Patient into a Bath of warm Water, to soften and supple the Parts, and make them more tractable; some small time after, they pressed the Jugular Veins, which made the Party so stupid, and insensible, that he fell into a kind of Apoplexy, and then the action could be performed with scarce any Pain at all to the Patient'. The fourth kind which Ollincan distinguishes were the *Spadones*.[8]

In the decadent period of Rome women found a new use for those who had lost only their testicles. Juvenal deplored the practice. They were regarded as ill-omened and according to Lucian in the second century they were so hated and suspected that when people saw them they would turn away or retreat into their houses rather than meet something so unlucky. In his *Dialogue of Eunuchs* Lucian relates the amusing story of the young nobleman of the court of the king of Syria who was obliged to go on a long voyage with the queen Stratonice. In order to avoid losing his life by intimacy with the queen he castrated himself and embalmed his genitals and presented them to the king in a sealed box before his departure. Events justified his precaution. But he was saved, and his intimate friends gelded themselves in order to keep him company in his disgrace and misery.

Of all the bizarre anecdotes which adorn the unhappy annals of castration two from Montaigne must be recorded. One relates of a young man who wanted a woman but who was unable to possess her. Therefore he castrated himself and sent his parts to his mistress as a bloody victim to atone for their offence. The other is of a peasant who cut off his genitals with a scythe to spite his wife—and threw them in her face. His wife was jealous.

The Byzantines revived the custom of using eunuchs. In fact castration for a boy or a young man in Byzantium was a certain step to success. There was no disgrace attached to it and even the nobility practised it. A eunuch could not become emperor but many important offices were open to him. Of course his main advantage was that he could produce no heirs.

Gibbon, invariably entertaining on anything which excites his scorn, deals with the eunuchs of Byzantium in passages which are irresistible. The triumph of the arms of Constantius, he says, 'served only to establish the reign of the eunuchs over the Roman world. Those unhappy beings, the ancient production of Oriental jealousy and despotism, were introduced into Greece and Rome by the contagion of Asiatic luxury. Their progress was rapid; and the eunuchs, who, in the time of Augustus, had been abhorred, as the monstrous retinue of an Egyptian queen, were gradually admitted into the families of matrons, of senators, and of the emperors themselves. Restrained by the severe edicts of Domitian and Nerva, cherished by the pride of Diocletian, reduced to an humble station by the prudence of Constantine, they multiplied in the palaces of his degenerate sons, and insensibly acquired the knowledge, and at length the direction, of the secret councils of Constantius.'

Gibbon contends that the aversion and contempt which men had 'for that imperfect species' degraded their character and rendered them almost as incapable as they were supposed to be of any 'generous sentiment' or 'worthy action'.

He goes on to explain that they were skilled in the arts of flattery and intrigue and that they 'alternately governed the mind of Constantius by his fears, his indolence, and his vanity'. While he deluded himself about the public prosperity he 'supinely permitted them to intercept the complaint of the injured provinces, to accumulate immense treasures by the sale of justice and of honours; to disgrace the most important dignities, by the promotion of those who had purchased at their hands the powers of oppression, and to gratify their resentment against the few independent spirits, who arrogantly refused to solicit the protection of slaves'.

One of the most famous eunuchs was Eutropius who flourished in the time of Arcadius (395–408). It was against Eutropius that Claudian delivered a vicious and lengthy attack. Gibbon, who followed the account of Claudian, is scarcely less acrimonious. In a magnificent passage he fires one perfectly primed salvo after another. Every order of state, he says, 'bowed to the new favourite; and their tame and obsequious submission encouraged him to insult the laws, and, what is still more difficult and dangerous, the manners of his country.'

Under the weakest of Arcadius' predecessors the reign of the eunuchs had been secret and they had gradually insinuated themselves into the suburbs of the emperor's affection. Ostensibly they were menials in and about the imperial chambers. They might, as Gibbon says, 'direct in a whisper, the public counsels, and blast, by their malicious suggestions, the fame and fortunes of the most illustrious citizens'; but they did not have public honour and power. Eutropius was the first of his 'artificial sex' to become a Roman magistrate and general.

Moving powerfully from terrace to terrace of his denunciation Gibbon describes the situation thus: 'Sometimes, in the presence of the blushing senate, he ascended the tribunal to pronounce judgment, or to repeat elaborate harangues; and, sometimes, appeared on horseback, at the head of his troops, in the dress and armour of a hero. The disregard of custom and decency always betrays a weak and ill-regulated mind;—[the authentic ring of Augustan decorum!] —nor does Eutropius seem to have compensated for the folly of the design by any superior merit or ability in the execution. His former habits of life had not introduced him to the study of the laws, or the exercises of the field; ... The subjects of Arcadius were exasperated by the recollection, that this deformed and decrepit eunuch, who so perversely mimicked the actions of a man, was born in the most abject condition of servitude; that before he entered the Imperial Palace, he had been successively sold and purchased by an hundred masters, who had exhausted his youthful strength in every mean and infamous office, and at length dismissed him, in his old age, to freedom and poverty.'

He became powerful and famous enough to be a patrician and a consul, and many statues of him were erected.

Narses, on the other hand, who lived in the time of Justinian, earned some praise, and Gibbon's treatment of him shows considerable discrimination and impartiality. He was ranked among the few who had rescued 'that unhappy name [eunuch] from the contempt and hatred of mankind'. His tiny body sheltered the soul and abilities of a statesman and a warrior.

'His youth', writes Gibbon, 'had been employed in the management of the loom and the distaff, in the cares of the household, and the service of female luxury; but while his hands were busy, he secretly exercised the faculties of a vigorous and discerning mind.' In the end he became a highly successful general.

The Turks adopted the use of eunuchs from the Byzantines in approximately the middle of the fifteenth century. Castration was forbidden by the Koran but this provision was usually eluded by performing the operation outside the city, a rather hypocritical expedient. Roughly speaking, the White Eunuchs looked after the *selâmlik*, and the Black cared for the *harem*. The quarters of the latter lay behind the Divan and the Treasury and between them and the *harem*. They had their dormitories, their common-room, their coffee-room and their own mosque. The senior eunuchs had bed-sitting rooms.

Their power was great and it increased as that of the White Eunuchs declined. They were given a long and intense training for their service. They were well paid and well dressed. The Chief Black Eunuch was a man of enormous wealth and influence. He was entitled to eunuchs and slaves of his own and when he retired he was given—like other senior eunuchs—a munificent pension.

It is one of the sadder ironies in the annals of sex that the urine of eunuchs was regarded as a potent aphrodisiac. Even worse is the fact that often, though deprived of the instruments of sexual intercourse, the desire for it was as strong as ever; even intensified by the deprivation. It was the punishment of a Tantalus to be surrounded by desirable women and to be incapable of possessing them. Some forms of intercourse were possible for them, but most of the methods were perversions and caricatures of the real thing. Insomnia, obesity, baldness, loss of sight and loss of memory were further afflictions which could overtake them as a result of the operation. On the other hand they were supposed to be immune to leprosy and gout, and they had power, riches and influence. A poor reward, some might think. Ollincan says that eunuchs were never bald 'because their Brains are more entire than those of other Men, who loose great Part by the use of Venus, the Seminal Juices deriving thence chiefly their Original'.

The later in life they were castrated the more the damage done—both physical and psychological. But at whatever stage, the operation made their characters and behaviour extremely variable: kind and cruel, suspicious and credulous, cunning and simple, and so on. They were fond of pets and children, sweets and music. They were neat but parsimonious. In his *Persian Letters* Montesquieu gives at some length what may well have been many of the feelings of a eunuch. It is a satirical correspondence between several Persians on a visit to Europe. Their letters go between each other and their friends in Ispahan.

The letters of the Chief Black Eunuch are almost unrelievedly sad. 'Shut up in a hideous prison,' he says, 'I am always surrounded by the same objects; there is no change even in what irritates me. Burdened by fifty years of care and annoyance I lament my wretched condition: all my life I have never passed a single untroubled day, or known a peaceful moment.' At first he thought the sacrifice of his passions would be more than repaid by ease and wealth, but whenever he entered the seraglio he was filled with hopeless longing for the women, and whenever he took a woman to his master's bed his heart was consumed with anger and his soul crowded with despair.

Eventually, in his age, when desire dispersed, he came to hate women and paid them back for their contempt and tormenting. He could not forget that he was born to command them and in the exercise of his authority he felt that he had recovered his lost manhood. He took pleasure in detecting and discussing all their weaknesses. He oppressed them and obstructed them and interfered with them. He spent his time reminding them of their duties, their chastity, their modesty. He willingly incurred all their hatred because that established him more firmly in his position.

In turn they annoyed him. 'Between us', he writes, 'there is a constant interchange of ascendancy and obedience. They are always putting upon me the meanest services; they affect a sublime contempt; and, regardless of my age, they make me get up ten times during the night for the merest trifles. I am run off my feet with everlasting commissions, orders, tasks, and caprices; one would think that they take it in turns to invent things for me to do. Often they amuse themselves by making me doubly watchful; they give me imaginary confidences. Sometimes I am told that a young man has been seen lurking round the walls, or that a startling noise has been heard, or that someone is about to receive a letter. All this annoys me and amuses them. They are delighted when they see me tormenting myself. Sometimes they hide me behind the door and keep me

standing there night and day. They know very well how to pretend
to be ill or to faint or to be frightened out of their wits: they are
never at a loss for some pretext to do what they want to me.'[9] It
does not sound like an ideal life whatever the rewards, but they are
still used to guard women in the *harems* that survive.

To qualify as a priest, to get into the kingdom of heaven more
easily, to obtain preferment in the world, to preserve a fine voice,
to avoid adultery, to spite jealous wives, to guard women and have
power and money—men have had their genitals cut off for all these
purposes, and probably for many more that are unrecorded. Absurd
and repellent such deeds and motives may seem, but how many
things as ridiculous and as unpleasant are still done in the world
every day, and for less worthy motives. Before we despise the eunuch
—if we ever do—we must remember that we have made abortion
scientific, that we are perfecting the techniques for destroying and
corrupting people's minds, that we are improving the methods of
wholesale murder, that we are practising racial persecution on a
colossal scale, and that hardly at any time in history perhaps has
human life and human dignity counted for so little.

★

Walking through the eunuch's quarters, a French-speaking Turk,
thin, unshaven, with a yellow, toothy smile, explained how the
Sultans always liked to have the ugliest possible Black Eunuchs, despite their emasculation, to guard their women. 'Always they were
medically inspected,' he said, 'lest a miracle had restored them.' The
yellow teeth wavered for a second.

Then we were upon the threshold of the *harem*, the most secret,
the most guarded, the most inaccessible of all the buildings in the
palace; and, for centuries, one of the most inaccessible buildings in
the world. It is an immense and truly labyrinthine structure. Cnossus
must have been a model of simplicity beside it. There is as much
difference between the two as there is between a crossword in the
Evening Standard and *Ximenes*.

It has been altered, added on to and adapted countless times. It
contains an astonishing profusion and confusion of architectural and
decorative styles: native and imported, Turkish and Italian, Persian
and French. Many rooms are still locked and boarded up. Staircases
are treacherous, floors rotten. Only a very small part has been opened

to the public, but hard work is being done to recover the rest. By dint of peering through cracks and keyholes and windows it is possible to get some idea of the still forbidden areas. Decay is common to most of them. Dimly lighted rooms are piled with furniture, with clocks, brocades and curtains, with china and glass and chandeliers. The dust of more than half a century has been accumulating on them. Plaster has crumbled, tiles have become tarnished, wood is riddled with worm. The death-watch beetles tap in the dark corridors and everywhere the spiders have spun their webs, the grey elegies and winding-sheets of an empire.

Sir Thomas Browne would have enjoyed visiting the Seraglio. He would have written a sequel to the *Urn Burial*: '. . . the inequity of oblivion blindly scattereth her poppy, and deals with the memory of men without distinction to the merit of perpetuity.' Webster and Tourneur might have been inspired to write their most gloomy tragedies about it. How Bosola and Vendice would have revelled in the intrigues of Sultans and eunuchs and concubines, devising ever more bizarre and quaint methods of luring people to their destruction. Death was the only subject on their syllabus, and murder their hobby. In what more sinister university than the Seraglio could they have written their macabre examinations?

We looked at the rooms of the head nurse and the chief laundress, the *harem* hospital and the suite of the Sultan Valide. Her apartments consisted of a waiting-room, a dining-room and a bedroom. The Sultan Valide, that is the Sultan's mother, was one of the most powerful people in the whole empire.

Then we took the Golden Road—to the *selâmlik*: the male quarters. The walls of this corridor were lined with exquisite tiles. We turned through the Valide's courtyard and then passed again into the honeycomb of rooms.

We went down heavily carpeted corridors and passages—a maze. There were doors and curtained doorways everywhere: draperies, brocades, arrases. It was cool and there was a faint smell of dust, a subtle aroma of pressed flowers and the shades of perfumes. A hanging was pushed aside.

'The school-room of the young princes,' said the Turk. Here the *hoca* was let in to tutor the Sultan's children. There were painted patterns on the walls and beautiful blue and green faïences and X-shaped desks for reading the Koran.

The young princes were kept in the Princes' Cage, the *Kafes*, a

building which Penzer describes in an excellent work on the *harem*
as the 'scene of more wanton cruelty, misery, and bloodshed than
any palace room in the whole of Europe'.

Murat III (1574–95) had 103 children and when he died twenty
sons and twenty-seven daughters were still living. His successor,
Mehmet III, the eldest of the twenty, had his nineteen brothers put
to death at once in order to remove all rivals and, to be on the
safe side, had seven of his father's concubines who were pregnant
drowned in the Bosphorus in case they were carrying further claim-
ants. After this holocaust it was decided not to kill the younger
brothers but to keep them locked up. Here they were kept year after
year with a few sterile women and deaf-mutes for their companions.
They were not properly educated. Some of them were incarcerated
for many years. For most of this period they lived in constant fear
of being murdered. When one of them emerged to ascend the throne
he was, as like as not, an illiterate imbecile. Thus were the Sultans
prepared to rule the Ottoman empire. It is no wonder that it declined.

We visited the Throne Room, the Vestibule of the Hearth, the
Vestibule of the Fountain and the Royal Saloon. Some walls were
tiled from floor to ceiling. Doors and carved panelling were inlaid
with mother-of-pearl. There were numerous gilt chairs, and grandfather clocks—all silent. Furniture was upholstered in opulent brocade and silk. Mirrors were carved. Rococo was mingled with
Turkish ceramic.

We entered the Sultan's apartments: one room leading into another, then another, then many more. There were not many windows
and those that there were had not been opened for many years. The
atmosphere was musty. Low divans upholstered in brocade and
velvet ran round three and sometimes four sides of the rooms. Most
of the walls were faced with extravagant mirrors, perhaps for the
inmates to see with ease everyone who came in; perhaps, also, as in
the imagined halls of Sir Epicure Mammon, to multiply the succubae. The Turk tapped a panel and opened a secret door: narrow
stairs ran upwards. 'Down here came the Sultan's women,' he said.
'Thus they could enter and leave without anybody but the Sultan
seeing them.' His yellow teeth flickered for an instant and he winked.
We could not go upstairs where the women used to live because the
rooms had not been used for many years: not, in fact, since 1908.

The *harem* was a highly organized realm of its own with its hierarchy and much complicated ritual and protocol—all of which the Sultan himself had to respect. It was ruled by the Sultan's mother. To become the mother of a Sultan, therefore, was the ambition of many of the concubines. The concubines were divided into those who were the official and regular favourites and those who merely shared the Grand Seigneur's bed occasionally. Obviously a girl's principal aim was to achieve the Sultan's bed, but if she never attained this low eminence she might yet advance herself to one of the many minor offices which were available: a member of the Valide's cabinet, Keeper of the Baths, Mistress of the Robes, Manageress of the Table Services, Reader of the Koran or even Chief Coffee-maker.

The right-hand man of the Sultan Valide was the Chief Black Eunuch with whom she worked in close conjunction. Below her was the Lady Controller, the second in command. Then came the Treasurer, then the minor posts mentioned above. In this brave old world the hatcheries and nurseries were highly organized. It was also, by most accounts, extremely difficult to see anything of them. Thomas Dallam, who took out an organ for the Sultan in 1599, was one of the first to see anything of the *harem* and he had a narrow escape. He was looking through a grating at thirty of the Sultan's concubines who were playing with a ball in a courtyard when four Black Eunuchs with drawn scimitars came running towards him. He also ran and lived to hear his organ played.

A girl who was lucky enough to catch the Sultan's attention was called *gözde* or 'in the eye' and she was at once segregated and given separate rooms and special attendants while she waited for the imperial summons. When that came there began a long and exhaustive process in order to make her acceptable for her master. In a similar fashion dogs, cats and horses are prepared for shows and joints for the table. When 'bedded' she was called *ikbal* and her visits to the royal sheets were kept secret. In 1595 Murat III had as many as twelve hundred women in his *harem*. History does not relate how many became *ikbal*.

Fifteen years later Edward Lithgow reports that the numbers had dropped to eight hundred, 'being the most part Emeeres, Bashawes, and Timariot's daughters'. He refers briefly to the *harem* which he describes as being 'well attended at all times with numbers of Eunuches, and other gelded officers.' He also gives an account of the Sultan's selection process, which seems to have varied a good deal:

in this instance it was that of Ahmet I. Every morning the odalisques were arraigned in a great hall on open seats. The Sultan
walked among them and selecting the youngest and fairest he 'touch-
eth her with a rod; and immediately she followeth him into his
cabine of leachery, where if any action be done, shee receiveth from
the Head-Clarke her approbation thereupon . . .'[10] Another method
of singling out the required girl was to throw a handkerchief to her,
as the Venetian Bon relates in the seventeenth century.

Life in the *harem* was often boring and there were only occasional
diversions. Unfortunately tedium would sometimes beget folly and
then the Chief Black Eunuch would hand over the victims to the
chief gardener who put them in sacks and weighted them with
stones and then threw them into the Bosphorus. Sometimes there
were wholesale drownings, and one Sultan, Ibrahim, in the middle
of the seventeenth century, actually drowned his complete *harem*
—a spring-clean as it were, because he was in need of a change. It
was a matter of about a thousand women. Even the Turk grimaced
at the enormity of such a deed. 'Once,' he said, 'a diver went down
off the Seraglio Point and found at the bottom numberless sacks,
bowing and swaying.' The sacks, needless to say, contained the
corpses of women, standing upright because of the weighted bottoms
and leaning to the beck of the currents.

From the time of Selim II, the 'Sot', in the middle of the sixteenth
century and for the best part of the next hundred and fifty years
the women of the Seraglio ruled the empire. A succession of Sultans
who were either imbeciles or drunkards or sexual maniacs brought
one catastrophe after another. Ibrahim aspired to and reached unimaginable heights, or depths, of depravity. One astounding de-
bauch followed upon another. Orgies which might have exceeded
the belief of even Belial and his sons followed orgies which would
have made Nero, Tiberius and Caligula turn away in shame. Ibrahim, when worn out with sexual indulgence, plied himself with
powerful aphrodisiacs and, naked and crazy with lust, charged to
and fro among his equally naked concubines like a mad bull in a
field full of heifers.

★

From the Sultan's 'cabine of leachery' we entered an exquisite vestibule adorned by a fountain. 'Here,' said the Turk briefly, 'the grandmother of Mehmet IV was stabbed to death. She was over eighty.' In fact she was not stabbed. When she had been dragged from the clothes-chest where she had been hiding her garments were torn off her and she was then strangled. It was one of many brutal and ghastly deeds. The method of despatch is of minor importance.

In almost every room a murder of varying degrees of callousness had been committed. The Sultan's bathroom, it seemed, was one of the few exceptions; yet clearly some crime was expected here as well. It was a lofty and capacious place made almost entirely of marble with sky-lights high above. The bath, in which a stallion could have stood with ease, was protected by a wrought-iron gate. Similar defences surrounded the stalls for the women and the Sultan's dressing apartment in which slippers, clothes, and toilet requisites of some majesty long since dead lay in opulent inutility. I turned on the tap in the bath. The water ran cool and I drank and rinsed my hands. It is not often that one has a drink in a Sultan's bathroom.

There were other and more magnificent baths and Evliya Efendi, who was personally entertained by Murat IV early in the seventeenth century, gives us a picture of one. 'The four sides of it', he writes 'are assigned to the use of the pages, and in the centre there is an enclosed bath for the emperor. Water rushes in on all sides from fountains and basins, through pipes of gold and silver; and the basins which receive the water are inlaid with the same metals. . . . The pavement is a beautiful mosaic of variegated stones which dazzle the eye. The walls are scented with roses, musk, and amber; and aloes is kept constantly burning in censors. The light is increased by the splendour and brilliancy of the windows. The walls are dry, the air temperate, and all the basins of fine white marble. The dressing-rooms are furnished with seats of gold and silver.'[11]

Beyond The Gate of Felicity, that guarded by the Gilbertian fireman, and immediately in front of it, was the Throne Room. It is reminiscent of a small pagoda. It dates from the fifteenth century and its walls were once panelled with sheets of gold. It contained, besides the throne, a fountain, the cascading water of which effectively prevented conversations being overheard.

The third court, in which this Throne Room lies, is small and peaceful. Lawns and trees decorate it. The ground slopes gently downwards to the north. There is a small library in the middle of it and another library to the side in what was once a little mosque. Beyond that, in a corner, and in part of the *selâmlik*, is the Pavilion of the Holy Mantle—a repository of sacred relics.

The footprints of the Prophet, like those of the Buddha and the Abominable Snowman, are reputed to have been found in many parts of India, and according to Charles White, who saw it in the middle of the nineteenth century, one of the Prophet's prints, on a piece of stone, is preserved in this Pavilion.

Sultan Selim I, a man who fluctuated between extremes of religious self-abasement and piety and secular self-aggrandizement and arrogance, stole the Prophet's mantle, standard and sword, among other things, from Cairo in 1517. In the course of this pious theft he had slaughtered fifty thousand of the inhabitants of that city.

It is not altogether certain what happened to the sword but it is reasonably sure that the mantle and the standard, plus the Prophet's beard and one of his teeth, are in the Pavilion. The beard is believed to have been shaved from him after his death by his favourite barber. It is said to be a brown beard, three inches long and without grey hairs. Hairy relics, indeed relics in general, have a habit of multiplying themselves, and portions of the Prophet's beard have turned up in a good many different places.

Naturally enough, lots of people want a relic and in the heyday of relic-collecting a saint had scarcely given up the ghost before the souvenir-collectors were swarming about the corpse. Now, the attentions of these voracious hunters are turned more often to film stars and rock 'n roll idols. For instance, recently my dentist took out one of Tommy Steele's teeth and within a few hours of the operation half the newspapers in Fleet Street were on the telephone asking after the patient and reminding him of the immense prices that could be got on the souvenir market for one of Mr Steele's teeth. It is only a year or so ago since another famous singer was almost dismembered by a fanatical crowd of admirers before he was removed unconscious for medical attention. But for prompt intervention by the police the fans might have had an involuntary martyr to publicity on their hands. Nowadays the souvenir-collectors do not even wait until their idol is dead.

One can see the point in collecting religious relics. Faith in their sanctity lends them therapeutic powers. A blessed hair or a beatified toe could be a potent talisman, a charm against baldness or a cure

for arthritis. But I doubt if even the most fervent of Mr Presley's
or Mr Liberace's worshippers would consider portions of their clothes
or persons effective against anything. Possession, in these cases, is all.

The tooth of the Prophet, unlike Mr Steele's, was acquired in
fairly exceptional circumstances. It is one of four knocked out by
a battle-axe in a battle in which the Prophet was aided by the
Archangel Gabriel and three thousand angels.

★

From the Pavilion of the Holy Mantle to the Hall of the Pantry is a
brief walk and en route, in what was the Hall of the Treasury, I
paused to look at a gallery of portraits, most of them painted during
the last fifty years. The majority were of famous men: Enver Pasha,
Atatürk, Inonou and others. Most of them were technically competent but aesthetically dull. An unimaginative naturalism ensured
'likeness' without revealing much of the essential character and per-
sonality of the sitter. They were like metaphors that have become
clichés: familiar but lifeless. About seventy per cent of them would
be assured of a hanging in the Academy.

But, after all, artists must live. The vanity and wealth of those
who wish to decorate their dining-rooms with portraits which flatter
without revealing, which will commemorate their physical virtues
while consigning to oblivion their spiritual vices, enable the needy
to survive. It must be one of the few examples of hypocrisy which,
in the long run, or, perhaps, more accurately, the short run, does
good.

The Hall of the Pantry, now offices of the director of the Seraglio,
was, in fact, a pantry; but a pantry of an exotic kind. Here was
stored everything from poison to marmalade, from aphrodisiacs to
ambergris. Aphrodisiacs, of course, in this woman-riddled domain,
were of great importance. The fillies had to be served and sometimes
the stallions ran short of stamina.

It is possible that part of the pharmacy was attached to the Pantry.
In the first half of the seventeenth century Michel Baudier of
Languedoc reported that there were eighteen apothecaries in the
Palace who were aided by three hundred boys. 'Four Masters,' he
says (the translation is by Grimstone), 'most expert in their Art are
Superiour to all those: they call them the Priors.' Their quarters
were spacious and they were abundantly furnished with all sorts of

'Oiles, Sirrops, Ointments, Waters, and other liquors proper for Physicke'. There were four 'goodly Chambers full of divers sorts of Drugs' and two others near the gardens, very likely those below the Hall of the Pantry, where they drew the essences and distilled the waters which were fit for physic.

Baudier concludes on a melancholy note. 'But in all these Vessels,' he writes, 'amidst these Drugs and divers Quintessences, they find not any remedy which can mortifie the amorous Passions of the Prince, wherewith hee is continually afflicted.' When we remember that the 'Prince' in question was very probably Ibrahim this gloomy reflection comes as no surprise. In a fine sentence Baudier goes on to explain the depredations of these passions. 'They devour his leisure,' he says, 'interrupt the exercises which are more worthy of his person; and deject him under that which hee is, and make him a slave to his slaves: for loving them desperately, he lives more in them then in himselfe.'[12]

When we recall the lecherous and barbaric antics of Ibrahim in his apartments we realize the delicacy of the Frenchman's account. 'He lives more in them than in himselfe'—what finesse for that naked monster scampering to and fro! And yet how accurate also. But if it was not he it was Murat IV, a drunken monster of almost unsurpassed brutality who, if somewhat less lascivious than Ibrahim, has had few equals as a tyrant and a murderer. In the last seven years of his life fifty thousand of his subjects were executed, many of them for trifling and non-existent offences. Like the Jew of Malta who walked abroad at night and poisoned wells and killed sick people groaning under walls, Murat took to the streets in disguise and murdered for sport those whom he did not fancy. The Sultanate went through some hard times.

While the 'Priors' and the apothecaries and their slaves laboured like Chaucer's cooks to turn 'substaunce into accident' to fulfil their master's 'likerous talent', preparing 'red beans' or 'Spanish Flies' or perhaps even eunuch's urine, to lend a new lease to their lord's virility, others of a numerous retinue waited closely upon him. He had a Turban Bearer, a Sword Bearer and a Carrier of the Royal Robe. There was a Chief Footman, a Water Carrier, a Chief Butler, a Chief Cutler, a Master Falconer and a Chief Launderer. There was the Controller of the Treasure and the First Secretary of State, not to mention the Chief Washer, the Chief Barber, the Chief Nail Parer, and the Chief Taster.

★

It must not be imagined that the Seraglio was constantly the scene of orgy and depravity. Such a conception belongs only to fiction, the *Arabian Nights* and sensational history books. Many of the Sultans were civilized men. Their lives were circumscribed but by no means tasteless. In many things they showed the most admirable discrimination. Even Murat IV had a keen eye for beauty and elegance as well as for the bottle and the bow-string.

In the fourth courtyard which overlooks the Bosphorus and the Horn is one of the most beautiful of all *kiosques*, the Baghdad Kiosque. Murat IV was responsible for it. It was based on a Persian original, like the Revan Kiosque which stands near it in what was the water garden. The Baghdad, standing on a terrace beneath which is the Lunar Park, is shaped as an octagon imposed on a cross, and it would be difficult to find anything of its kind more light and graceful and yet at the same time more sumptuous and ornate. The central room is domed with a rose-coloured ceiling. Its four transepts have golden ceilings. The most exquisite blue and white tiling covers the walls: Turkish ceramic at its best. The fireplaces are of bronze, the woodwork inlaid with ivory. Rich carpets lie on the floor and stained-glass windows alchemize the light—claret and pavonine. Outside the broad overhanging roof is supported by an arcaded cloister.

Nearby is the Mustafa Pasha Kiosque. The ceiling of this is of fretted gold. The walls are pink with bands of green and dark blue high above. Low sofas run round the sides. There is comfort here, ease and elegance. It would please the most fastidious hedonist, calm the most neurotic philistine.

This *kiosque* lies in the middle of the Tulip Garden. It is still quite a fine garden for the Turks are accomplished gardeners and have always been, the Sultans included. Lilacs, carnations, roses and hyacinths used to abound. In the eighteenth century, during the reigns of Ahmet III and Mahmut I, there was an age of what Mr Liddell has called 'tulipomania, almost of tulipolatry'. Ahmet III created yet another post in the palace—the Master of the Flowers; and there were frequent fêtes in the gardens. When the moon was full in April and the beds were filled with thousands of Dutch and Persian tulips the festivities began. Shelves were erected and vases containing tulips were arranged on them, all in the form of an amphitheatre. There were lamps between the vases. Above them hung cages of canaries and glass balls full of coloured waters. The *kadins* and concubines, for whom this was a great occasion, were let out of the *harem*, and, dressed and made up with all the art of which they were capable, they paraded in the gardens, all of them competing, so Flachat the French historian says, to outdo each other in an incomparable display of voluptuous charm and coquetry. Platoons of ravishing women displayed themselves, dancing and throwing golden balls from one to another while tortoises with lighted candles fixed to their backs ambled among the flower-beds. Meanwhile, the Sultan looked on.

The moon shone, music played and—who was to know?—some anonymous and aspiring virgin might catch the eye of the Shadow of God on Earth, the Lord of the Black, Red and White Seas, the Grand Seigneur, might have the inestimable privilege of being invited to share his bed and submit to his caresses, and might, all being well, if she pleased and the Sultan's apothecaries had not failed him, add yet another prince to the swollen ranks of the nursery and, it must not be forgotten, the Prison. From this, years hence and if he were not strangled, he might emerge once more and ascend the throne. And the girl? She might become the Sultan Valide, the most powerful woman in the empire. There were so many possibilities, so many hazards, so many ifs and buts and ands. After all, if something went wrong, if she perhaps or the apothecaries failed, by breakfast-time her head might be in the chief executioner's basket or her body at the bottom of the Bosphorus. It had happened before. It might happen again.

I stood one day with the yellow-toothed Turk by another small *kiosque* on a terrace overlooking the Bosphorus in the furthest corner of the Tulip Gardens. We had been talking about the fêtes and I remembered 'la belle Héaulmière', the wizened old lady in black silk with her canaries and her cats, the old lady whose beauty flowered more than half a century ago.

> Was a lady such a lady, cheeks so round and lips so red,—
> On her neck the small face buoyant, like a bell-flower on
> its bed,
> O'er the breast's superb abundance where a man might
> base his head?

So Browning wrote on a toccata of Gallupi's. But all that was over. The Prince's Prison, the Gate of Felicity, the Hall of the Treasury, the *kiosques* of Revan, Mustafa and Baghdad, the Garden of Tulips itself—all were now deserted. All was still. Silence unfurled itself. Shadows beneath trees shook and unfolded. The sun spread and below the parapets and battlements the Bosphorus sparkled blue, breezes doodling whitely upon it. Beyond that the shores of Asia were a brown mist laden with heat.

The Turk turned and looked at me. His yellow teeth shuffled between his lips. 'It is all very beautiful,' he said.

'Yes,' I replied, and thought of the smooth brown neck of some royal youth condemned for being alive and the jerk of the silken cord.

NOTES

1. Nicolas de Nicolay, *Quatre Premiers Livres*. Lyon, 1567.
2. Tournefort, *Voyage into the Levant*. London, 1741.
3. Sandys, *A Relation of a Journey Begun An: Dom: 1610*. London, 1615.
4. Evliya Efendi, op. cit.
5. A. de la Motraye, *Travels through Europe, Asia and into part of Africa*. London, 1723.
6. Ibid.
7. Xenophon, *Cyropaedia*, Bk. VII.
8. Ollincan, op. cit.
9. Montesquieu, *Persian Letters*. London, 1899.
10. Lithgow, op. cit.
11. Evliya Efendi, op. cit.
12. Michel Baudier, op, cit.

CHAPTER SEVEN

The City (III)

'IF I should minutely describe all the pleasure-places, gardens,
yallis, and koshks, it would be a long work; therefore according
to my narrow intellect I have given only the most famous of all
the buildings, foundations, pilgrimages and walks.'

EVLIYA EFENDI, *Narrative of Travels*. 2 vols. Trans. by
J. Von Hammer. London, 1834

I lay on the bed and watched the flies darting and circling, landing
and taking off, and I marvelled at the astounding capacity that flies
have for repeating themselves. The air was hazy with invisible patterns as they wove and wound and unwound and rewound spool
after spool of airy thread.

I got up and walked to and fro, measuring the drab territory of
my room and its few properties, a room acquired in emergency and
also because it was cheap and central. There was an iron bed, a
chair, a worm-eaten chest of drawers and a corner cupboard full of
old paint-brushes and rags. I had always intended to have them
removed, but had always forgotten to ask. Over the bed hung the
familiar and repulsive oleograph of Mustafa Kemal.

I opened the glass door and stood out on the balcony. It was late
evening. Below, in the narrow, cobbled street, the guests and land-
lords of other hotels had begun to sit out by their doors; some of
them clad in pyjama tops, some in pyjama bottoms. They talked and
sipped their glasses of pale-brown tea. At this hour a thousand different streets would reveal a similar scene.

Like nearly all side-streets in Istanbul it was permanently littered
with refuse: rags, peach-stones, melon-rinds—green and red—cardboard, paper and a substratum of unidentifiable filth. One might

194

suppose it to be a city infested by rats, especially as it is a large port, and no doubt there are many; but for every rat there must be at least two cats. There are thousands and thousands of them and even as I surveyed this small street there were nearly a dozen lean, efficient-looking scavengers reconnoitring the garbage with the fastidious care of inveterate gourmets. Later, when it was safer, the cockroaches would come out and feast on the rancid agglomerations of many weeks.

Opposite was a café where I occasionally dined. At night the waiters slept half-clothed on the table-tops wrapped in the dirty cloths and napkins. From everywhere I could hear the perpetual lament of Turkish music: garish and absonant. In the end it destroys all other sounds by sheer tenacity. It takes some time to get used to it and then you can live for weeks without it really troubling you. Then, one day, without warning, as if its full discordance has been gathering behind your back, it suddenly springs upon you and exasperates beyond all measure; perhaps at six in the morning. For a minute or two you wonder if you can tolerate it any longer. Then custom reinoculates the aural system.

Soon I became aware that every movement commented on a growing tedium. I felt as if I were waiting for something to happen, and all the time knowing that nothing could happen. It was reminiscent of the state of Vladimir and Estragon.

Prolonged purposelessness is dangerous. Inertia becomes like the repetitions of the flies, leads to the horrible analyses of *La Nausée*, the arid depths of *Huis Clos*. I did not understand either work fully until I was in Istanbul.

It was the first time I had been there and I had begun to get the feeling that I had been there too long, pottering indeterminately among familiar ruins. From time to time a gap of idleness would promote the desire to move on somewhere else. Both the plan and the replenishment of energy for this would be a relief; but usually lack of will found falsehoods and insufficiences in the plan and new activities dissipated the energy. Once, it is true, I travelled up the Black Sea, and another time went to Troy, on a third occasion to Bursa (Broussa), but they were expeditions long considered and often postponed. It was pleasant to loiter, gestating schemes and then finding reasons for finding them unworkable. This may seem foolish but Istanbul is one of those places which has this effect. One of the few, fortunately, that I know.

June had passed, then July—and now August was well advanced.
I had intended to leave and go south to Damascus and Baghdad,
but now it would be too hot further south and in any case there was
little incentive to leave. There never is an incentive to leave Istanbul. It is beautiful and desolate, enlivening and depressing. It is the
civic equivalent of Cleopatra in whose purlieus one is always compelled to remain just a little longer, to catch one more glimpse, one
more expression or posture.

After a time a feeling began to take shape. Tentatively I looked
it over. It shifted uneasily at a corner of the brain. It was vaguely
familiar and soon became fully recognizable. It was an old companion. Every club is reputed to have its bore. Every palace has its
Polonius. Every city has its ennui; or, perhaps more accurately, it is
in the city that a person finds a particular kind.

Ennui is one of the oddest and most inexplicable conditions.
Desire and life seem to have cyclical movements, and at the
apogee the desire for life is deserted by the source of life. Ennui
comes for no apparent reason. People say, and no doubt with justice,
that this is foolish—and so it is in some respects. It is the result of
self-interest, too much introspection, they aver. It is unhealthy.
Take a good walk, read a good book, do something. Such remedies
do not really work. It is something which has to be combatted in a
different fashion. If you run away from it by distraction it remains
as strong as ever, as insidious and as poisonous as ever. It comes,
settles, infiltrates, overpowers; it has the potence of volumes of
water, the weight and insistence of profound and immense silence.
It silts up the will, muffles and deadens the mind, numbs the limbs,
reduces the whole system to a dead, futile, paralysed passivity. The
roots of sorrow are squeezed in a steel grip, and the soul is as dry
as a cactus beset by hot winds, as hard and as dry as a viper's
scales, tinder and wood-rot and ashes and sand; most horrible—and
frightening. You awake and feel 'the fell of dark, not day':

> Selfyeast of spirit a dull dough sours. I see
> The lost are like this, and their scourge to be
> As I am mine, their sweating selves; but worse.

It leads, I think, it is almost bound to lead if you allow it measure,
to a despair, to the vacuum in the spirit, where out of nothing, in a
core of nihilism, the germ of suicide, the need and the despair for

it, begins to grow. Hope shrivels and the germ grows, and the rich evil blooms overcast the mansion. There is self-love and self-hatred and self-pity in it, all manner of diabolical inventions:

Odi, nec possum cupiens esse quod odi.

To put it in another way—the chaos is within. As the earthquake has its epicentre so the human has its anarchical nucleus from which, in desperation, cussion brings repercussion and the widening rings of shock shudder through the whole being, and the turbulent desolation, that same which lay not far behind the mocking smile and the jocular fisticuffs of Mephistopheles in Marlowe's *Faustus*, that turbulent desolation of the central hell explodes in the very core of the heart of the core. Later the calm falls, like the calm that lies in the pupil of a hurricane's eye—and there is nothing there. In that strange novel by Bernanos, *Sous le Soleil de Satan*, just before Mouchette commits suicide, the calm fell. 'He [i.e. Satan] came at once, abruptly, with no fluttering of wings, dreadfully peaceful and sure. However far he strains his likeness to God, no joy can proceed from him; yet, far superior to the pleasures which move only the entrails, his masterwork is a dumb peace, lonely, icy, comparable to the delight of nothingness. When this gift is offered and received, the angel who watches us, astounded, turns away his face.' At the moment of his coming 'Mouchette's turmoil miraculously ceased...'

He who finds the world repulsive, hates life, and sees his own corruption and futility reflected at every turn, like the grotesques of distorting mirrors, is in the Satanic predicament all over again. In his solitude he blames the world, and we see why he blames the world when we read the Devil's soliloquies in *Paradise Lost*.

But there are others whose cry is not motivated by a sense of personal loss but rather by a realization of the inadequacy of this world and their method of living in it, the expression of the man who is struggling rather than yielding, whose protest against the world and for the world and for the sadness of this life is the complaint for the huge, unbridgeable breach which lies between man's capabilities and man's achievements. 'Bunk!' replies the extrovert— but who is to know how many people have their seasons in hell and never return from it? In *Religio Medici* Thomas Browne wrote of that Satanic condition in a man which is probably less uncommon than we might like to believe. 'The heart of man is the place the Devils dwell in,' he writes, 'I feel sometimes a Hell within myself;

Lucifer keeps his court in my breast. Legion is revived in me. There are as many Hells, as Anaxagoris conceited worlds. There was more than one Hell in Magdalene, when there were seven Devils, for every Devil is an Hell unto himself; he holds enough of torture in his own ubi, and needs not the misery of circumference to afflict him: and thus a distracted Conscience here, is a shadow or introduction unto Hell hereafter.'

Every man has it in him to be an Iago as well as an à Becket, and ennui with its related states is a condition that promotes the closer knowledge of the diabolical as well as the divine condition of a man, of his nothingness, of his appalling powerlessness in the face of immense forces. There are the dark nights and the darker days, the days when we see that the sum of human joy is merely the remainder of the quotient of human misery. In the shallow depths of one's own limited experience and even more limited understanding one attempts to approach to some idea of the meaning and suffering of the great minds, the great writers, those who have seen and felt and summed up on behalf of those less articulate: Sophocles, Chaucer, who is an astoundingly sad poet much of the time, Pascal, Villon, Shakespeare, La Rochefoucald, Johnson, Swift, Baudelaire, Hopkins, Hardy and Leopardi. They have known despair and anger and ennui, and it is when we read them and also when we read of and participate in the spiritual struggles of men such as St Augustine, Donne, St John of the Cross and Hopkins again that we realize how trivial are our own sufferings. Is there anything to match St Augustine's conflict, or rather the culmination of his conflict, in company with Alypius, in the garden at night? What a fight for the liberation of the spirit, from the dross and itches of the world, the passing through fire, the cleansing through flame, the exquisite and excruciating pain of being purged and tempered, purified and wrought again in the immaculating blaze of divine love.

Of ennui and spleen many have written. Perhaps, in poetry, Hopkins' *Leaden Echo* is the finest expression, and how amazing and instructive it is to compare this with Lady Winchelsea's Pindaric Ode on the same theme and, more still, Matthew Green's. In a way the contrasts are too great but they show the interesting difference of period and outlook as well as of character, Green's tripping complacencies are almost ludicrous:

If spleen-fogs rise at close of day,
I clear my evening with a play,
Or to some concert take my way.
The company, the shine of lights,
The scenes of humour, music's flights,
Adjust and set the soul to rights.

'Adjust and set the soul to rights!' It is on the same level as 'An apple a day keeps the doctor away.' Nowadays we probably take an 'oblovon' or a tonic wine. And again Green writes:

In rainy days keep double guard,
Or Spleen will surely be too hard.

How like a commercial it sounds! And now let us turn to Pascal who lived in a time when even the worst of versifiers would have been incapable of such inanities and who provides, in prose, what is perhaps the best account, but without, like Green, offering remedies: '*Rien n'est si insupportable à l'homme,*' he wrote, '*que d'être dans un plein repos, sans passions, sans affaire, sans divertissement, sans application. Il sent alors on néant, son insuffisance, sa dépendance, son impuissance, son vide. Incontinent il sortira du fond de son âme l'ennui, la noirceur, la tristesse, le chagrin, le dépit, le désespoir.*' There is as great a gulf between Green and Pascal as there is between ordinary mortals and St Augustine, but perhaps these comparisons are not fair and perhaps Green was right after all. Take plain food, drink water, hunt, talk with women, 'chat away the gloomy fit', make jokes—

To cure the mind's wrong bias, Spleen,
Some recommend the bowling green;
Some, hilly walks; all, exercise;
Fling but a stone, the giant dies.
Laugh and be well.

'Laugh and be well', I suppose, is not a bad slogan. Let's have another round of drinks, let's play golf tomorrow, let's forget—everybody must have their own remedy. I left my room and went downstairs.

★

At the bottom was the reception office and a short broad passage. At the end of it the boy who did night duty slept. His bed remained permanently made and was never remade. The proprietor, a round square-headed man, sat on the steps and brooded aimlessly, hour after hour. Like many Turks he was taciturn but kindhearted. Years before he had left his village in the Anatolian plain and come to the big city. He was proud of his hotel, and in his red striped pyjamas, a solid figure planted on too small a chair, he surveyed the traffic of the street with the air of one conscious of his domain. Periodically a boy would slip along to a café and get a little tray of tea for him.

From time to time a man would come up and ask for a bed and Mustafa would, in all probability, with that slight upward and backward motion of the head which accompanies every negation in Turkish, say '*Yok*'. It takes a long time to get used to that one word *yok*. It seemes to sound more final than any other negative can be in any other language. It is a full-stop, an impassable barrier, a stone-hard, clearly chiselled word that, like a pebble, has become smooth and round and unbreakable as the tongues and lips of millions have shaped and rolled and smoothed it until it has acquired an eloquence, a brevity and an economy which is as depressing as it is admirable.

It neither needs nor receives the slightest appendage, no alleviating or exaggerating phrase to mollify or assist its effect. It is never accompanied by a smile or a hint of apology. Like a fixed bayonet or a bolted door it denies admission and banishes reprieve. Often the word is never actually said. It is, as it were, mimed by the upward and backward gesture of the head, and in this form it is even more formidable. It is an action that must take its place alongside those others, indispensable and infinitely expressive, the shrugged shoulders, the outspread hands, the raised eyebrows. It is extraordinary really, and rather pleasant as well, that such perfect and effective simplicity can prevail.

Mustafa raised his hand to his brow as I passed him. 'You're always moving,' he said. 'Why don't you sit down and take it easy like me?'

I thought of the last two hours, the uncertainty, the inaction, the fluctuations. I smiled and looked at his growing bulk. 'When I am fifty,' I said, 'I shall sit down.' I felt a little dishonest.

I went out into the main thoroughfare which led down to the square and the station in Sirkeci, and was at once absorbed in the

crowds. They rolled ponderously towards me, about and past, over-
flowing the narrow pavements, straggling across the road. The trams,
crammed and bulging, bodies clinging at the sides and ends, bells
ringing, ground past, dust swirling, paper jigging in their wakes.
Their wheels skirled as they braked.

The countless cafés, full of bare marble-topped tables, were
crowded with men drinking their inevitable glasses of tea and fruit-
juice, talking, reading newspapers, playing interminable games of
whist and backgammon. Water-sellers, doubled under their enormous
canisters from which long spouts projected, forged along the densely
laden sidewalks, rattling their glasses and saucers together, crying
out in their peculiar and rather melancholy voices, 'Soo . . . Souk
. . . Soo.' Vendors opened suitcases at random on the pavements,
spreading out pyjamas, lurid shirts and even more violent underwear.
Round these coloured reefs the crowds wavered, lapped and rolled on.

In the square outside the station was the row of bootblacks who
sat late into the night, often sleeping on their pitches. They squatted
there all day, doing a brisk trade. Their livelihood and often their
only property was contained in their heavy and intricately ornamented boxes. They were importunate and imperative, banging
their brushes on their boxes and throwing accusing eyes at anyone
with dirty shoes who ignored them. I walked down to the Lunar
Park.

★

The Lunar Park is reminiscent of Battersea Park, though much
better equipped. It lies at the ankles of the great walls of the Sultan's
Seraglio and at night becomes one of the principal recreation grounds
of the city. A long avenue of trees is flanked by shops, open-air
restaurants, side-shows, *kiosques*, bars, fun-fairs and, in one place, a
rather pathetic zoo.

The zoo consisted of two horses, two deer, some monkeys, an infinitely old and chagrined elephant bored by the futile attentions of
men, some ornamental birds, some snakes and two mangy lions in
small cages on wheels. The lions had long since lost interest in roaring and the proprietor had installed a gramophone to simulate this
noise and attract customers.

The manager of the snake-pit exhibit looked as if he had been
waiting for a local Godot for a long time. Beneath a hat adjusted

half-way back his head a lean, unrazored face topped a thin body in a threadbare suit. He leant on the top of his rostrum like a silent preacher. There was no need for him to speak. Above, enormous letters proclaimed: SNAKE-PIT—SLAVE GIRL. Occasionally he turned and encouraged tardy spectators.

I paid my entrance and he received it like a tithe overdue. Inside a raised walk ran round a wire-mesh cage. Beneath it, quite deep, was the 'pit'—upholstered in red satin. Lying full length in this, nine-tenths naked, was the slave girl. Her immobile face revealed irrepressible boredom. Disposed about her motionless white limbs was a profusion of snakes—python and anaconda. They lay in coils, rolls and bars, like sober but richly decorated brocade mottled and inlaid with patterns in buff, orange and yellow. They lay with that uncanny inertness that reptiles alone command. Every minute or so the girl stretched out an arm and touched the heap. There was a ripple of movement, the liquefaction of scales shifting over steel sinews.

The spectators shuffled round, curiosity chasing astonishment and repulsion across their faces.

I called in once some years later but the slave girl had gone. The manager was reduced to her role and the 'pit' had turned into an ordinary wire cage on wheels. He sat in it fingering his beads and trying to give the crowd their money's worth.

The zoo is a feeble shadow of the expansive days of the Sultanate. When Thomas Gainsford was there at the beginning of the seventeenth century he saw a *kiosque* not far away down by the Seraglio Point, 'a quadrant of seven arches on a side cloyster wise, like the *Rialto* walke in *Venice*; in the midst riseth a core of three or four roomes with chimneys, whose mantell trees are of silver, the windows curiously glazed, & besides protected with an iron grate all guilt over most gloriously: the whole frame so set with opals, rubies, emeralds, burnisht with golde, painted with flowers, and graced with inlayed worke of porphery, marble, iet, iasper, and delicate stones, that I am perswaded there is not such a bird cage in the world. Vnder the walls are stables for sea horses called *Hippopatami*, which is a monstrous beast taken in *Nilus*, Elephants, Tygres, and Dolphines: sometimes they have Crocadiles and Rhinoceros: within are Roebuckes, white Partridges, and Turtles, the bird of *Arabia*, and many beasts and fowles of *Affrica* and *India*.'[1]

At one end of the park, that which abuts on to the Golden Horn and the Bosphorus, there are larger tents containing boxing-booths and stages where third-rate singers and dancers line up on chairs and await their turn to deliver yet another dissonant Turkish song.

Outside one, by way of attracting attention, a young man stood on a platform with a dwarf sitting in the crook of his arm. The creature was antique with a brown wrinkled face, like a very old apple, and rheumy eyes. It appeared sexless—if anything more like a woman. It may well have been a eunuch, but more than anything else it was like a decrepit monkey, defenceless and withered. Its tiny wizened hands played with a set of beads and sometimes it spoke in a minute, quavering voice.

A crowd was gathering to examine this grotesque reduced to the task of luring curiosity without ever being able to satisfy it. It was merely a blurb to the leg-show within.

The overcrowded tent was foetid with stale smoke. Boys ran up and down with lemonade and tea. A ragtime band performed monotonously. An all but naked rubber-limbed woman curveted and waddled about the stage. Each distortion of her body was greeted by rapturous applause, and encores. In the middle of one of them a man in the row behind me had an epileptic fit. There was a crash of chairs and the dancer was forgotten. The man lay on the floor, his trunk rigid and hard, twitching and kicking. A thin froth surfed his lips. Two eager helpers were promptly lashed in the face. Another was kicked in the stomach. In the end it took eight men to carry him out and in a matter of seconds most of the remaining two hundred-odd had left the tent. An epileptic was more interesting any day than any Egyptian dancer, however salacious.

From an adjacent tent came the high-powered roar of a motor-bicycle being revved. Banners and posters proclaimed trilingually: 'THE WALL OF DEATH.' I paid fifty kuruş to a woman the other side of a hole in a box and walked in. The noise of the engine reached an intolerable pitch, obliterating my ears. Wooden stairs rose steeply for about twenty feet and at the top a circular platform ran round the arena—a strong wooden cylinder about thirty feet in diameter. It was like looking into a large silo or an enormous cheese-vat. Six inches from the top a red band had been painted—the danger line. There was no protection except a thick wire cable round the perimeter. In the middle of the floor at the bottom stood the bicycle: a rakish machine, brightly coloured. The engine had just been stopped while the owner went out to bring in customers. I leant over the edge and became aware of a man looking at me: a Turk of sullen mien. I knew he wanted to say something. Soon he did.

'English?' he asked. I nodded.

'Why do you come here?'

'Just passing an hour or two.'

'I mean—why do you come to Turkey?' he said impatiently.

'I find it interesting.' A safe reply. He grunted and there was a pause. I could see him digging about for a method of saying something. He had a matter to get off his chest.

'The English are not popular now,' he went on at last.

'No. I know,' I said. 'I'm sorry about that.'

'Your government very foolish,' he said. Now we're off, I thought. Has any government ever been anything else? I wondered how I was going to avoid the argument which never gets anywhere.

'Turkey and England always good friends,' said the man, anxious not to appear rude.

I smiled. 'Of course—'

'But your government must be careful,' he admonished.

At that moment a door below opened and a Turk walked in in a check shirt and trousers. He mounted the bicycle and revved it vigorously. It had no silencer and the noise shattered the air as it crashed round the confining cylinder. Then it slowed so that single explosions came rapidly; the detonations of a hoarse Bren-gun. He did this several times to bring in the stragglers.

The man nudged me, 'Like Cyprus,' he said, and laughed sourly. Suddenly the man below waved, mounted the machine, kicked off, went half-way round, ran on to a slope at the base and, in one gesture, swept to the top: the wheels racing along the red line. The spectators recoiled and the whole cylinder shuddered horribly. I was certain that it was only a matter of seconds before he took off from the wall. Round and round he went, faster and faster. Then— DOWN . . . in a swoop. Then—UP. The spectators reeled again. In a fraction of a split second he went from top to bottom and up again. He went past a foot away: a blur of body, steel, chromium, wheels and white and gold teeth flashing. Then he slowed and went round and round climbing gradually. The audience relaxed and craned fowards. Then he shot to the top with a burst. The audience swayed back.

He did this for about three minutes, soaring, plunging, climbing, rolling—all with bewildering rapidity and ease. The frame of the cylinder shook and the thunder of the sound increased and expanded until it seemed the very air would burst with the strain of it.

Then in full career he whipped out a large red handkerchief, put one corner in his teeth and let the rest blow back over his face. Then he did the same routine: racing round and round on the red ring at the top, plummeting violently to the very bottom. All the heads of the spectators went round in little circles, then forwards, then back. The Turk beside me was smiling now and pleased that I was impressed. 'Very good, eh?' he bellowed. 'Yes,' I shouted at him.

Without faltering the rider took both hands off the handlebars and steered the bicycle with his body, arms outstretched, crucified on the rushing air, the red handkerchief like a pennant in the slipstream. He looked like some avenger, one of the mechanized Eumenides sprung from a Cocteau underworld. The crowd goggled. He vaulted to the rim, then dropped like a stone to the base; sideslipping, lurching, weaving. Then he heeled over so that he was parallel to and three feet from the floor. A jerk of the body and he was flying round the red-edged lip. As he dived I exhaled, and my stomach seemed to drop as I leant forward. As he rose I breathed in again and momentarily my stomach hoisted itself again.

Nonchalantly, without hesitating for a second in his headlong and furious circling of the cylinder, he crossed one leg over the other as if he were sitting in an armchair, and rode the bicycle side-saddle. Blindfolded, handless and side-saddle, the man and the machine zoomed in circles making a haze of patterns and a continuous swirl of colour.

Suddenly he dropped to the floor in a half-roll, braked, flicked off the engine, dismounted, waved briefly to the crowd and stepped through the door. The thunderous noise was amputated at a stroke. The ensuing silence was almost deafening. I took a breath and walked unsteadily down the stairs. The Turk followed, importunate. Outside he took me by the arm. 'I would like to buy you a drink,' he said. It seemed an opportunity for good-will not to be missed. 'You must not think that I do not like the English,' he went on.

'That's very kind of you,' I replied.

'But when the landlord makes a mess,' he continued, 'the tenant objects, eh?' He was a long time getting to the point so I saved him the trouble and asked him what he would do in Cyprus. 'It belongs to Turkey,' he said emphatically. I had put the coin in and the machine worked. Whichever way we looked at it he couldn't see

any point of view but his own and Turkey's and what his government had told him. It is much the same in any country. People
repeat what they are told to believe.

Soon I lost interest. Some Turks are not good at arguing and they
are every bit as obstinate as Englishmen; but not as bad as the
Irish.

Over by the other tent the men were helping the epileptic into an
ambulance which had at last arrived, and beyond that the Golden
Horn and the Bosphorus glittered in the wake of the moon: the
slenderest silver bow imaginable. That rather unpleasant man
D'Annunzio early in his life wrote a stanza describing such a bow,
a hypnotically beautiful stanza which does for all new moons:

> O falce di luna calante
> che brilli su l'acque deserte,
> o falce d'argento, qual messe di sogni
> ondeggia a 'l tuo mite chiarore qua giù!

★

I walked back. The coloured lights hung like bright fruit in the trees.
Stalls were being packed up. The men would sleep in them and on
them. I went out of the park and into the streets. There was life
and activity everywhere; men everywhere, dark heads and black
moustaches, a round blotch of darkness and a smear of black beneath it, white all round. Occasionally there was a copper-head or a
blond. Everywhere people were in trousers and shirt-sleeves, white
and dark again, all colour being ironed out in the artificial light.
Men sat in rows on the edges of the pavements, squatted against the
walls, and went to sleep propped in doorways and against boxes.
Hamals still working trudged by folded in two under huge loads:
bales, cases of fruit and vegetables, furniture. Boys cooked maize
over charcoal braziers and ran to and fro with trays of tea. There
was a persistent and powerful but subdued roar of activity: wirelesses
everywhere, wailing and moaning and groaning; people laughing
and shouting and talking; dozens of games of cards going on; backgammon counters banging and clapping; horns eructing; trams grating. Noise. Nothing but noise and movement.

Suddenly all the lights failed. This is a regular occurrence. There
was a momentary blow of silence. Trams pulled up, wirelesses
stopped. At one stroke everything was immersed in intense blackness.

Within a minute candles were lighted. The card games and the backgammon went on, under the flapping, waggling flames, while huge shadows swayed and capered across walls and ceilings. A couple of minutes later the lights went up again, very quickly like a sheet of lightning. Then they dimmed and pulsed uncertainly as if there were a terrific strain on them. The bulbs breathed in and out with light, a kind of aching light as if they were being blown upon or as if someone at the power station were actually pumping life into them with rhythmical spasms. The bulbs expanded and contracted for a minute or so and the trams started and stopped awkwardly, hiccoughing.

I got back to the hotel and on the landing found the majority of the guests praying: a dozen or more bodies kneeling and bowing and rising again, making their evening obeisance to Mecca. The building was filled with the restrained murmur of chanting, mingled with the minute clicking of beads. I made my way through the swaying bodies and headed for the basin and the lavatory. There were two basins and two lavatories for about thirty people. The basins were always unusable and the lavatories perilous, perilous by any standards. I have only known one other lavatory comparable in its hazards and that was—and perhaps still is—in a cell in Abergavenny police station where I once involuntarily spent a night. It was necessary in this hotel to time things precisely, with one hand on the chain and one on the latch of the door. Thus the pull and the exit were, ideally, almost simultaneous. It was a piece of synchronization which required great dexterity, Sometimes the chain would not work, sometimes the latch, sometimes both. Then you would be left oscillating awkwardly between the reluctance to stay and the difficulty of departure. Meanwhile a miscellaneous tide swirled about the feet.

The prayers finished. Silence began to creep over the city. Cats went about their business. All the things of the night began to come forth, the rats in the shadows and the cockroaches running along the pavements among the refuse. I lay on my bed and read Leopardi —*Coro di morti*, a great poem:

> Profonda notte
> nella confusa mente
> il pensier grave oscura;

The arid spirit feels the will to hope and to desire failing . . .

208

Che fummo?
che fu quel punto acerbo
che di vita ebbe nome?

But the bright salesman with the cure for sorrow is knocking at the door, he has the packet of pills that will banish care. 'Good morning, sir,' he says breezily. 'Laugh and be well.' Matthew Green would have made money as a copy-writer.

★

Some of the most remarkable things to be seen in Istanbul are the cisterns. As many as eighty covered cisterns have been discovered and the most accessible of these is the Yerebatan Saray which lies quite close to St Sophia.

Of course it is now exploited for the tourist trade and a small ticket office and shop have been set up at the entrance. From there steps lead down about thirty feet and bring you to a landing within the cistern—from which point more steps lead to the water's edge. At once it is cool, delightfully and cleanly cool after the heat and dust of the streets. Some lighting has been arranged and for some distance all is clear. Rows of high Corinthian pillars stretch away into the aqueous twilight and support the bricked domes of the roof. Two or three feet of icy, pellucid water still lie on the sandy floor. By straining my eyes I was just able to distinguish the far end and part of one side of the cistern. I looked down the long, symmetrical colonnades of three hundred and thirty-six identical noble columns. They converged and crossed in long and diagonal perspectives and multiplied themselves in countless reflections. Magnificent.

The cistern has been there for over sixteen centuries. It was built by Constantine and enlarged by Justinian and it would be difficult to find a place where the domain of silence and tranquillity is more complete. As the reverberations of the city receded from my ears the veils of noiselessness descended. The water lay like flawless black glass merging in the areas of light to a pale buff, and the aisles of the pillars and the arches went down depthlessly into the dark water. Then, after a minute, a sound began: the distant and almost metallic sound of water dripping; frail precise drops falling truly twenty or more feet and each one striking out a pure and delicate note, limpid. They almost pinged on the water as if a wire had been touched.

Various improbable stories are told of this cistern. In 1830 two Englishmen rowed a boat across it and are alleged to have disappeared. Much later another Englishman took a boat and afterwards swore that he had travelled for two hours in a straight line and had seen nothing but water and line upon line of columns. It was concluded that the cistern extended over many square miles beneath the city. In fact it is a hundred and forty metres long and seventy wide.

The Spanish traveller Pero Tafur, who was there in the fourth decade of the fifteenth century, refers to a cistern beneath St Sophia which was probably this one, which 'could contain a ship of 3000 botas in full sail, the breadth, height and depth of water being all sufficient'.[2] Forty years earlier a fellow countryman, Gonzalez de Clavijo, maintained that ten galleys could float there.[3] I do not think that either is really possible. It is not quite high enough.

Almost as big, but inaccessible, is the cistern of Philoxenus, variously ascribed to the ages of Constantine and Justinian. It lies not far to the west of the site of the ancient Hippodrome and is believed to have held enough water to supply a population of 360,000 for ten or twelve days. Much of this great underground cavern is now filled with rubble and soil. For many years it was used by the silk-weavers because the atmosphere was ideal for this process. Many travellers visited it during this period when it must have looked more like a department of the bazaar. Sanderson records his wonder at the end of the sixteenth century: 'One thinge resteth, in my judgment to be mervailed at,' he writes, 'and the most noteable in this place; which is that it is all hollowe underneth and houlden up with pillors of ritch marble, with thier foundation and toppgarnishing all wrought in brainches. They ar said to passe the nomber of 1000; and underneath it is light and fresh water. Ther ar also instruments or great wheeles that they use to spinne silke with.'[4]

Other comparable cisterns are those of Theodosius, Pantocrator and Pantopopte, not to mention those named Phocas and Pulcheria, the cold cistern under the south-west end of the Hippodrome, one at the Laleli mosque and yet another near the Bodrum mosque.

There were also open storage reservoirs. There is a gigantic one next to the mosque of Sultan Selim, now filled with houses and gardens, a spacious green and fertile well thirty or forty feet down. It was constructed as long ago as A.D. 459 by a Gothic general called Aspar who was in the service of the emperor. There is another,

almost as large, in the north-west quarter of the city off Çevdet Paşa
street and this, like that of Aspar, contains a village and gardens.
An even bigger one lies a few hundred yards from the Adrianople
Gate. It was a vast arena, very deep and very long, and was named
after a prefect Aetius. It was built in 421. It is now used by a school
as a playing-field and takes a full-sized soccer pitch with plenty to
spare. It is Sanderson again who refers also to these open reservoirs
in a rather interesting connection. 'There is to be seen also in the
citie . . .' he writes, 'certaine very great places, of the auntients
cauled Numathia, which they filled with water and shewed theron
battailes of thier navi, to delight the people; which at this time is
full of orchards.'[5]

They have certainly made very successful sunken villages and,
naturally enough, fruit, especially figs and peaches, grows well in
the protection of their walls.

Water-supply for the city was always a problem and, from the
time of Hadrian, emperors and sultans tried to ensure a regular
quantity by bringing it from a distance. Formerly it was brought
from Lake Derkos near the Black Sea and there were three main
systems. An aqueduct attributed to Constantine brought water from
streams at the west of the city. This was improved by Valens shortly
after Constantine in the fourth century, who built the great aqueduct named after him which still strides gigantically across the valley
between the third and fourth hills and over the long sweeping rise of
the Atatürk boulevard. The immense arches, in a double tier, look
like the empty windows in the skeletal wall of some huge palace. It
wears easily its sixteen centuries of life and so far as I can see there
is nothing to prevent it from standing for as long again. Water was
also brought from reservoirs near Belgrade—the forest about fifteen
miles away—by a series of aqueducts which vault the intervening
valleys.

I was coming out of the Yerebatan Saray one May afternoon
when I passed a drove of well-upholstered German tourists in their
bush shirts and *Lederhosen* and festooned with cameras and light-
gauges. English with a treacly, laryngeal accent came into my ear. I
turned to find a startlingly beautiful girl: dark with dark-blue eyes—
a young Jewess. She wanted to know the way to St Sophia.

It is easy to laugh at other people's manner of speaking your
language and I am always finding it necessary to remember my own
lamentable shortcomings at foreign tongues. But Rachel's English

was astounding. It was, in a manner of speaking, 'fluent' but quite often her enthusiasm trapped her into incredible statements like 'I muzzed go to end my shoppings.' But no print can capture the elusive euphony of her speech, its rhythms at once harsh and sweet, its curiously discordant tunefulness, its husky and glottal inflexions. Her accent was, in fact, fascinating, and this, plus her ability to invent syntactically outrageous and grammatically ramshackle sentences, formed an exercise in mental and aural agility.

They would start crisply and formally, open out, gather speed, and then, like an ailing engine or battery, begin to stumble and hop, and sometimes stop dead. Improvisation, at which she was expert, would come to the rescue. Participles were transformed into nouns, weak verbs were jerked out of oblivion or created for temporary service, prepositions and adverbs performed the oddest antics. Then she would be away again, patching her grammar en route.

Once we went to a museum—there is no pattern of reason or consistency behind their hours of opening and shutting and this one was shut. 'Oh,' she said, then mixed her French, 'they are always fermed when you do not will it.'

I imagined that after a time the strain of listening to one's tongue being massacred, albeit with charming and uninhibited abandon, would be too much. But her resources were manifold and her wit irrepressible.

I admired her a good deal for being bold enough to travel single from Israel to Turkey and then on to Greece where I met her again by accident in Athens. As I say—she was a beauty, and to walk down a crowded street—or even an uncrowded street—with her verged on the embarassing. Hundreds of eyes were all boring in one direction. I began to realize, very vicariously, what it must be like to be famous, to be the Queen or Miss Loren or Lady Docker, what it must be like to be the owner of breasts and legs which are reproduced and plastered round the walls of the world. But this meant little or 'nuzzing' to her.

Sartorially she was a complete failure. But she was blissfully unaware of this also. It could not be said that her clothes were out of fashion. They had never been in it. They were neither old nor outmoded. They were as original as her genders and as freakish as her tenses. In addition her limbs clinked and rattled with some of the most gaudy and tasteless jewellery which it would be possible to conceive or devise.

Somehow she got away with everything. She had only to smile and twang off some linguistic monstrosity and things happened. Keys were found, and doors unlocked which had not been opened for years, tables were emptied, taxis materialized, forms were forgotten, officials succumbed. It was like being in the wake of a very modern Titania, and it was all done without effort and with disarming innocence. This I take to be glamour, in the proper sense of the word: magic, throwing dust in people's eyes.

She covered a lot of ground and changed her escorts with sensible regularity: about every three days. 'Three days is enough,' she said. 'They get too heated.' She might have been talking about ovens or electric blankets. Being an Englishman I proved an exception. It is distressing how traditions and reputations pursue one; disheartening to realize that one is expected to live up to them. This has been a stock joke for a long time, but, like a great many stock jokes, it is a symptom of something. Some forms of English education and upbringing are to be regretted; not least those forms which make it difficult to be at ease with strangers and talk to women without introduction. The boarding-school, and the attitude towards women which life in it generates, can be extremely harmful and its effects may persist for a long time, quite apart from the absurd fictions of men sowing middle-aged oats in Paris, a place which is still regarded by a large number of people as a Mecca of erotic practices and a place for working off inhibitions and frustrations. Because they are afraid of women, many English boys (and men)—a good many years in boarding-schools, the army and rugby clubs have left me in little doubt about this—attempt to protect and unify themselves against women by laughing at them, by developing what they believe to be a superiority cult. Anything which smacks remotely of sensitivity, effeminateness or sentimentality is persecuted and derided. Even a healthy virility is regarded as 'not quite the thing'. By men, in women, dullness, respectability and cloistered (but not religious) virtue are prized, even nourished. England is supposed to be full of bored and unsatisfied women. This may be another fiction but it is a belief widely held, and so it is believed that Englishmen spend much of their time trying to turn their women into men, or wishing that they were. The women, on the other hand, are meanwhile spending much of their time hoping, if not trying, to turn their men into men: at any rate *qua* women.

'Why can't a woman be more like a man?' sings Higgins. 'Show me!' sings Eliza to Eynsford-Hill. There are the two sides of the coin.

I remember once being greatly startled when an eminent and beautiful and, as I thought, relatively cold-blooded lady said, quite soberly, that sometimes she felt that she would like to be dragged out by the hair and raped by a Sheik. The choice of a Sheik was immaterial. It was the rape that was relevant. On the whole, of course, rape is not something to be encouraged or condoned—but it is quite easy to see what she meant. Oppressed by well-bred protective gallantries, padded about by the clichés of a luke-warm chivalry, misled by lack of decision and embarrassed by excess of apology and consideration, she suddenly had a strong desire to be treated, even if violently, as a creature of flesh and blood.

The English attitude to women, if there is still such a thing— perhaps there are changes now—has produced an attitude beyond the island to Englishmen. The mirth of the world has ossified the alleged characteristic attitude into an immutable symbol. The English have turned it into a virtue. There was nothing else we could do. We have cut our losses but we have talked ourselves into it by half. That is how bogus reputations are made. Inhibitions are transmuted into noble and gentlemanly qualities. We can congratulate ourselves that we can laugh at ourselves and do not mind being mocked. Telling a joke against oneself or sustaining it is a simple form of self-flattery and self-protection. In the world the shares of opinion fluctuate but humour is steady. The rule seems to be pretty generally proved by exceptions, but this circle cannot be dignified by 'vicious.' It is the product of too much imagined virtue for that.

So Rachel volunteered that she never expected the English to behave 'cadly' as she put it. But, in any case, when you are twenty, every grey hair is an old tune, the signature on a fading photograph.

For long it never really occurred to me that she might do some work. I never associated her with 'work'. She was the kind of person for whom everything was done. She belonged to the Utopian and illusory world of the labourless and untrammelled. I still find it virtually impossible to believe that she taught in the Tel-Aviv equivalent of a comprehensive school. And she taught, of all things, English. Some children have remarkably mixed blessings.

Her reaction to St Sophia was roughly what might be expected:

a kind of astonished ignorance. It is without doubt the most notable monument in Istanbul and one of the most notable in the world. It was the great church, the East Roman equivalent of St Peter's.

It began as a church, became a mosque and is now a museum. Externally it is not at all symmetrical because of innumerable additions, alterations and repairs which render it a confused mixture of buttresses and superfluous domes, some of which are covered by saffron-coloured plaster. But it stands solid, immense and dignified and, in its way, beautiful. It has stood there for over fifteen centuries.

Three buildings have had the name and approximate site of this sanctuary. First there was a basilica with a wooden roof probably founded by Constantine and completed by his successor and son. It was dedicated in 360. But in 404 it was burnt down following the disturbances caused by the exile of St John Chrysostom. A new church rose from the ashes and was dedicated in 415 by Theodosius II. This in turn was burnt down during the seditious riots of Nika in 532. Justinian began rebuilding it forty years later and it was rededicated after nearly six years in 537. At intervals afterwards various disasters befell it. In 558 the great dome and the eastern dome fell in; and in 975 an earthquake brought down more of the roof. Another earthquake in 1346 did great damage.

After Justinian's restoration it became the place of the most solemn ceremonies of Church and State.

A number of legends gathered about it, about some of which Paul the Silentiary wrote. A hundred architects were supposed to have superintended its construction, each of whom was in command of a hundred masons. Five thousand masons worked on the right-hand side and five thousand on the left according to a plan outlined by an angel who appeared to the emperor in a dream.

This angel appeared a second time—as a eunuch, curiously enough—and ordered a boy who was guarding the masons' tools to call them immediately to get on with the building. The boy declined and the angel, understandably angry, swore by the word of God that he would not leave until the boy obeyed. The boy was brought before the emperor who realized, with admirable perception, that the eunuch was in fact an angel and he resolved to dedicate the church to the Word of God—the Divine Wisdom.

When the church was finished as far as the cupola there was insufficient money to go on. But the angel rose to the occasion, appeared as a eunuch again, led the treasury mules to a subterranean vault and loaded them with eight hundredweight of gold.

The walls and arches were made of bricks and revetted with marble of great variety and magnificence. Every kind of marble, porphyry and granite was used: Phrygian white marble streaked with rose-coloured stripes; green marble from Laconia; blue from Libya; black Celtic marble with white veins; white Bosphorus marble with black veins; Egyptian granite and Saitic porphyry. Material was carried from many distant parts: Troas, Cyzicus, Athens and the Cyclades.

During the empire the church was filled with the most fabulous wealth and ornamentation which it would now be tedious to chronicle. There was also reputed to be a large number of relics.

At the very beginning of the fifteenth century Gonzalez de Clavijo claimed to have seen the arms of St John, some of Christ's blood and some of His beard and the sop of bread which Jesus gave to Judas at the Last Supper. Forty years later Pero Tafur also saw a number of relics: the lance which pierced our Lord's side; the coat without a seam, violet but grown grey with age; one of the nails; some thorns from the Crown, some wood from the Cross, and the pillar at which Christ was scourged. Not to mention several belongings of the Virgin and the grid-iron upon which St Lawrence was roasted. Other travellers reported the existence of the red marble cradle of Jesus and the basin in which he was said to have been washed—both from Bethlehem. In addition there were His swaddling clothes and the table at which He celebrated the Last Supper.

It was also holy in the Muslim regard. The doors were said to have been made from wood of the Ark. There was a well covered with a stone from the Well of Samaria which was supposed to cure palpitations. And there is still the Sweating Column which is believed to effect miraculous cures.

When you enter the immense narthex floored by huge flagstones and flanked by colossal doors you at once realize the magnitude of the church. Once within, the eye traverses the great floor, circles the arcades, rests upon the enormous pillars and then ascends. It climbs the four principal supporting piers. Then, head bent right back, you look at last at the huge dome which, as Procopius put it in his *Aedifices*, 'seems not to rest upon solid masonry, but to cover the space with its golden dome . . . suspended from heaven'.[6] Half-domes extend to the east and west and widen the space. The ceilings were covered with gold, and the marble columns are tinted with purple and green, splayed with red, feathered with white. The colours form extraordinary patterns and figures. Much is now faded but the mosaic-work is being restored gradually.

At the conquest, of course, all mosaics and paintings were obscured by whitewash and plaster; but there are still more obvious signs of its use as a mosque. The *mihrab* and the steps of the sanctuary are askew so that the eye shall be directed towards Mecca. There are also green medallions like enormous shields which hang high above and are inscribed with the names of Allah, the Prophet, the first Caliphs and the first *Imams* in large gold script.

St Sophia is such an astounding building that to attempt even a partial analysis and description would be both presumptuous on my part as well as inconsistent with the scope of this book. It would be like trying to analyse the structure of *Aeneid* or the *Divine Comedy* in a weekly picture paper. It has already been dealt with very thoroughly by many authorities and when you see it, as Procopius wrote, the vision 'constantly shifts . . . for the beholder is utterly unable to select which particular detail he should admire more than the others. But even so, though they turn their attention to every side and look with contracted brows upon every detail, observers are still unable to understand the skilful craftsmanship, but they always depart from there overwhelmed by the bewildering sight.'[7]

It was in their architecture and in their internal decoration that the Byzantine artists achieved their finest expression. Their main contribution to architecture was the discovery of how to balance a dome over a square. The architects who managed this were mainly Greeks and Armenians. They employed two methods: firstly, pendentives, that is, triangles at the corners of the square which curved inwards to join a circle; secondly, squinches—these were apsidal vaults over the angles of the square. The pendentive was used at St Sophia. Their mosaic-work was rich and magnificent. It was direct but not simple and it satisfied an emotional need. Gold provided the principal element and the richest materials were always used. Expense, therefore, curtailed excess. A mass of highly organized and intricate detail produced an overall purity and beauty. Quite often the effect was one of sombre splendour. But decoration did not obtrude and was subservient and contributory to the harmony of the building. The building itself was the text and bulk of the sermon in stone, the mosaics were the *exempla*.

★

Water, to the man of the East, is the symbol of the principle of life. 'By water everything lives.' These words from the Koran are often to be found inscribed on fountains, and they are written on the fountain of Ahmet III which lies just beyond St Sophia and in front of the Imperial Gate to the Seraglio. It is a beautiful one with carved arabesques and inscriptions in gold letters on blue and green backgrounds, and surrounded by borders of faïence. It is dry now and the blown dust accumulates in it in miniature dunes. One day in summer I was sitting on the edge of the fountain wondering rather aimlessly what to do next when a curious figure came into sight through the Imperial Gate of the Seraglio. It moved as an abandoned newspaper does in a spasmodic breeze.

I saw him spot me, waver for a moment and then plot a more certain course. He was clad in a russet suit (of linen I found a little later), and white shoes. His clothes drooped and flapped round his spare frame. He appeared to move edgeways and in a straight line, a shuffling, sidling walk. Under his arm was a zip-up brief-case.

He arrived, sideways and forwards. He smiled. 'Vous-êtes anglais?' His smile was a tentative reconnaissance of good-will and would have been attractive; or was still—just. But it consisted of an ancient barrier of decaying, filthy teeth, umbered, broken and gapped. They were the dental equivalent of the city walls. His 's's' were sluiced through the apertures. He was hawk-nosed and grey-eyed beneath short pepper-and-salt hair.

I braced myself involuntarily. Mad? Drunk? A confidence trickster? A tramp? British reserve can be a harmful habit. Blessedly, it can also be extremely useful. But either way it often distresses me to find how deeply engrained it is. I am always regretting how often I suspect the worst motives when accosted by strangers.

'Je suis un poète turque,' he said. It was refreshingly direct and unexpected. After the prefatory moment I relaxed a little.

'Moi aussi—anglais.'

His fine but filthy and calloused hands fidgeted awkwardly with his jacket and kept on clambering round the edges of his brief-case as if they did not belong to him and as if they were searching for something to hang on to. Then one came out, a scarred talon, and plucked my sleeve. 'Je m'appelle Kasim. Venez et buvez?'

Some people have an infallible gift for the right suggestion. I felt the outer bonds of conservatism slacken perceptibly. We went to a little shop a few yards away. He talked thirty to the dozen and I was usually the verbal equivalent of a paragraph and a half in arrears.

Poet he was. Soon the marble-topped table was littered with script: some published work—newspaper articles and poems as stained as his teeth and as frayed as his clothes. Then sheet after sheet of typed and written work came out, much of it in French, a lot in Turkish, some translated from Persian, some in Persian. His brief-case was like a conjurer's hat.

'I must introduce you to people,' he said. 'Writers, publishers.' Then he plunged his hand into the case and pulled out another battered lyric. He reminded me of a mad newsvendor I once knew in London who prowled the streets of Bloomsbury like some deranged and rejected Jude the Obscure. He had educated himself, as he averred, out of newspapers for half a century. He had the face of a Roman and the eyes of a drug-addict and was prepared to lecture you—and indeed did with astounding tenacity and eloquence—on anything from the Gracchi to Palmerston.

I began to feel uneasy. Kasim had captured his audience, paid for entrance with the drinks, and now I had to listen. With returning misgivings I saw another sheaf pulled forth. His restless fingers fiddled with the pages. He embarked on a long Persian epic, translating extempore into French. I lost the thread at once. It was like missing the first line of one of Arnold's long Miltonic similes in *Sohrab*. Something was coming down a long defile in the mountain-side. It was 'comme' something. I concentrated hard. A baggage train? A wild animal? A posse of bandits? I never discovered. Suddenly he shovelled all the paper back into the case. 'C'est trop long,' he said. 'Allons-nous.' I was vastly relieved.

We went to visit the Istanbul 'Fleet Street' near St Sophia. All the editors he knew were away. Then I had to leave to keep an appointment. Two hours had passed very agreeably and I was to spend a good many more in his company. He was a very kind man and introduced me to many interesting people. His thought was exuberant, discursive; and he was amazingly energetic for fifty-six. Sleep and food were always secondary considerations. Unlike most

Turks he nearly always walked everywhere, perhaps from poverty rather than wish.

He loped away—edgewise, forwards; his horny hands beginning again their nervous explorations, an ageing bird in dun and tattered plumage.

Many such solitary scavengers rove the earth. They may be failures as the world counts success. They may have made a virtue of necessity. But they have tried to do something by themselves and for themselves and are content to give pleasure to others without ulterior motive and their lives do not hang hinged on habit and subservient to all the petty disciplines and regular motions of bureaucracy and small-mindedness.

★

A minute's walk from St Sophia is the At Meydani (or Square of Horses) a name which derives from the fact that it was used as a *cirit* (polo field), now a long, rectangular garden with well-watered lawns and flower-beds. On one side rises the mosque of Sultan Ahmet; the other is flanked by large, decaying offices and commercial buildings. At the end furthest from the Great Church is a small café hidden by chestnuts and plane-trees: a cool and secluded place for lunch where tourists never go.

Beneath these gardens lay the Hippodrome, the focal point of Byzantine life, begun as long ago as A.D. 203 by Septimus Severus. He had already destroyed much of the city as a reprisal for rebellion, and by this gift to the people sought to reclaim their affection. Constantine completed the work in 330.

Enormous, lavishly decorated, the Hippodrome was the scene of entertainment and barbarity. Sometimes revolts broke out there and already dangerous and violent spectacles deteriorated into large-scale butcheries. The spectators were divided into two factions which were largely political. They sat on different sides of the arena.

Originally the people of the city were organized at an unknown date into four groups: Blue, Green, White and Red. In time the Blue and Green absorbed the others. They were municipal organizations. The Blues and Greens were civil and political, the others military. The principal event in the Hippodrome was chariot-racing and this went on all day, the charioteers wearing the colours of the factions. It was exciting and extremely dangerous. Accidents were frequent and fair play unheard of. Partizanship was violent. The entertainment was free and forty thousand people could be seated there.

To the east of the Hippodrome the ground fell away, as it still does, and it had to be levelled by building huge arches which gave on to the stabling and accommodation. Some of these chambers survive and are lived in from time to time by the homeless. Gradually the Hippodrome. fell into disuse and from the middle of the twelfth century until the conquest it was deserted.

I often lunched in the little café at the end of the gardens and usually had the place to myself plus half a dozen rapacious cats. They were veteran, independent scavengers who fought, stole and survived according to jungle law. The food was not good but it was adequate, a kind of *kebab* called *köfte* with flat, thick pancakes like tortillas and a tomato and paprika salad. What I couldn't eat went under the table for the cats. From beneath the vine I had an excellent view of the gardens, St Sophia in the distance and the 'Blue Mosque' almost opposite. Even better than the view was the amount of silence available.

It is only a matter of time before silence, or at any rate an absence of noticeable and obtrusive noise, will be extremely difficult to attain. We shall have to have sound-proof areas, peace reserves on the same principle as national parks and trust regions, into which we can retire and avoid the appalling and ever-increasing bedlam which rules the air. You can already make a handsome living out of selling time and selling space. It cannot be long now before some enterprising commercial concern will make a big turnover out of selling silence: one hour's relief at ten shillings, and cheap at the price, in a sound-proof cubicle.

It is a feature of some communist-controlled countries that even small villages are fixed up with a radio and loudspeaker system which makes constant and largely meaningless noises all day long. It is one method of preventing people from thinking for themselves. Silence and solitude are two of the enemies of totalitarianism.

At the moment many of us have to travel miles into the country to find both of them. All silence is harmony, but most noise is discord. The monks of enclosed orders have the boon of silence, and all those, and they are relatively few, who have the advantage of living in remote and unblemished natural surroundings. We have become so used to noise that silence is a source of embarrassment, is construed as a sign of stupidity and dullness. It is regarded with suspicion and distaste. It exasperates. It is elusive. It gives nothing away. There is no answer to it. When in doubt, to fill the awkward pause, put on the wireless, the television, the gramophone, sing, dance, shout, anything must be done to repel the alarming nakedness of silence. The silent man is unsociable, uncouth, an enemy. Silence is the bleak sentence of scorn and disregard. It will remind us of things of which we do not wish to be reminded.

The removal of external noise enables people to hear other sounds which they can less easily understand, which frighten them. They are the noises of the mind and the imagination, the persistent sound of the will and the desire. These are the sounds which clamour for attention when external silence falls. They are dangerous and, what could be more distressing, through these sounds will come the clear, tireless, invincible tones of the conscience and 'better self' giving orders and repeating all those tiresome 'do's' and don'ts' which prevent us from going on thinking that we are enjoying ourselves. It is external noise and diversion which prevent us from coming to grips with the unpleasant agglomeration of sins and urges and evil thoughts which press chaotically against the bars, grimacing, mouthing, howling to be let loose; the mobs of lust and malice and hate jabbering stridently, flocking up in droves from the sewers and tunnels and back-alleys of the brain, reminding us of what we are and what we have done and not done, disrupting the artificial and dubious lulls of self-satisfaction like the sheeted dead that squeaked and gibbered in the streets of Rome before the fall of Caesar.

Discord springs from hell, the gates of which always lean wide open. When silence falls those of heaven are ajar. But there, in a trice, to prevent us from taking advantage of the situation are all the subtle and alluring displays of misdeeds and imagined delight and, hiding behind them, gesticulating wildly for attention, the horrible spectres of things we thought we had forgotten, hoped we could and wished we had. The Faustian pageants of the desirable perform their delectable and fascinating charades. Fabulous women uncover soft breasts and silken thighs and melt the marrow; magically, prospects and vistas of power and riches (it may be a matter only of commanding a servant or making a few pounds) unfold, and we are entertained by the ingenious promptings of hypocrisy and vanity, the pleasing itches of self-justification and self-love. Beyond them are the pale, agonized ghosts of sins still unadmitted, still unconfessed, still unpardoned and still unatoned.

We know them when we see them. But turn the wireless on and let us think that they go. They do not. They slip back down the cracks and the gratings, slithering back into the sewers. There they sap away the vitality of the soul. It is there that they are dangerous.

★

In the middle of the gardens are three famous objects which are supposed to stand on what was the *spina*, the low dividing wall which ran the length of the Hippodrome. They are the Egyptian Obelisk, the Colossus of Constantine Porphyrogenitus and the Serpent Column.

The obelisk is precisely the same today as it was fifteen hundred years before Christ was born. It is a piece of granite that the Pharaoh Thutmose III (1549–03 B.C.) had cut and shaped in a quarry of the Upper Nile and it was first erected at Karnak. In A.D. 390 it was raised on four corner cubes to the honour and glory of Theodosius the Great. The hieroglyphics cut on it—and these are as clear as on the day when they were first carved for there is no sign anywhere of the effects of three and a half thousand years of weather—were described by Lady Mary Montagu with something less than her usual good sense as 'mere antient puns'. In fact they represent a prayer of Thutmose to his god.

It rests upon a sculptured base which depicts the emperor enthroned amidst a gathering of courtiers and guards on one side, waiting for the games to start in the Hippodrome; the imperial household watching their progress on another side, the giving of a reward to the victor on a third, and the reception of homage from the defeated Goths on a fourth. Inscriptions in Greek and Latin record the great difficulties involved in raising the column.

Very close by is the sadly pitted and weathered pillar of Constantine Porphyrogenitus. It was once clad in burnished brass plate which the troops of the fourth Crusade ripped off and melted down. The holes made by the nails and bolts are plain. It looks extraordinarily vulnerable to wind and storm but somehow it survives, a hundred and one feet of melancholy monument—and to what? Nothing.

Much more interesting is the Serpent Column which was brought by Constantine from the sacred precinct of Delphi. Originally it was an offering to Apollo from the thirty-one cities which were represented at the battles of Salamis and Plataea. It was a triple-headed serpent but the heads have gone and only a short green coil of bronze remains. Pero Tafur, the Spanish traveller, came across it and described it, inaccurately, as consisting of two snakes entwined in gilded brass. The inhabitants told him that wine poured from the mouth of one and milk from the other. 'But,' he adds prudently, 'no one can remember this, and it seems to me that too much credit must not be attached to the story.'[8]

Evliya Efendi also mentions it as an image of a triple-headed dragon which was erected to destroy all scorpions, serpents, lizards and 'similar poisonous reptiles'. He records that Sultan Selim II knocked off the lower jaw of the head of the dragon which looked to the west and as a result snakes then made their appearance on the western side of the city and became common in that quarter. Evliya adds that if the remaining heads should be destroyed, 'Islambol will be completely eaten up with vermin.' They have been and it is not. Though small scorpions, snakes and lizards are quite common out in the country I have, in fact, never seen any such creatures actually in the city. In the past numerous travellers have seen many such things. Busbecq, the French diplomat who spent some years there in the middle of the sixteenth century and who was by no means a credulous man, saw what he thought was at least one dragon. He actually accumulated a small zoo and saw a variety of wild beasts in the town: lynxes, wild cats, panthers, leopards and lions, also a dancing elephant and a hyena. Some of these were loose and some were not.[9] The chances of a lion whelping by the capitol seem to have been not inconsiderable. He also saw a giraffe by dint of having its bones dug up for his inspection.

The Serpent Column was one of many talismans enumerated by Evliya. Theodosius the Great had another pillar to the east of the Seraglio in what became, in Evliya's time, the poultry market. He says that one of the later Constantines placed a talisman on top of it which was in the shape of a starling. This versatile bird clapped its wings once a year and brought all the birds in the neighbourhood to the spot, each carrying three olives in its beak and talons. On top of another column, one, Socrates, placed a brazen cock which clapped its wings and crowed once in every twenty-four hours. At this signal all the cocks of Istanbul began to crow. By contrast, to the south of St Sophia, there were four lofty columns of white marble which bore the statues of four cherubs which faced the four points of the compass. Each of these clapped his wings once a year and thereby fore-

boded desolation, war, famine or pestilence. On yet another pillar
there was the bronze figure of a wolf which protected pasturing
flocks. Domestic strife might be solved by clasping the brass figures of
a youth and his mistress in close embrace.

There were also sea talismans. One of them stood near the
emperor's palace and spat fire and burnt the ships of any enemy which
approached from the Marmara Sea. There was another in the form
of a triple-headed brazen dragon on the Seraglio Point which
belched fire and ignited hostile ships approaching from the Bosphorus. The harbour was exceptionally well protected. There was a
brazen ship which, once a year, when the cold winter nights had set
in, embarked all the witches of the city and set sail until morning
to guard the White Sea. The Black Sea was guarded by another
brazen ship which contained all the wizards and conjurers. Evliya
concludes his extensive section on talismans by reference to a further
twenty-four colums which were spaced round the city. 'All could be
visited by a man in one day,' he writes, 'provided it was a day of
fifteen hours: now the longest day at Islambol, from sun-rise to sunset, is fifteen hours and a half. That city is situated in the middle of
the fifth climate, and enjoys excellent air and water.' Few would
dispute his opinion of the air and water.[10]

We may smile a little at talismanic superstition of this kind nowadays. We have grown blasé about the prenatural and the miraculous, about, as the Catechism puts it, 'charms, omens, dreams and
suchlike fooleries'. But it is quite extraordinary how scepticism is
banished by an apparently inexplicable event. The stigmata, for
instance, has so far defied all scientific analysis and explanation.
Periodically the blind do see, the lame walk, and the defective are
made whole. We can rationalize to our heart's content, but ratiocina-
tion turns to discontent, for here and there, if we are honest, we have
to admit the apparently impossible.

In *The Everlasting Man* Chesterton recalls how he once defended
the religious tradition against a whole luncheon-table full of distinguished agnostics. Before the end of the conversation every one
of them had brought forth some charm or talisman from which he
admitted that he was never parted. Chesterton was the only person
without one. 'Superstition', he wrote, 'recurs in a rationalist age
because it rests on something which, if not identical with rationalism,
is not unconnected with scepticism. It is at least very closely connected with agnosticism. It rests on something which is really a very

human and intelligible sentiment, like the local invocations of the numen in popular paganism. But it is an agnostic sentiment, for it rests on two feelings; first that we do not really know the laws of the universe; and second that they may be very different from all that we call reason.'

The size of the talismans in Constantinople is not really relevant. They were public rather than private. They had to be visible. Now talismans tend to be private and portable. The use of the blue bead against the evil eye is a widespread custom. The Jews have their phylacteries. The Arabs have abraxas stones. Thousands of Christians carry hidden charms. With diligent faith and make-believe the most improbable objects can be invested with potency. Again potency does not depend upon size. And one of the reasons for the survival of the potency is that people tend to forget the failures, remember the apparently coincidental successes.

Who can say when and how the potency is a product of the faith rather than the faith being the product of the potency? One might suppose that an object is not potent of itself, but by arrogating power to it, faith elicits a power beyond it. Above all the talisman is a reminder.

The strange, the inexplicable, is always quickly relegated to the domain of the preternatural. When the bicycle and the telephone first arrived in Turkey they were regarded as instruments of the Devil. Now people think nothing of them. Towards the end of the eighteenth century Burke, in *A Vindication of Natural Society*, wrote that 'The fabric of superstition has in our age and nation received much ruder shocks than it has ever felt before; and through the chinks and breaches of our prison we see such glimmerings of light, and feel such refreshing airs of liberty, as daily raise our ardour for more.' Perhaps, perhaps, but *Old Moore's Almanac* still sells three million copies a year in England. We may know more but we understand as little as ever.

★

By the main gateway of the 'Blue Mosque'—that of Sultan Ahmet —there lounged an unofficial guide. He was wearing a broad-brimmed black hat, red shirt, bell-bottomed trousers and patent-leather buckled shoes. He looked as if he had strayed off the set of a bad Hollywood film about Mexican bandits. He spoke American with a Turkish accent and was alternately insolent and servile. When a possible client approached he would buttonhole him brashly and brandish a card under his nose: a card which said that he was an official guide to the mosques.

Inside the courtyard, as at Beyazit and elsewhere, pigeons waddled and strutted: the mosque fowls which are unlucky in houses and which it is a pious act to feed. Some old women were selling seed for the purpose but it looked as if it would have been an act of piety to feed them instead. On the other hand, if you fed the pigeons, you might expect to hear news of absent friends.

Inside the cloister a cripple was selling picture postcards and beads, and cheap medallions and china. At the big fountain and at the taps men were rolling up their trousers and washing their feet before praying. High above, on the little balconies of the slender minarets, the *muezzins* were still calling the faithful to prayer. They walked round the balconies, stopping periodically to lean over, cupping their hands to make a megaphone. Their voices reached out over the city. People began to stop work and fall silent.

The mosque was built between 1609 and 1616, with the usual dependences of theological college, kitchens for the poor and so on. It has six minarets—a rarity—and the story is that Ahmet was reproached by the *Imam* of Mecca for glorifying it in this manner when the same number of minarets was reserved for the mosque of the Kaaba. The Sultan is then supposed to have given a seventh minaret by way of reparation. In fact it now seems that the seventh minaret of the Kaaba was built some time before Ahmet's mosque.

I turned a deaf ear to the truculent unctions of the guide. Judging by his tone, business had been especially poor. I left my shoes with the doorkeeper and slid my feet into a pair of big leather slippers— about size 19—which are provided for the use of 'infidels'. I shuffled in, feet flapping grotesquely like a circus clown's. Acres of floor stretched away, a great expanse of unimpeded praying-ground, covered with magnificent carpets laid upon rush matting. Some of them were sixty to eighty feet long and proportionately broad.

A few had already entered and had begun the ritual of prayer. Away to the left, in a separate enclosure, were a group of women. They were black humps cross-legged. I watched one man. He faced the *mihrab*: that semicircular recess which takes the place of the altar and which is focused on Mecca. He stood and said inaudibly the number of bowings that he would perform. Then he opened his hands and touched the lobes of his ears with his thumbs, and began to recite the prayers which go with the bowings. He lowered his hands and folded them, the left within the right, and recited the *Fatiha*, the first chapter of the Koran:

> Praise be to Allah, the Lord of the Creation,
> The Compassionate, the Merciful,
> King of the Day of Judgment.
> You alone we worship, and to You alone
> We pray for help.
> Guide us to the straight path,
> The path of those whom You have favoured,
> Not of those who have incurred Your anger,
> Nor of those who have gone astray.

Other verses followed. Then he bowed from the hips with his hands on his knees. He went on murmuring. Then he sank to his knees, placed his hands upon the ground, then his nose and face. He repeated the words. Then he sat on his heels and made a second prostration. Then he pronounced the credo, looked over his right shoulder, said 'Peace be upon you and the mercy of God', and afterwards said the same words over his right shoulder.

It was all done with great speed and alacrity; beautiful to watch. The exercise has the added advantage of keeping limbs and joints extremely supple and I have seen old men going through all these motions with the ease of youths.

The great flat floors of the mosques allow that equality of position among men before the Creator which is a fundamental part of Muslim teaching. In all Christian churches the contours of the floor are graduated in an ascending scale leading to the altar and thence to the tabernacle or cross. The step is an important feature of this worship. The eyes are practised to look straight towards where the altar is, the focal point, and it is a long time before one becomes accustomed to its absence.

To the right of the *mihrab* is the pulpit (or *mimber*). This lies at the top of a long, straight, narrow staircase closed in at the sides. Nearby the Koran lies upon a lectern.

The mosque of Sultan Ahmet is famous for its marvellous blue faïences which decorate much of its interior. Because of the beauty which these impart it is a mosque often visited by tourists at the expense of some believed to be still finer but a little off the beaten track. The experts complain. They point out the spurious effects of blue stencilling, indistinguishable, except at very close quarters, from the genuine blue tiling. But even the blue tiles are boring after a time if you stand too close to them. They also complain at the lack of stained glass and they remark the monotony of the square ground-plan and the repetitive spacing of identical numbers of windows. Of the outside, on the other hand, no complaint can be made. It is magnificent in its huge simplicity.

I squatted unobtrusively at the back and thought the interior also to be incomparably fine. But I did not have the disadvantage of knowing that much of the blueness was 'bogus'. I had not stood so close to it that I could see nothing else except the defects which made the virtues invisible. But I have often seen people examining the signatures of artists before coming to conclusions about the paintings.

More and more men began to come in, carrying their shoes. They left them in the little racks and troughs provided. Then they went towards the *mihrab*, selected a spot, and began to pray. The un-affected humility of all their movements was a delight to watch. They were extraordinarily graceful: a pleasing change from the clumsy sprawling and genuflecting, all the half-hearted bobbing and self-conscious curtseying so often noticeable in Christian churches. So many Christians seem to be afraid to go on their knees. If only they knew how ungainly they look as they compromise between comfort and self-abasement, with comfort getting the upper hand as time goes on.

Soon there were several hundred present and prayers began; the *Imam* intoning, the congregation assisting, bowing and rising, bow-ing and rising—their movements matching the melodious rhythms of the chants. The voice of the *Imam* rose:

'In the Name of God, the Compassionate, the Merciful . . .'

The great building was filled with a murmur, undulating, swelling and dying, the suppliance of Islam.

'O Thou, enwrapped in thy mantle!
Arise and warn
Thy Lord—magnify Him.'

Soon the smell of several hundred pairs of exposed feet, albeit washed, became noticeable. In half an hour it was all over. Outside the unofficial guide was still sitting on the wall, swinging his legs and waiting for a gullible customer.

★

Prayer is one of the five principal moral duties of every Muslim; the others being belief in the One God, almsgiving, pilgrimage and fasting. Alms are of two kinds: obligatory and voluntary. By Muslim canon law everyone had to set aside one-fortieth of his income. Now alms are virtually all voluntary—certainly, so far as I know, in Turkey. The giving is dictated by the conscience and on my observation it is done a great deal. Every Muslim is obliged to make a pilgrimage to Mecca once in a lifetime. Fasting is *de rigueur* for the faithful Muslim in the month of Ramadan, which may fall in any season for it is calculated by the lunar year. If the injunctions are obeyed fully no one may eat, drink or smoke between sunrise and sunset. The sick and travellers are exempted but they are expected to fulfil their duties when they can.

The Prophet said that during Ramadan the gates of Paradise are open and the gates of Hell closed and the devils chained by the leg, therefore it is prudent to take advantage of the beneficence which may flow down from the liberal hand of God.

When the cannon boom and the drums roll at the end of the day then they may eat and drink. The penalties for breaking the fast used to be considerable and Sanderson records about 1600 that if a Muslim were careless enough to be found drunk in the streets in the month of Ramadan then he had to melt a ladle full of lead and pour it down his throat. But, on the whole, there seems to have been a good deal of variability in the attitude towards the fast. Many stayed at home and pretended. Lithgow, later than Sanderson, formed a very poor opinion of the Turks during Ramadan. He reported that they did what they liked, 'counting that best devotion, which is most sutable to their dispositions; allotting fancy to follow their folly, and blindnesse, to overtop the ignorance of nature', and then, in a splendid Jacobean phrase which might have been penned by Jeremy Taylor or Thomas Browne he concludes, 'drawing all their drifts within the circle of destruction'.[11]

The feast of Seker Bayram follows immediately upon Ramadan.

It is the Candy Feast: the equivalent, in a way, of the Easter celebration after the Lenten privation. The other principal holiday is the Kurban Bayram, a sacrificial festival when every good Muslim is supposed to slaughter a sheep and give most of the meat to the poor. This, of course, commemorates the delivery of Isaac. In the past the markets of Istanbul were thronged with sheep a few days before Kurban Bayram, each beast bearing a dab of red paint to signify its sacrificial role. The sheep thus sacrificed is supposed to carry every good Muslim over the bridge which, as narrow as a hair, leads to Paradise. Those whose burdens of sins are light are able to make this perilous trip. This holiday lasts four days but now fewer sheep are killed, especially in the large towns.

On the whole the religious situation is comparable with that in England (though the comparison is detrimental to the Muslim) where a large number of Christians do not attend church or pray regularly but still quote the Bible, observe the rituals for marriage and death and christening and keep the Christmas and Easter festivals, which are both opportunities for a bout, more uninhibited than usual, of over-drinking and over-eating.

On Christmas Eve the public-houses stay open until twelve o'clock which enables the Catholics to fortify themselves for midnight Mass and the non-church-goers to get themselves into the right frame of mind for commemorating the birth of Christ.

In Turkey these corybantic releases are much less noticeable, and adherence to established Muslim practice is more firmly founded. The faith manifests itself more practically. It is not taken out once a week, or when someone dies or when someone gets married, like a piece of cherished china or a best suit, to be dusted and carefully put away again.

★

Periodically I explored the area to the east of the 'Blue Mosque' and up to the Seraglio Point. Alongside the mosque is a large square of hard, dusty ground used occasionally as a football-field. Beneath it, but inaccessible, are parts of buildings connected with the Hippodrome and these joined the great imperial palace. At one time, the best part of a thousand years ago, much of the broad end of the peninsula which juts out into the Marmara and the Bosphorus was covered by this palace. It was enormous and complicated: a maze of gardens, courts and buildings. It began to fall into disrepair when the Comnene emperors moved to the Palace of Blachernae during the eleventh century.

Early in the fourteenth century Pero Tafur recorded rather gloomily that the 'Emperor's Palace must have been very magnificent, but now it is in such a state that both it and the city show well the evils which the people have suffered and still endure'.[12] Five hundred years later the relentless processes of decay and neglect have left a region full of patches of waste land joined by rough tracks and roads thick with dust or mud according to season. Slowly disintegrating wooden houses, shacks, hovels and Byzantine ruins are mingled with the occasional modern building, stables, barracks, disused fountains and crumbling tombs. There is half a century's labour here for archaeologists, but I doubt if it ever can or will be undertaken. The expense would be colossal and the work unimaginable.

One part of the palace, however, has been recovered: a magnificent mosaic pavement—the floor of a colonnade. It lies almost immediately below the eastern end of the 'Blue Mosque'. The section revealed is about fifty yards long and varies in width: between five and ten yards. The area has been roofed and it is possible to examine it all at close quarters by using wooden foot-walks and cemented areas. It dates from the fifth or sixth century.

A little middle-aged Turk showed me round whenever I went. He had picked up a few words of English and he had a well-developed gift for pointing out the obvious, or nearly so. 'There', he would say, pointing emphatically, 'a man.' And, sure enough, there was. The lineaments of an admirably depicted donkey never deceived him. Two men hunting a tiger, however, were firmly described as 'Men chase leopard'. A bacchanalian scene was faithfully mimed by swigging gestures and a melancholy smile.

> What men or gods are these? . . .
> What mad pursuit? What struggle to escape?
> What pipes and timbrels? What wild ecstasy?

He was very anxious that all should know the importance of his charge. Certainly the mosaic is splendidly done and remarkably well preserved despite the fact that the pavement has many small hummocks and valleys in it due, perhaps, to earthquakes and other upheavals. The colours are bright and the figures animated.

When Peter Mundy visited the palace some time between 1617 and 1620 he saw, among other animals, a 'terrible great lyon (somwhat tame) playing with a little dog'. Now diversions are less sensational and the nearest I drew to a survivor of those distant and roaming menageries was a flat stony lion with an eagle's beak spread across the colonnade floor. As the lovers at Pompeii lived ossified in the postures of desire overwhelmed and the figures on Keats's *Grecian Urn* were for ever loving, for ever fair, so the fifth-century tiger survives the steel of the poised lances, children play with their toys and the undulating tableau of the pavement unfolds the silent procession of a receding glory.

There is a small museum of other pieces of mosaic and statuary near by and stacks of finely made and unblemished tiles bearing the monogram of Constantine.

I was leaving the museum one day and walking along a street flanked by vaulted brick chambers which once belonged to the Hippodrome when a young man stopped me and pushed a printed sheet into my hand. Perfunctory pen and ink sketches were scrawled round it. It was headed 'DAMPING—Agenzia di Viaggi'. Then followed a long and mellifluous tirade on what 'Damping' offered. It guaranteed you to know *nel più breve periodo di tempo la città di Istanbul come un nativo.* The guides would defend your interests in any *situazione imbarazzante.* They would provide lawyers, interpreters and pen-friends and so on.

I cannot but be depressed by the remarkably low standard of tourist 'literature'. It is yet another branch of the mass appeal to the masses; a highly organized stunt to tell people what to think and to curtail individual choice.

The advertizing techniques are, on the whole, poor. One has only to read the relevant material for one's own country to realize how poor they can be. Cliché-ridden and dishonest tourist 'literature' standardizes every country, irons them out, into the modern counterparts of the mythical Isles of the Blessed and the Happy Lands; but they are isles and lands conjured by the cheap wand of a Hollywood nurtured magician, a tedious succession of plushy hotels, picturesque ruins and views and slinky night-clubs, and everywhere all the vaunted facilities which will ensure that people shall not be embarrassed and discomforted by the unfamiliar. Travel is becoming the equivalent of a temporarily sedating drug, a series of stiff drinks, a purgative visit to a brothel; in fact a kind of escape. Often the escape is from the 'self'. But, alas, the 'self' is not to be shaken off so easily, not to be deceived so naïvely. Some photographs, a souvenir or two, a conversational gambit and a tan are the most tangible products of travel, but one supposes that the 'change' does people good, and however rapid and cursory it may be (and 'Damping' was ready for this: *si propone di farvi acquistare con una spesa minima i più bei e caratteristici 'ricordi' di Istanbul*), and it often has to be rapid, travel does help to disperse insularity and dispel illusions. I have talked to people who thought Istanbul to be a country still ruled by a Sultan; to others who firmly believed that posses of bandits still roam the Bulgarian countryside robbing voyagers; to others who thought Albania to be a democracy ruled by a king, or, alternatively, a place invented by Evelyn Waugh in one of his novels. People with a secondary school and university background were among them.

Travel will help to break down barriers which are erected by politicians and it will also help people to realize the appalling poverty and hardship under which so many of the world's peoples suffer and die. But 'shop-window' travelling, the kind promoted by much tourist 'literature', will only serve to make knowledge selective and understanding distorted.

★

Allah, who, as the Koran says, is closer to a man than the vein in his neck, saw, I hope, the man beating his apprentice with a steel rod in his workshop as I went by. The boy had damaged a tyre while taking it off its rim and, as sometimes happens, with incredible rapidity, the master had gone off the deep end. On the whole Turks have a fairly phlegmatic nature, they are patient and can be very well disciplined, but it is true that when roused they are extremely dangerous. Under the blows the boy was comparatively unmoved: a little frightened but quite fearless. It was a painful incident to witness for there are few things so ugly as a man's temper out of control. More than most powerful emotions anger produces the most alarming distortion of the features. People become quite unrecognizable. Happily intervention came, and then peace once more.

I was on my way to the church of SS Sergius and Bacchus which lies to the south of the 'Blue Mosque', on the shore of the Marmara and right up against the railway line. Electric trains rush past within a few feet of its windows, windows made as long ago as A.D. 527.

I went down steep twisting streets, among old houses and shops. It was a hot day and the shadows lay solidly black in blades and wedges, sharp across white dust. Doorways were dark and cool. A derelict taxi stood wheelless on orange-boxes. Hornets zoomed round a fruit-stall and a cat stalked an imaginary prey along a garden wall. Some men were stretched out in patches of shade. There was a small courtyard of beaten earth before the church, which is now a mosque, and some children were playing desultory games of hopscotch and football. Behind railings alongside the church and beneath yew and cypress there were old cracked sarcophagi and tombstones huddled and tilted in disorder. Two men were asleep in the Turkish portico which has replaced the narthex.

It is a very small church, and very beautiful: an octagon inscribed in a square. Eight piers subtend eight arches which directly support the dome. There are marble pillars between the main piers. It was built by Justinian and was the prototype of St Sophia. The monograms of the emperor and Theodora are clearly visible. The gleam of stones and the abundance of gold which Procopius remarked in his *Aedifices* are dimmed now and mosaic is plastered over, but for the magnificence there are the great compensations of peace and unpretentitious harmony. Whenever I go into a church that has become a mosque, and nearly always when I go into a mosque, I am aware, because I am not a Muslim, of what Chesterton neatly described as the 'presence of the absence of God'. One becomes used to the Sacrament in the tabernacle, the focal point, but in this church I found the presence of absence less marked than anywhere else. I am sure that this may seem very foolish but that is the feeling, feeling which is as much the product of familiarity with the presence of the presence as it is of the shortcomings of the imagination.

I walked round on tiptoe carrying my shoes. It was the quietest place in the whole city. A big grandfather clock ticked. A Pope once hid there, and another celebrated Mass. The emperors worshipped there regularly. A boy began to chant from the Koran, then a train roared by and vanquished the melody. Fracted light shivered on glass and crystal as the building shook. Then silence fell again and the chant picked up, growing, now higher, now lower. I stood there holding my shoes and listened for a long time

From there I wandered along the inside of the walls below the railway. I clambered up on them and used footpaths that wound over mounded earth and refuse, through nettle and dock and disintegrating stone. The narrow streets came down to the embankment. Women in shawls were washing, men sitting. Paprikas in ragged bunches were turning orange and vermilion. Wooden houses were blistered and cracked and peeling. Twisted ironwork threw crooked shadows on shutters. Beyond was the sea: milky-coloured, acres of pale glass with dark strands grazed by breeze and change of current. Fishing-boats were scattered miles out like little brown bugs and lozenges. Beyond them were the Princes' Islands, smoky blue shadows, a just discernible bulk in the opaline haze.

Soon I came to Justinian's palace, or what remains of it: big windows like a colonnade rising above the top of the sea-wall. It was full of pigeons, rock doves, Senegal doves, warbling and fussing. Refuse dump, playground, temporary home, lavatory—the palace has been used for everything. A man came out of one of the recesses doing up his trousers as if to prove the point.

It was very still, very hot. The light lay in sheets on the water, ritulant, blinding, and the track of the sun was brazen, a golden fire burning, like all Yeats's 'complexities of fury'—

> Dying into a dance,
> An agony of trance,
> An agony of flame that cannot singe a sleeve.

But there is little or nothing of Yeats's Byzantium left. It is one of the receding 'unpurged images', and down there at night there is nothing except the slabs of the moonlight falling through the tall windows, marbling stone and revetment, the sound of the water lipping and nuzzling the rocks, the scurrying of rats in the garbage; and across the water, through the ruins, over the tottering wooden houses, the twisting streets, the broad courtyards, the desolate cemeteries, there comes the belling and the pealing of the owls, the watch-song of the owls, and all Caesars dead.

NOTES

1. Gainsford, op. cit.
2. Pero Tafur, op, cit.
3. Gonzalez de Clavijo, op. cit.
4. Sanderson, op. cit.
5. Sanderson, op. cit.
6. Procopius, *Aedifices*. Loeb Class. Lib., vol. 7.
7. Ibid.
8. Pero Tafur, op. cit.
9. Busbecq, op. cit.
10. Evliya Efendi, op cit.
11. Lithgow, op. cit.
12. Pero Tafur, op. cit.

Appendix

In Turkish the vowels are pronounced as in French or German: that is, *a* as in *rather*, *e* as in *met*, *i* as in *machine*, *o* as in *oh*, *u* as in *mute*. There are three other vowels which don't occur in English: these are *ı* (withouth a dot) pronounced as the *u* in *but*, *ö* as in German or as *oy* in *annoy*, *ü* as in German or as *ui* in *suit*.

Consonants are the same as in English, except the following:

c as *j* in *jam*

ç as *ch* in *chat*

g as in *get*

ğ is almost silent and tends to lengthen the preceding vowel.

ş as in *sugar*

The following is a short list of Turkish words which may be helpful:

cami—mosque

çarşi—market or bazaar

çeşme—fountain

dağ—mountain

dershane—lecture hall in an Islamic theological school

hamam—turkish bath

han (or kervansaray)—inn or hostel for merchants and travellers, with accommodation for animals and merchandise.

hisar—castle or fortress

imam—a 'clergyman' who presides over public prayers in a mosque

iskele—quay

kale—castle of fortress

kapi—gate or door

kilise—church

köprü—bridge

köy—village

külliye—a complex of buildings which includes a mosque, medrese etc.

medrese—Islamic school of theology

mektep—Ottoman primary school

mescit—small mosque or place of prayer

—meydan—square or town centre

mihrab—embrasure or niche in a mosque indicating the direction of Mecca

mimber—pulpit in a mosque

müezzin—the man who gives the call to prayer from the minaret of a mosque

pazar—bazaar or market

şadirvan—a mosque fountain for ritual ablution

saray—palace

sebil—street fountain for drinking water

şehir—town

sokak—street

tekke—Dervish monastery

türbe—mausoleum, tomb

yeni—new

Index

Index

241